fotofeis

fotofeis 95

INTERNATIONAL FESTIVAL OF PHOTOGRAPHY IN SCOTLAND

5 OCTOBER – 5 NOVEMBER 1995

PUBLISHER

Fotofeis Ltd
58–59 Timberbush, Edinburgh EH6 6QH
First edition of 3,000 copies
published September 1995
ISBN 0 9521396 2 6

DISTRIBUTION

Art Data, 12 Bell Industrial Estate,
50 Cunnington Street, London W4 5HB

CATALOGUE

Edited by Alasdair Foster, Ken Gill and Euan McArthur
Designed and typeset in FF Quadraat by Dalrymple
Cover by Derek Watson at Shaw Marketing & Design
Fotofeis logo by Tayburn Strategic Design
Printed by BAS Printers Ltd, Over Wallop

Sponsor's Foreword

THROUGHOUT 1995 BECK'S has been celebrating ten years of Arts Sponsorship in Great Britain, and has during this time helped to bring challenging and exciting work in the areas of dance, theatre and the visual arts to new audiences. Beck's are therefore proud to be the Major Festival Sponsors of *Fotofeis* '95, and are delighted to be involved in bringing to Scotland photographic art from around the world.

The mix of exhibitions which are held in galleries and museums alongside photo-performances and on-street projections, encompass a wide variety of photographic art, making *Fotofeis* '95 a unique Festival

We hope that visitors to and residents of Scotland will take this opportunity to explore the many facets of *Fotofeis* '95 – a truly international event.

BRIAN SHARP
Brands Director, Scottish Courage Ltd

BECK'S 10

CELEBRATING 10 YEARS
OF ARTS SPONSORSHIP

Introduction

Welcome to *Fotofeis* '95, the second international festival of photography in Scotland. Now the leading photographic festival in the UK, Fotofeis spans Scotland, with over one hundred exhibitions in venues from Dumfries in the south to Unst, in the far north. Taking in the cities of Glasgow, Edinburgh and Aberdeen the festival features exhibitions at many of the major museums and galleries in the country. It also includes a lively and diverse community programme and a number of innovative presentations outside the traditional gallery environment. For Fotofeis is, perhaps more than any other such festival in the world, a celebration of the photo-based arts in all their many and diverse forms.

Fotofeis '95 has three themes – *Mortality*, *Migration* and *City* – each inextricably linked with the medium of photography in the late 20th century. These are muster points for the ideas explored in the various exhibitions and events, but not their containing vessels. In giving structure to the programme we do not seek to dictate the way in which the work of each artist is viewed. Even the introductory essays are in the form of personal musings rather than authoritative instructions on what to think – animating but not didactic. There is space here for personal interpretation and no one point of view has precedence over another.

Mortality

As the French writer, Roland Barthes, has observed, photographs must always remind us of death for they can only ever show us things which have past and gone forever. While photography was invented at a time when an acceptance of mortality was woven deep into the social fabric, in the late 20th century and in the West we live in a social and cultural fools' paradise which seeks to deny death, or at least to avert our gaze from it. These twin facts – the medium's affinity with death and our society's denial of it – ensure that mortality is a fertile subject for photographic artists. From the baroque tableaux of Joel-Peter Witkin to the sensual imagery of Andrea Fisher; from the moral outrage of Lucinda Devlin to the psychedelic exuberance of Robert Flack – the exhibitions confront the temporal nature of individual existence from many points of view – some quite surprising.

Migration

If photographs show us times past, they also bring alive memories of places where once we lived. For the emigré such images are particularly charged for they are the key to an identity which is no longer rooted in the place they inhabit. Migration brings with it a cultural synthesis, as the immigrant negotiates the hybridization of their past culture and that of their new home. The exhibitions in this theme reflect the hope and the confusion which surround such migrations: the pioneering spirit of those who sought a new life in the Americas and the desperation of those forced there through economic necessity; the enrichment of the cultural melting-pot and the violence borne of racial intolerance.

City

Cities, which began as centres of trade and learning and, in the 19th Century grew up around industry and transport, have in the late 20th century become mediated spaces whose reality lies as much in the pages of a magazine or the screen of a television, as it does on the paving stones of their streets. The contemporary city is a cacophony of rhythms, fantasies and information. The photographers and curators whose exhibitions are included in this section of the festival are drawn to the city as a collection of signs and facades, as a place where appearance and experience are layered like the skins of an onion. There is no ultimate truth nestling at the core, only the relation of one layer of meaning with another.

Complementing these three thematic ideas, the festival includes two sections which address the practice and process of making photographs. The *Emergent* section brings together an eclectic selection of artists whose work is little known outside their own country, while *Collaboration* features work created in a range of artistic partnerships including that of the artist with the community. This latter section takes in a number of specially commissioned exhibitions and others can be found throughout the programme, ensuring that there is a freshness to the festival as a whole.

In addition to these themes and sections, there are five projects which stand alone. These *Feature* exhibitions which begin the catalogue, include a major new survey of American photography, a series of artist interventions in Scotland's museum and art collections, and an exhibition of photo-based multiples which is at the centre of a range of public art projects and community workshops around the country. *The European Face* is an ambitious exhibition bringing together portraiture by artists from all fifteen member states of the European Community, while the three festival themes are explored in specially selected programmes of experimental film and video put together by the *New Visions* team.

Broad as it is, *Fotofeis* '95 does not attempt to be a comprehensive review of contemporary photography, nor does it address itself solely to the *cognoscenti*. By locating elements of the festival across the country the festival actively encourages the involvement of not one, but many local audiences. In a world so heterogeneous and diverse we cannot assume that the photographic arts have a unified audience or a single canon of excellence. We must learn to recognize quality *of its kind* and value each area of practice and each viewer on their own terms.

While the programme is presented in this catalogue as a series of themes and sections, it is easy to see that other threads can be drawn between the constituent exhibitions and projects. There are some strong examples of artistic intervention – from the museological hide and seek of *Whispers* to the very public manifestations involved in Micah Lexier's bus shelter exhibits and Jane Brettle's modification of the National Monument. We are also delighted to have so many Canadian artists participating in the festival. Their work can be found in every aspect of the programme, demonstrating the vibrancy and variety of the photo-based arts in that country.

Fotofeis '95 is a collective enterprise. It has taken, first and foremost, the vision, talent and sheer hard graft of the many artists without whose work there would simply be no festival. It has involved the knowledge and analytical skills of the curators who have grouped and interpreted this work. It has taken the enterprise and enthusiasm of the gallery administrators and arts-workers who strive to maintain the venues at which many of these exhibitions have been staged. It has taken the generosity of the public funders and commercial sponsors, both in the UK and overseas, who support the festival and its many constituent projects. In particular I would like to acknowledge our major festival sponsor, Beck's, whose support has greatly benefitted this year's event. And, finally, it has been enriched by the advice and ideas so freely offered by our colleagues and friends in Scotland and around the world.

There is much to see and lots to do. I hope that you will find the festival stimulating, thought provoking, challenging, but most of all, enjoyable.

ALASDAIR FOSTER
Director

American Photography 1890–1965

Scottish National Gallery of Modern Art

BELFORD ROAD
EDINBURGH

UK PREMIERE

23 SEPTEMBER – 26 NOVEMBER

American photography from the end of the 19th century through to the period following World War II is considered one of the richest and most innovative traditions in the history of the medium. This great tradition is most fully represented in the collection of the Museum of Modern Art, New York (MOMA).

Curated by Peter Galassi, Chief Curator of Photography at MOMA, this exhibition explores the development of American photography during that period as reflected in the rift between 'art' and 'vernacular' photography. The exhibition locates the origin of the schism at the very point at which photography became ubiquitous. It is particularly evident in the aggressively aesthetic rhetoric of the Photo-Secession, led by Alfred Stieglitz, which sought to establish photography as art and to distance that from common or functional photography which served other ends. From this point the exhibition traces the various accommodations and influences that passed between the two traditions through the work of around fifty of this century's most outstanding photographers.

While frequently antagonistic, the perceived distinction was also a source of dynamic cross-fertilisation. The exhibition pursues the hypothesis that "the contentions created by the divide, as well as the animating sparks that leapt across it, propelled the ceaseless renewal of modern American photography".

The artists exhibited include: Berenice Abbott, Ansel Adams, Diane Arbus, Richard Avedon, Ernest J. Bellocq, Margaret Bourke-White, Harry Callahan, Paul Caponigro, Imogen Cunningham, Bruce Davidson, Elliot Erwitt, Walker Evans, Robert Frank, Lee Friedlander, Lewis Hine, William Klein, Dorothea Lange, Helen Levitt, Lisette Model, Paul Outerbridge, Irving Penn, Aaron Siskind, Edward Steichen, Alfred Stieglitz, Paul Strand, James Van Der Zee, Weegee (Arthur Fellig), Edward Weston, Minor White and many more. This exhibition was organized under the auspices of The International Council of the Museum of Modern Art, New York.

Curated by Peter Galassi, Chief Curator of the Department of Photography, Museum of Modern Art, New York

Presented by the Scottish National Gallery of Modern Art

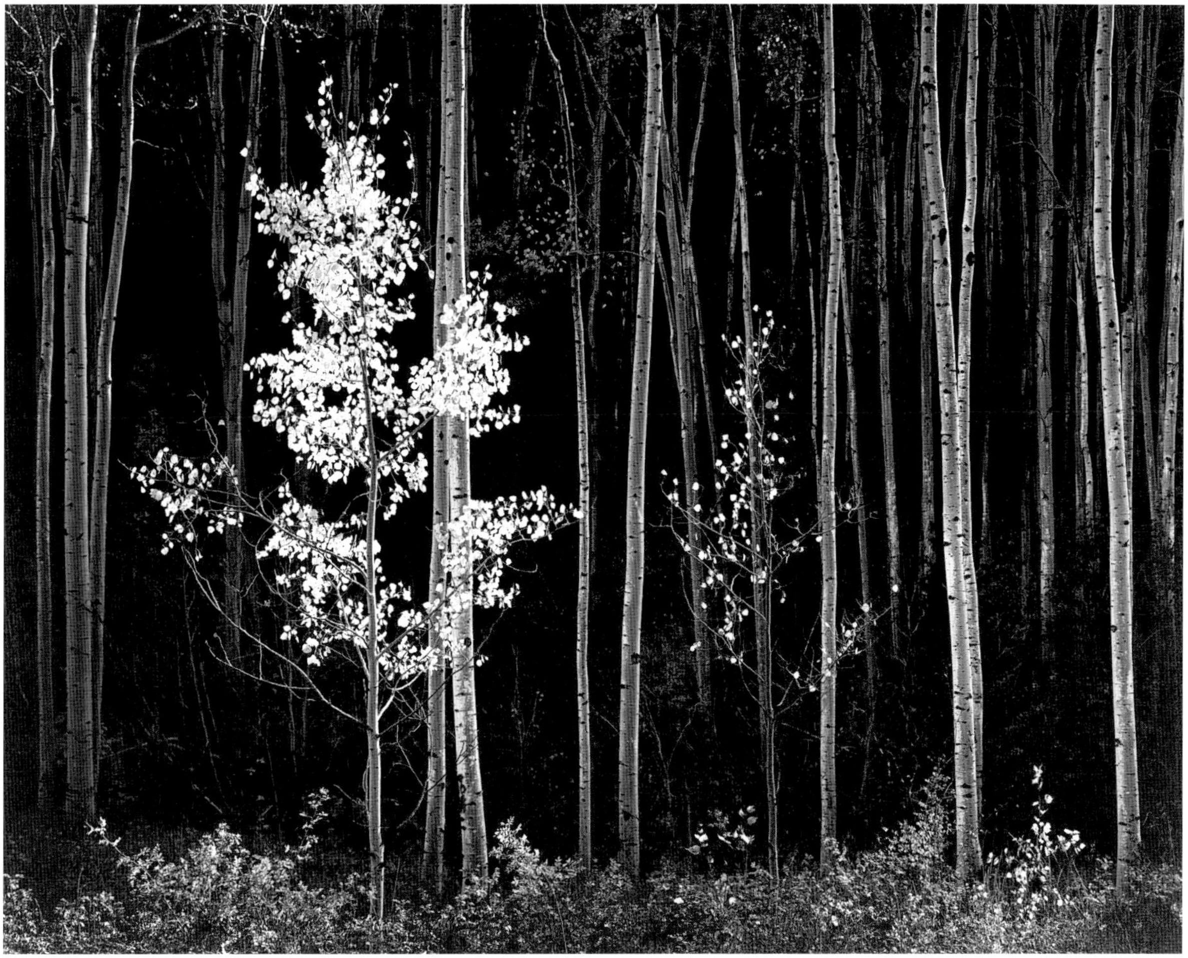

Ansel Adams Aspens, Northern New Mexico 1958 *silver-gelatin print (courtesy of The Museum of Modern Art, New York)*

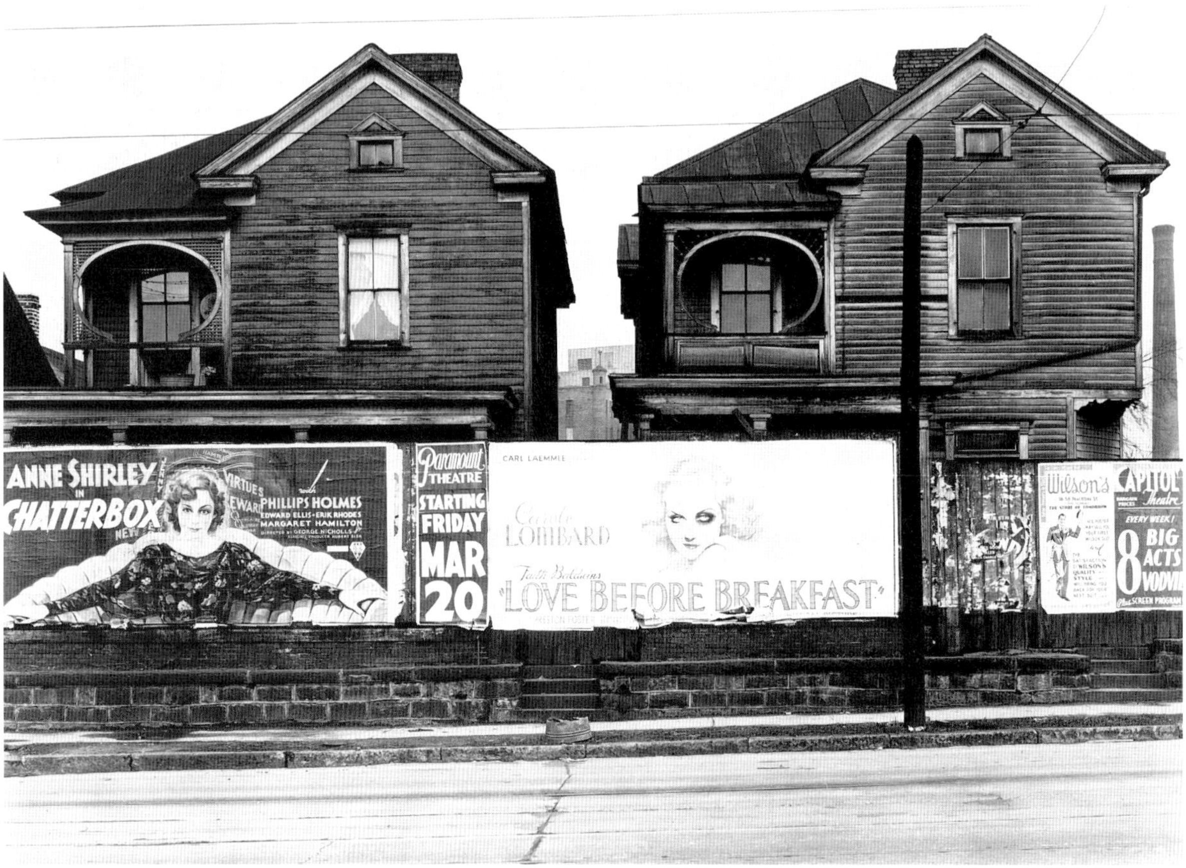

Walker Evans Houses and Billboards in Atlanta 1936 *silver-gelatin print (courtesy of The Museum of Modern Art, New York)*

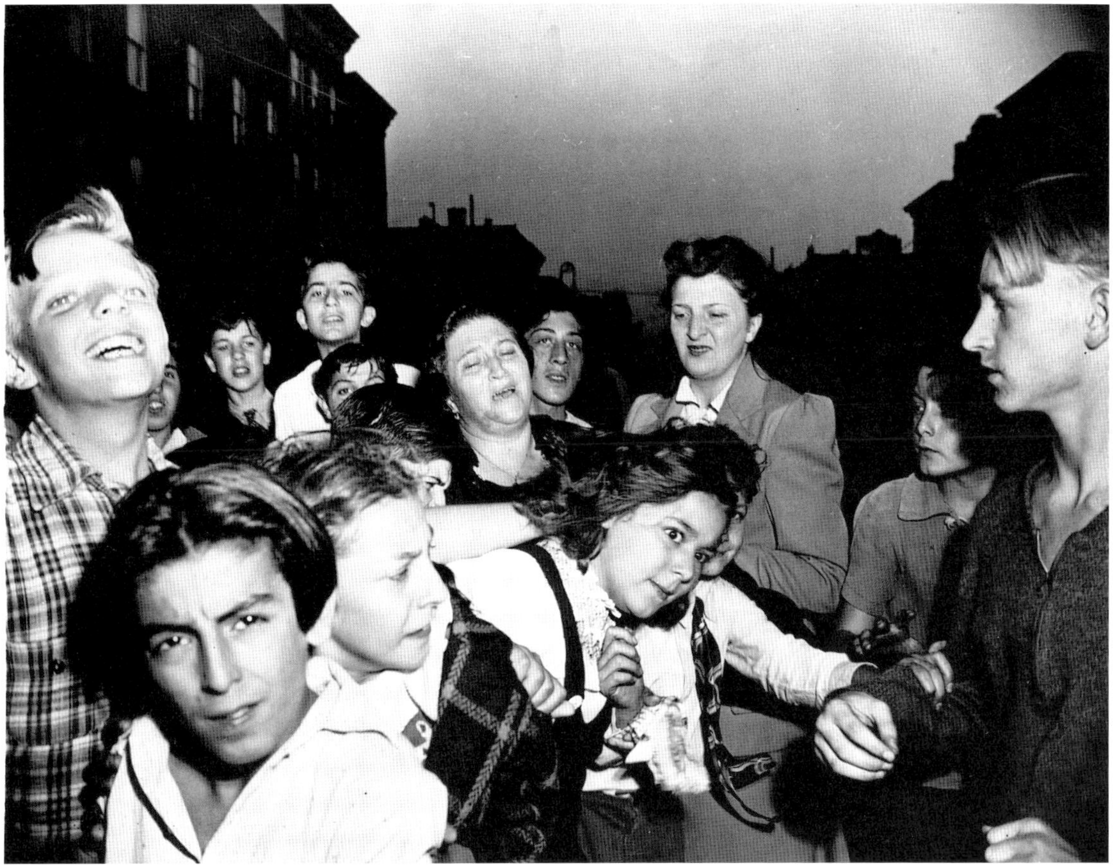

Weegee (Arthur Fellig) Brooklyn School Children See Gambler Murdered in Street 1941 *silver-gelatin print (courtesy of The Museum of Modern Art, New York)*

Fairy Tale in the Supermarket

The Scotland Street Museum

225 SCOTLAND STREET
GLASGOW

PREMIERE

7 OCTOBER – 5 NOVEMBER

Ordinary life is so dull that I get out of it as much as possible.

STEVE JONES, a Sex Pistol, quoted in *Melody Maker*

Sometimes an artistic movement or a mode of working makes a fissure in the fabric of normal cultural production and consumption (like Punk in the late Seventies). It challenges perceived assumptions of what and how things should be made and mediated, and how one should respond. It questions how things function and opens up ways of working in the world of real life: the world of going to work, of signing on, of shopping, of eating, of going to the movies, of buying records, of playing records, of voting, of lobbying, of protesting, of watching television, of talking or not talking, of drinking, of being with friends or on your own, of making love, of making lists, of living.

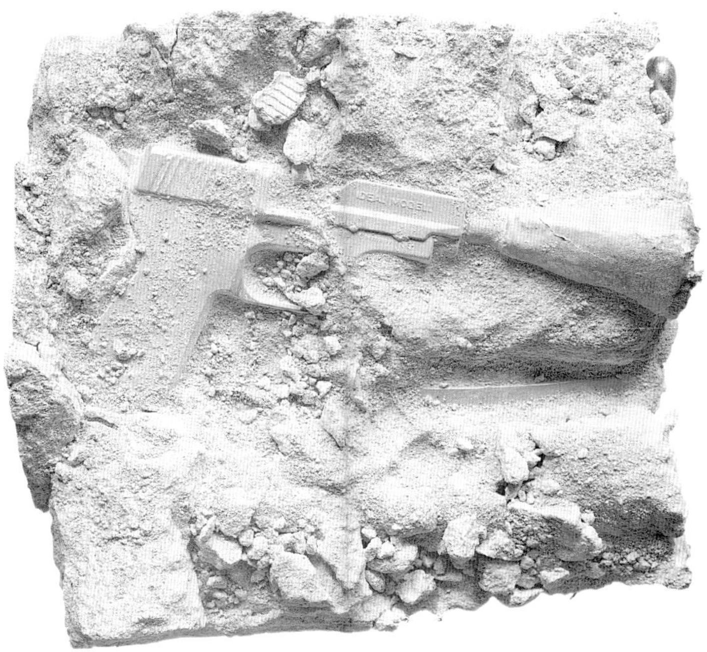

Simon Starling Cast aluminium replica of a toy pistol found on the 18th of January 1994 in the grounds of the Weissenhof Housing Project, Stuttgart *lithographic reproduction in an edition of 3,000*

Curated by Judith Findlay and Kirsty Ogg

Glasgow City Council

A&C Catering Equipment

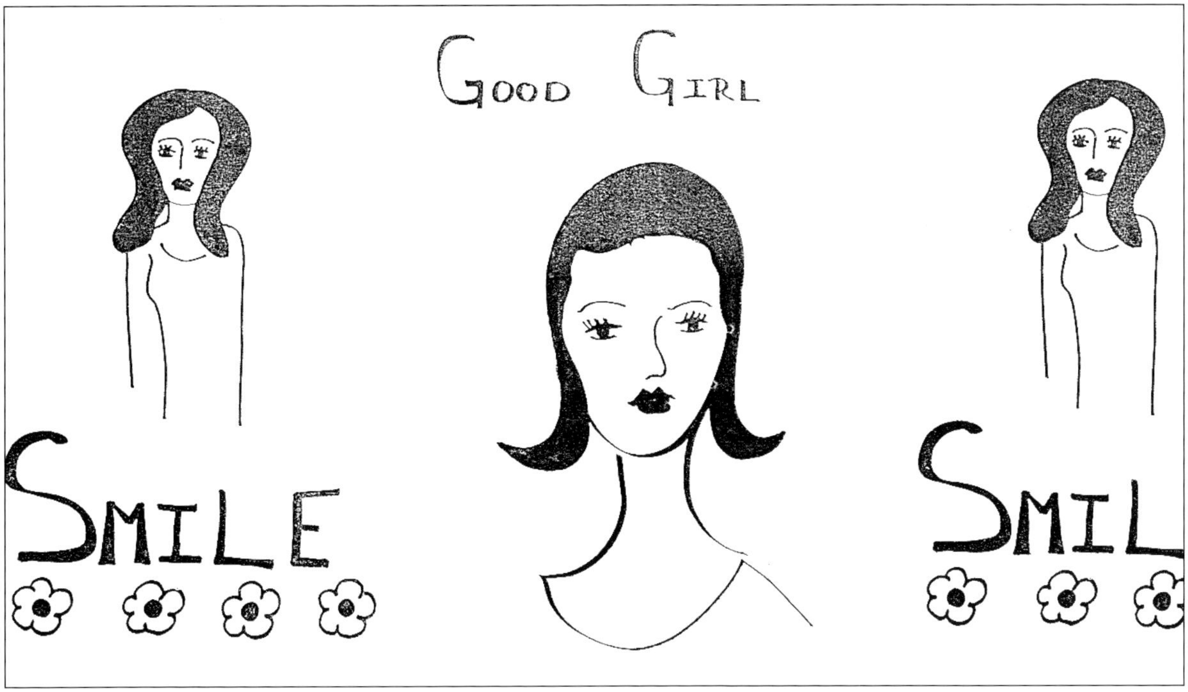

Pam Butler detail from Good Girl Project 1993 *photocopies on laser paper*

That is what the works in *Fairy Tale in the Supermarket* do. As multiple artifacts, they connect the acts of producing and consuming art with every other act of production and consumption, questioning everything from the most mundane purchase to the apparent authority of Art History. The fissure they make in the art milieu opens into the field of everyday life.

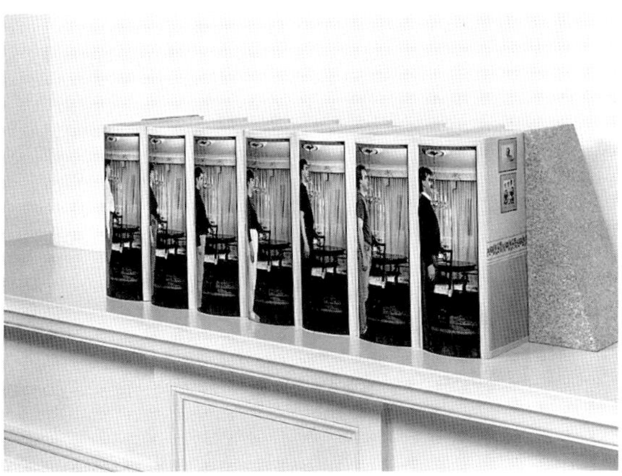
Micah Lexier Set of Seven (Siblings) 1993 *photographs mounted on custom-made books, Barre Granite bookends (installation photograph by Peter MacCallum, courtesy of Jack Shainman Gallery, New York)*

Fairy Tale in the Supermarket puts works on display which use, whether literally or conceptually, the technology of photography. They are fluid and flexible, they are produced in numerous forms and they are controlled by artists: posters, flyers, books, magazines, stickers, signs, packaging, tee-shirts ... the list is endless. The practices range from the social action of guerrilla tactics to the creation of more poetic and finely crafted artifacts.

The works are by artists based in Europe and North America. They include John Baldessari (USA), Barbara Bloom (USA), Pam Butler (USA), Jacqueline Donachie (Scotland), General Idea (Canada), Richard Hamilton (England), Ken Lum (Canada), Jonathan Monk (Scotland), Mark Pawson (England), Cindy Sherman (USA), David Shrigley (Scotland), Ross Sinclair (Scotland), William Wegman (USA), Gavin Weston (Northern Ireland) and many more.

Commissioned and presented by Fotofeis

Other Real Stories / d'autre fictions

The Scotsman *and* Scotland on Sunday

PREMIERE

EDUARDO ACQUINO
Quebec Saturday 7 October

JOSÉE BERNARD
Quebec Sunday 8 October

ANDREW CARLISLE
British Columbia Saturday 14 October

MICHAEL FERNANDES
Nova Scotia Sunday 15 October

NELSON HENRICKS
Quebec Saturday 21 October

ANDRÉ MARTIN
Quebec Sunday 22 October

RITA MCKEOUGH
New Brunswick Saturday 28 October

MARY WONG
Quebec Sunday 29 October

Curated by Marie-Josée Lafortune and Stephen Horne

Newspapers and magazines embrace the immediacy of the present. They are, by definition, vehicles for current information and debate that will be eventually indexed and archived on microfilm. In this project, eight Canadian artists will make works specifically for two Scottish broadsheets, *The Scotsman* and *Scotland on Sunday* (to appear, one artist per paper, on each weekend during *Fotofeis* '95), to propose an alternative form of curatorship to that of the museum or gallery. By appropriating the public space of the newspaper they will exploit another, less common site of exhibition, whilst integrating art within existing systems of classification and codification.

The newspapers will determine the background against which the works may be seen as art and, given the artists' subject matter (violence, Media, money, homelessness, identity/gender, community) the news of the day will offer a highly specific, if short-lived, historical context. This very ephemerality of the works will, in turn, reflect on a culture permeated by mass mediation and the notion of visual art as in some way more permanent. Ultimately, they question the role and meaning of photography within the Media whilst challenging the reader to reconsider her or his definition of a work of art.

Commissioned by Harbour Magazine/Burning Books and Galerie Optica, Montreal in collaboration with Fotofeis

THE SCOTSMAN
SCOTLAND *on* SUNDAY

CONSEIL DES ARTS ET DES LETTRES DU QUÉBEC

The Canada Council
Conseil des Arts du Canada

Conseil des Arts de la Communauté Urbaine de Montréal

EVA ROTHSCHILD *Eire* and JANIE NICOLL *Scotland*

Public Artworks

Glasgow Underground and across Scotland

PREMIERE

OCTOBER – NOVEMBER

Glasgow City Council

Adshel

PRIMESIGHT

FUJIFILM

B&S VISUAL TECHNOLOGIES LIMITED

Glasgow Print Studios

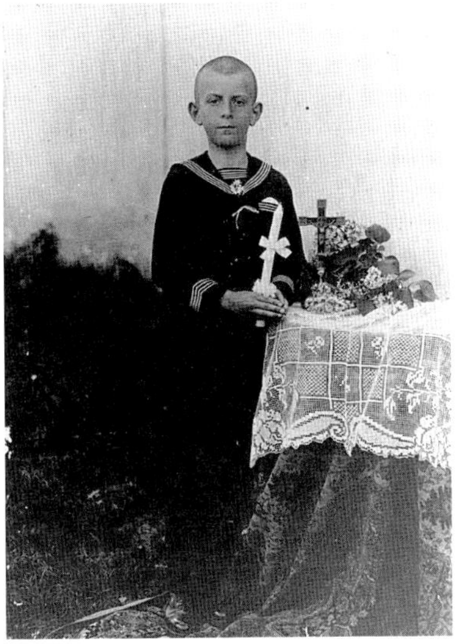

Janie Nicoll and Eva Rothschild present large works on billboards in different places across Scotland – some rural, some urban– which exploit the unexpected conjunction of personal content, feeling and mythologies with the highly legible, rhetorical space of public advertising. They assert the presence of the many private realities by which public space is invisibly animated. Janie Nicoll uses images of social propaganda and manipulation to explore her personal experiences of bereavement. Eva Rothschild deals with similar issues, if from a different perspective. Her imagery draws on popular culture and the mass Media, most recently presenting the city as uninhabited – an empty, elegiac landscape of the future. **An artist-run project**

Blatant, Obvious, True

Glasgow & Edinburgh

PREMIERE

OCTOBER – NOVEMBER

Organised by Valerie Hodgkinson and Margaret Mitchell

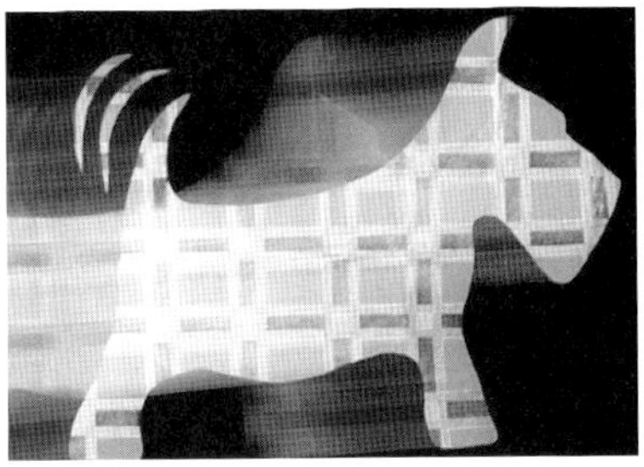

Postcards are familiar disseminators of photographs, whether seen on the streets, pinned to the bedroom wall or sent to a distant friend. *Blatant, Obvious, True* is a photographic postcard project which seeks to intervene in this process. Scottish artists from every photographic discipline have been invited to participate. The cards are available free from a variety of public locations in Edinburgh and Glasgow throughout *Fotofeis* '95.

above *Eva Rothschild & Janie Nicoll* untitled image from public artwork 1995

below *Deitch* untitled 1995 *postcard (original in colour)*

VARIOUS ARTISTS *from the member states of the European Union*

The European Face

Talbot Rice Gallery

UNIVERSITY OF EDINBURGH
OLD COLLEGE
SOUTH BRIDGE
EDINBURGH

PREMIERE

9 OCTOBER – 4 NOVEMBER

Curated by Duncan Macmillan and Gail Boardman

THE CITY OF EDINBURGH DISTRICT COUNCIL

with the support and cooperation of the member states of the European Union

The *European Face* consists of work by fifteen photographers in the genre of portraiture, one artist selected by each member state of the European Union. Taking the notion of the metaphorical face (or faces) of Europe the exhibition is, on one level, a simple celebration of the art of photographic portraiture, while, on another, it illustrates the very diversity which is at the heart of the Union.

This diversity is heightened by the personal preoccupations of the artists themselves. For some the concentration is on a single individual, for others it is the exploration of a group. Some artists focus on friends, others make images of famous people, some make portraits of the anonymous 'person in the street' while others photograph themselves. The range of the exhibition challenges any simple interpretation of the word 'portrait' just as much as it questions any simple understanding of the term 'European' and invites a more considered contemplation of the photographic representation of the human face.

The European Union Cultural Forum is a body made up of representatives from national cultural institutes or embassies in Scotland who meet and co-operate with representatives of the Scottish cultural community and undertake projects of a multilateral European character.

Presented by the European Union Cultural Forum in collaboration with Talbot Rice Gallery

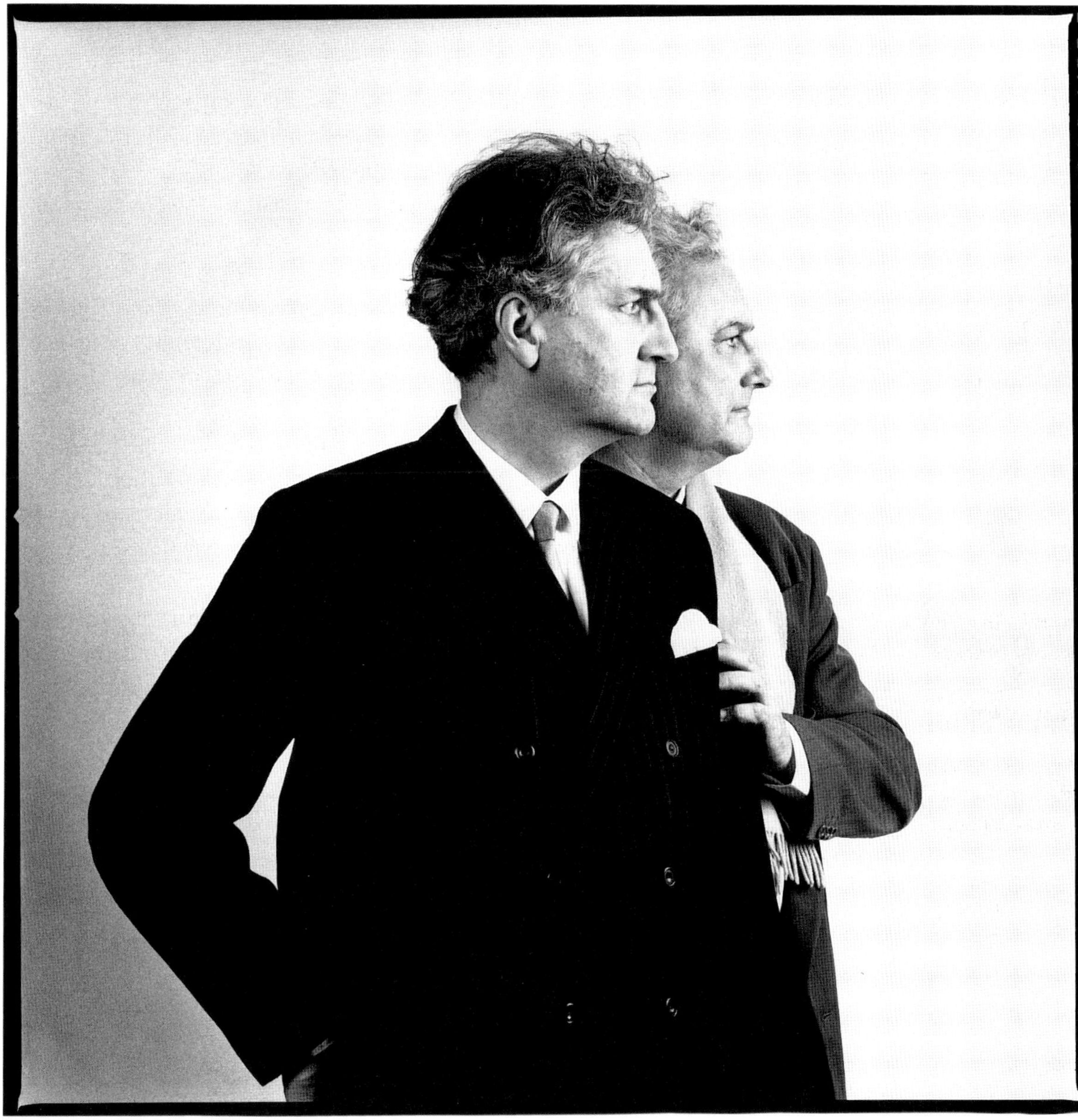

Marianne Majerus Léon and Robert Krier 1995 *silver-gelatin print*

Whispers

Edinburgh & Glasgow

5 OCTOBER – 5 NOVEMBER

To whisper is to communicate in a low and hushed voice, to speak with articulation but without vocal vibration. Accordingly, the work on view in this exhibition which focuses on the context of the museum, works with this idea asserting its presence by way of a disseminated undercurrent of signs and images which gain their resonance through an interactive dialogue with both historical artifacts and the public institutions which accord them their status.

The title however, also evokes an additional subversive undertone which reflects the artists' desire to question the accepted modes of presenting the past as a concrete given, and to suggest instead that through reinterpretation and representation other histories may be written.

Although the participating artists are diverse and use a variety of styles and approaches, they here share a commitment to explore the traditional connections and separations between the past and present, and to raise questions relating to the way the past becomes History, through an array of creations both aesthetic and conceptual.

Text by Peter Rimmer

Some installations are large-scale and highly visible, whilst others are hidden and must be sought out by the visitor. *Whispers* is a museological game – a cultural hide and seek.

Presented by the Institut Français d'Ecosse

Curated by Martine Beugnet

With thanks to Martha McCulloch, Street Level Gallery

Association Française d'Action Artistique

THE CITY OF EDINBURGH DISTRICT COUNCIL

THE SCOTTISH ARTS COUNCIL

Glasgow City Council

André Clément and Barbara Claus *Canada*

HUNTERIAN MUSEUM, UNIVERSITY AVENUE, GLASGOW, AND INSTITUT FRANÇAIS D'ECOSSE, 13 RANDOLPH CRESCENT, EDINBURGH

Claus and Clément's work recreates the features of the room in which it is installed, hinting at its hidden architecture and history, suggesting invisible memories which may still be entrapped in the fabric of the place. In this way an evocative and haunting environment is created from large negative prints of stones, walls, columns and fossils.

opposite *André Clément and Barbara Claus detail from* Limbe(s) *1993 installation* >

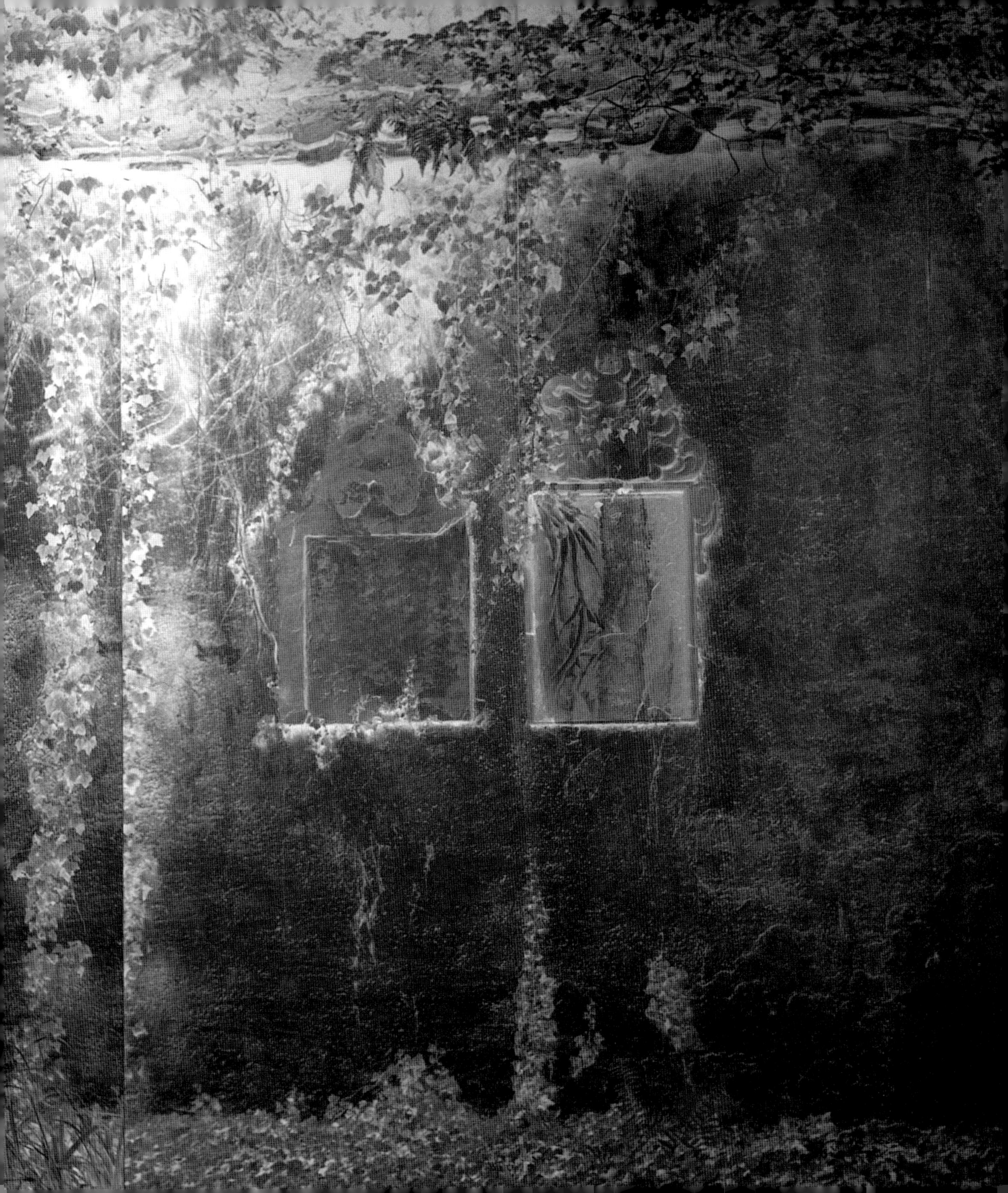

Jason Bowman *Scotland*

MUSEUM OF THE ROYAL COLLEGE OF SURGEONS
8 NICOLSON STREET, EDINBURGH

Jason Bowman's work, *You have been reduced into an historical site*, has slipped into the secluded Museum of the Royal College of Surgeons.

Peter McCaughey *Scotland*

HUNTERIAN MUSEUM, UNIVERSITY AVENUE, GLASGOW

Peter McCaughey is known for his video and film work. Inspired by the Hunterian Museum's collection of early X-rays, the artist has built a multimedia installation, using computer animation, sound and video projection. His work is concerned with ways of looking and how they can imply comprehension of the past and of the present.

Colonel (Thierry Geoffroy) *France/Denmark*

INSTITUT FRANÇAIS D'ECOSSE, 13 RANDOLPH CRESCENT, EDINBURGH

Artist and performer, Colonel (Thierry Geoffroy) is himself a museum. It may be necessary to obtain a ticket or complete an application form to gain access to the images presented on and inside his clothing. In line with the rules of *Whispers* the artist/museum will be exhibiting himself in the gallery of the Institut Français d'Ecosse along with artifacts representing the other participating museums.

Marie Jesus Diaz *France*

ROYAL SCOTTISH MUSEUM, 44 CHAMBERS STREET, EDINBURGH

Marie Jesus Diaz's installation builds a mysterious museum vitrine from large-scale photographs, seeking, through her art, to create a door onto another reality.

Colonel (Thierry Geoffroy)
Untitled (Coat) *photocopy*

Martine Neddam *France/Netherlands*

NATIONAL GALLERY OF SCOTLAND, THE MOUND, PRINCES STREET, EDINBURGH

Martine Neddam is concerned with language – with 'making sense'. Her use of text and computer manipulated images is cunning and challenging. For *Whispers* she has focused on the National Gallery and on the Reverend Walker ...

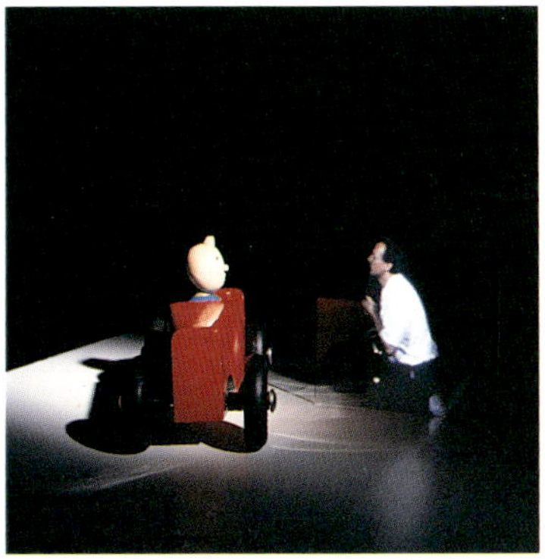

Wyn Geleynse *version of* All The Objects Have Meanings and Hierarchies 1995 *wooden toy, ground glass and 16mm film loop*

Wyn Geleynse *Canada*

MUSEUM OF CHILDHOOD, 42 HIGH STREET, EDINBURGH AND ART GALLERY & MUSEUM, KELVINGROVE, GLASGOW

Wyn Geleynse works with film. His minute, projected characters appear to be barely moving, but are so detailed and perfectly formed that each appears to have life and substance. Placed in the Museum of Childhood and the Art Gallery & Museum at Kelvingrove, his installations set a new context for a given artefact, imbuing it with reverential significance and spurring the imagination.

Patrick Bailley Maître-Grand *France*

MUSEUM OF TRANSPORT, KELVINHALL, 1 BUNHOUSE ROAD, GLASGOW

A former scientist, Patrick Bailley Maître-Grand has established a reputation as a photographer who relentlessly questions and experiments with conventional representation. His work is installed at the Museum of Transport, a large ghostly silhouette of shadows and light suggesting motion.

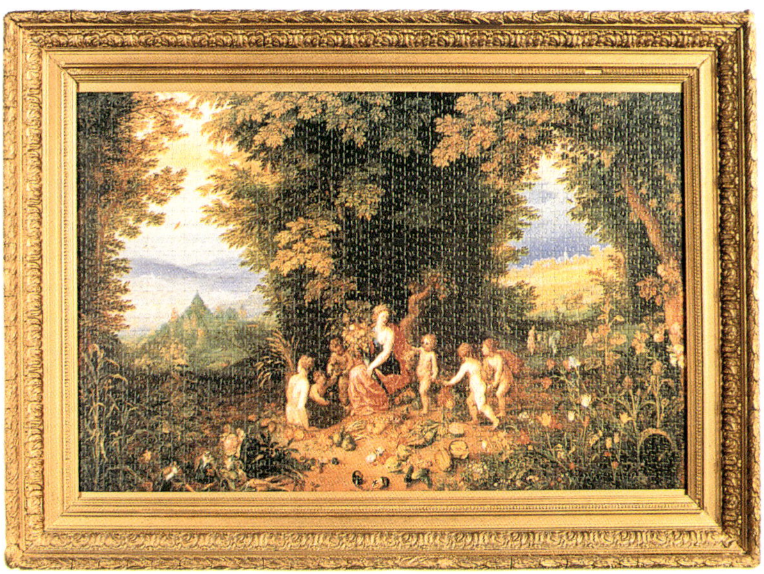

Gérard Collin-Thiébaut *France*

ART GALLERY AND MUSEUM, KELVINGROVE, GLASGOW

Gérard Collin-Thiébaut is one of the most respected contemporary photographers in France. Often controversial, his work explores the very edges of artistic practice. A couple of his *transcriptions* of the great masters may be found lurking amongst the Kelvingrove's collection of fine paintings – a challenge to the discerning viewer.

Gérard Collin-Thiébaut Transcription 1994 *framed photographic jigsaw*

JANE BRETTLE *Scotland*

Allegorical Blueprint

SITEWORK AND WHITESPACE INSTALLATIONS

National Monument & City Observatory

CALTON HILL
EDINBURGH

PREMIERE

30 SEPTEMBER – 5 NOVEMBER

Allegorical Blueprint develops strategies used in the artist's previous work in which the temporal and spatial qualities intrinsic to the medium of photography are employed to question the encoding of gender, which, being implicit within the ideology of western architecture, is consequently at work in the contemporary city. Intervening in both public and private space and time in a direct and physical way, this work attempts to disrupt the historically determined project of architecture, which, through written discourse, has traditionally placed women on the outside, as 'other'. These installations represent a meeting point between the concerns with light and space in classical and modern architecture.

Notions of reflection and mirroring are historically central to debates concerning the foundation of philosophy and the structure of western ideology since Plato. The mirror is fundamental to the mechanism of the Camera Obscura which commands a strategic place in the history of neo-classical Edinburgh. And the contemporary 35mm reflex camera relies on a mirror to deflect the image so it may be perceived through the viewfinder – by reflection. Historically, a re-organisation of architectural space was managed by the use of both painting and mirrors, particularly in the Neo-Classical buildings of the 17th and 18th centuries, where an illusion was created which suggested that the building could transcend its very structure. Nature, in the form of a *trompe l'oeil* representation of the heavens, was in turn brought inside the building. To contrast this, in contemporary architecture the mirrored building reflects nature and the sky externally, arguably itself creating the equivalent of a sitework.

An Artist-run project in collaboration with Independent Public Arts

IPA
INDEPENDENT PUBLIC ARTS LTD

THE SCOTTISH ARTS COUNCIL

UNIVERSITY of NORTHUMBRIA at NEWCASTLE

The Hope Scott Trust

Lothian and Edinburgh Enterprise Limited

MACRO ART

SRS Scotia Rigging Services

McGARRIE

Edinburgh COLLEGE of ART

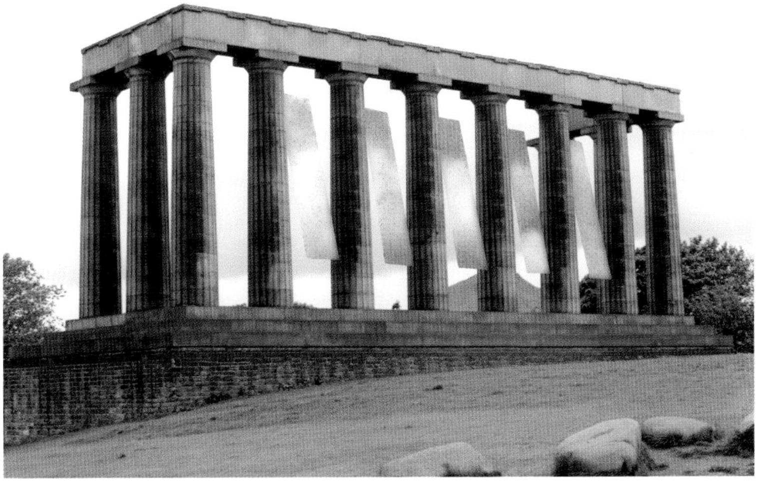

SITEWORK INSTALLATION – The National Monument

Five metallic banners are inclined between the Doric columns of the monument, creating a double sided mirrored surface which reflects the sky from above and the structure of the monument from below. At night the Monument is flooded with blue light.

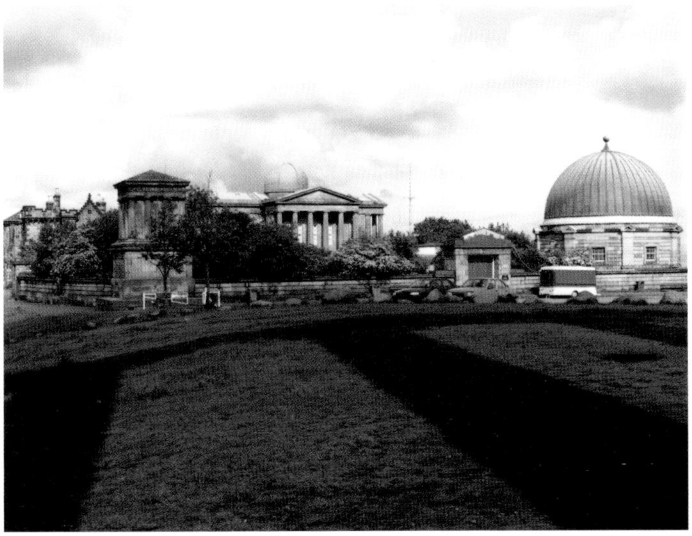

WHITE SPACE INSTALLATION – The City Observatory, Calton Hill
(Architect, William Playfair, 1822)

Two banner photographs lean out from the wall between the Doric half columns at either end of the central room housing the base for the telescope. These reflect into mirrors placed on the floor directly underneath.

New Visions for Fotofeis

Touring Scotland during Fotofeis '95

PREMIERE

OCTOBER – NOVEMBER

Beyond commercial cinema and television, an industry that includes independent production, there is the well developed area of low and no budget film and video making. Free of the commercial constraints of the mainstream, the work is diverse, rich and idiosyncratic. Whilst practice in this area is mature and broad ranging in Scotland, with a lively international dialogue, distribution and regular screenings are generally limited to Edinburgh and Glasgow.

New Visions has curated three international packages which offer a great opportunity for a broad audience to discover new forms and approaches in film and video making. The packages complement the festival themes of Fotofeis and are being screened in urban and rural venues throughout Scotland, often with an introductory speaker to animate discussion afterwards.

Twenty-five works are featured. Included in the *Migration* programme is *Darwish* by Shafeeq Vellani, together with Emma Davies' *Seaview*. Both are impressionistic semi-documentary works which address themes of home and place from the position of their respective cultural identities (Sufi and Scottish). The dynamics of urban life are explored in the *City* strand. Carol Morley's *I'm Not Here*, gives a subversive and humorous voice to the 'check out' girl, exploited on the one hand by chainstores and disregarded by the general public on the other. In the *Mortality* section, German artist Knut Gerwers' *Der Tod Ist* offers an iconoclastic view, a speeding collage of death and destruction featuring a dark, fragmented monologue from Klaus Kinski.

Balancing a mix of style, genre and format, these video compilations demonstrate the diverse range of personal vision that characterise this area of the visual arts: thought-provoking *and* entertaining; sometimes difficult, often challenging, but always compulsive viewing.

THE SCOTTISH ARTS COUNCIL

Presented by New Visions

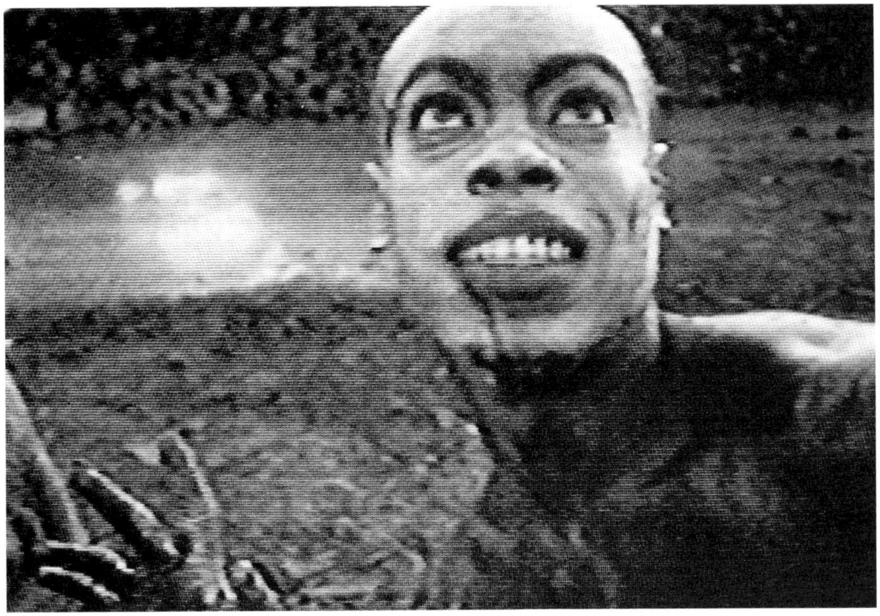

Isvan Kantor *from* Babylon 1994 *video still*

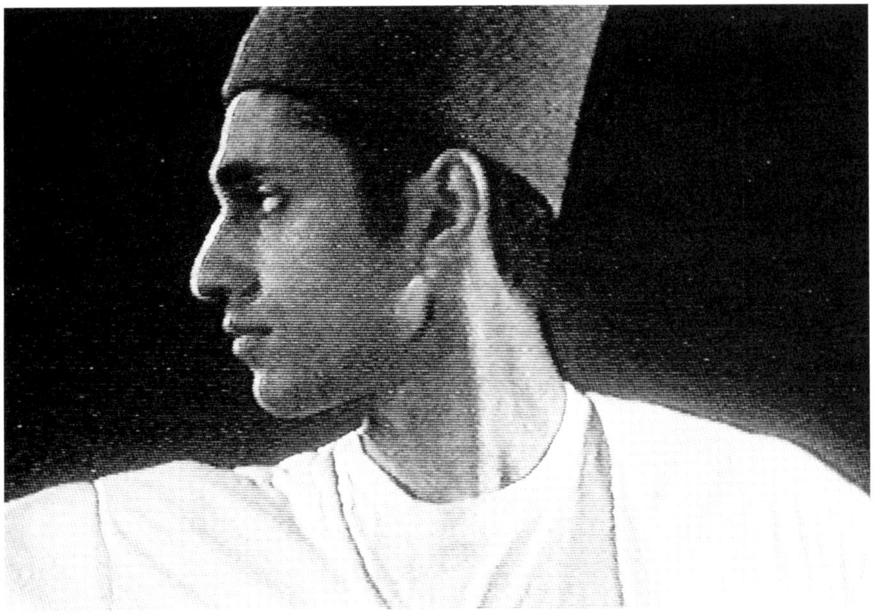

Shafeeq Vellani *from* Darwish 1994 *video still*

Mortality

FINDING A CONTINUUM

ALLEN FRAME

When I first started photographing, at the age of twenty, I was studying art history in college, and the painter that most captivated me was Caravaggio. In his early paintings of indolent androgynes, the *Self-Portrait as Bacchus*, *Boy With a Basket of Fruit*, *Concert of Youths*, and *Boy Bitten by a Lizard*, from around 1593–94, there is a strange atmosphere, erotic and melancholic, charged with foreboding. The young men of his paintings, sometimes impish, are also knowing – seers, angels, and whores all in one.

Their promiscuous gaze offers dark advice: everything is *not* going to work out alright. That implicit warning escalates to outright horror in later works. The pretty boy becomes a crazed Medusa in a painting of 1597, or, still as youthful, becomes Isaac, contorted with fear, his father's knife to his throat, in *Sacrifice of Abraham*, 1603. In *Judith Beheading Holofernes*, from 1598, the youth has turned into Judith, strangely distanced from her own bloody deed, as the artist's identification shifts to the older figure, Holofernes, a self-portrait, his head severed but preserving an expression of anguish and shock.

In *David With the Head of Goliath* from 1609–10, the artist inhabits both major roles – conqueror and victim, hero and villain. David is an echo of Caravaggio's earlier androgynous youth, and Goliath is the artist grown up, raging against dire circumstances. There is a strong demonstration of existential alienation in this split between youth and experience, life and death. As in the early, tender *Ecstasy of St Francis*, in which an angel hovers over the transfixed, supine Francis, there is a clear sense of the artist contemplating his own mortality and its psychosexual underpinnings.

In my early twenties, I was adrift, like Caravaggio's queer lads, with no grounding in the practical world and a lack of definition sexually. Entertaining fantasies of suicide, I romanticized the lives of artists. Diane Arbus had just killed herself, and I thought I understood why. She had squarely faced the most poignant contradictions in the human psyche and found them unbearable. I wanted to see the abyss for myself – and then check out.

My first model, synthesizing my young self with a version projected into middle age, was my mother. When I looked at her with my camera, I saw the same knowingness of Caravaggio's youths and a hint of the discontent of the middle-age man. She had an air of preoccupation, focused on a distant view beyond the immediate situation, and what she seemed to see was not a pretty picture. She appeared disturbed, disillusioned, or profoundly disappointed, as she looked back over her shoulder, walking through the yard with my grandmother, or picking figs, or standing in the garden.

She was 49 years old, an age I'm fast approaching, and things had not quite turned out as hoped – her children, for instance, and maybe her husband of thirty years. She was assessing and reassessing. At the time, in the early to mid-1970's, I was sure I was going to die by the time I was 30, and I wanted to witness life's extremes first. Without realizing it, I started to chronicle a friend's life in pictures. I started with a portrait and kept coming back, through a roller coaster experience of ups and downs as he swerved between the life of a demon and a saint. A few years older than I was, he was adrift, like me, but more profoundly so, or without brakes. His life over the time I witnessed it was not unlike Caravaggio's in the 17th century – moving constantly: a year in prison, a number of lovers from ex-cons to mafiosi, and with many nights of drunken carousing. Through it all, he could never find a place for himself until finally, the one he chose was with his mother, a fatal mistake. Being too much alike, they dragged each other down and both died within a couple of years of each other. I chose a tragic subject unconsciously, drawn to my friend David Kain's intensity, sensuality, and the drama of his struggle. He spent six months in hospital and died a few months after he was released, on Christmas Eve 1981, of cancer.

And that experience, of my close friend's early death, was the experience that ushered in the Eighties. I was now living in New York, taking pictures of a gay demi-monde that barely hinted at the terrible undertow that would sweep most of them away by the end of the decade. By the Nineties I had looked at death, loss, suffering, tragedy, horror, over and over. As many people with AIDS have reported, suffering is hardly the only dimension of their experience. I discovered layers and layers of complexity in illness and its politics, with much to learn from and much to despair of.

Now when I think of art that represents a sense of mortality acutely in the way I have come to perceive it myself, Caravaggio is less compelling to me. That mystery of which he speaks has been unveiled. Instead, I have found another, earlier model, Pieter Bruegel the Elder. Although I discovered his work at the same time I was introduced to Caravaggio, it was only recently that I came to treasure it for what it says of mortality. A few years ago, passing through Vienna, I saw the fifteen Bruegels in the museum there and was moved. His vision conveys the transience and folly of human existence, but with complete acceptance, and without sadness – in fact, with humour and robustness, hardly the usual companions to the subject of mortality.

Unlike painters of the Renaissance just before him who staged their main subjects as the central event, large and in the foreground, Bruegel subverted tradition, drawing the curtain back on his conception of an earthly continuum, a cosmic mosaic crowned with incident, in which figures of historical magnitude, like Joseph and Mary arriving in Bethlehem, can be easily overlooked as part of the multitude of constant flux. And when he paints him falling into the sea, Icarus barely makes a splash in a landscape unaware of his plight, with the emphasis in the painting being on a farmer ploughing in the foreground. There is irony but no distress over this farmer's attention to the everyday at the cost of missing an event of mythological significance. That's just how things are.

Even when Bruegel catalogues the mores of his day in the painting *Proverbs* in which scores of figures act out all the Flemish proverbs, the potential for a heavy righteousness is mitigated by the larger cosmic view that even ample moral commentary is but a passing phenomenon, just a depiction of the shifting values of a particular time.

Whereas Caravaggio's sense of life's impermanence is suffused with sadness, Bruegel finds affirmation in his depiction of mortality. Life is fleeting, humans can be blind, selfish and stupid, but solace is in the flow of endless variety. Life doesn't end with you or me, and what satisfaction we don't find in individual experience can be found in a recognition of the larger continuum.

Allen Frame is an artist, writer and curator living in New York

Joel-Peter Witkin USA

Stills Gallery

23 COCKBURN STREET
EDINBURGH

UK PREMIERE

3 OCTOBER – 18 NOVEMBER

I have devoted my soul to the philosophical and artistic investigation of what it means to be human. JOEL-PETER WITKIN

Joel-Peter Witkin's work, the visual remnants of his personal exploration of life's pains and pleasures, goes beyond the provocative. The images cease to be literal portraits of humans in extreme situations. Both attraction and repulsion are fundamentally embodied in the work. His grotesque tableaux are not just scenes, but invitations to accept the repulsive, to contemplate the unknown and to face the horrific. Joel-Peter Witkin exploits the condition of being human (of being mortal and capable of accepting or denying that inevitable end) with an emphatic personal involvement. His work is a philosophical study of abjection in which the power of horror becomes a tool he uses to expose the inescapable truth of human destiny.

His work melds the base and contemptible with the sublime and the peaceful. Horror is not contained purely in the aesthetic, rather, it is the fact of its possibility that both terrifies and attracts the viewer. He pushes forward towards realities which the viewer might prefer thrust aside but which must be faced in order to live honestly.

Ignorance is a privilege (and if not, then denial certainly is) when approaching issues of fearful contemplation. Joel-Peter Witkin's imagery reaches beyond its own shock value. His vision, coupled with a dark imagination, expands upon and seeks to transcend, the repulsive attributes of his subject matter.

Based on a text by Stephanie Sehlach, Tuscon

THE SCOTTISH ARTS COUNCIL

Presented by Stills Gallery in collaboration with Fotofeis

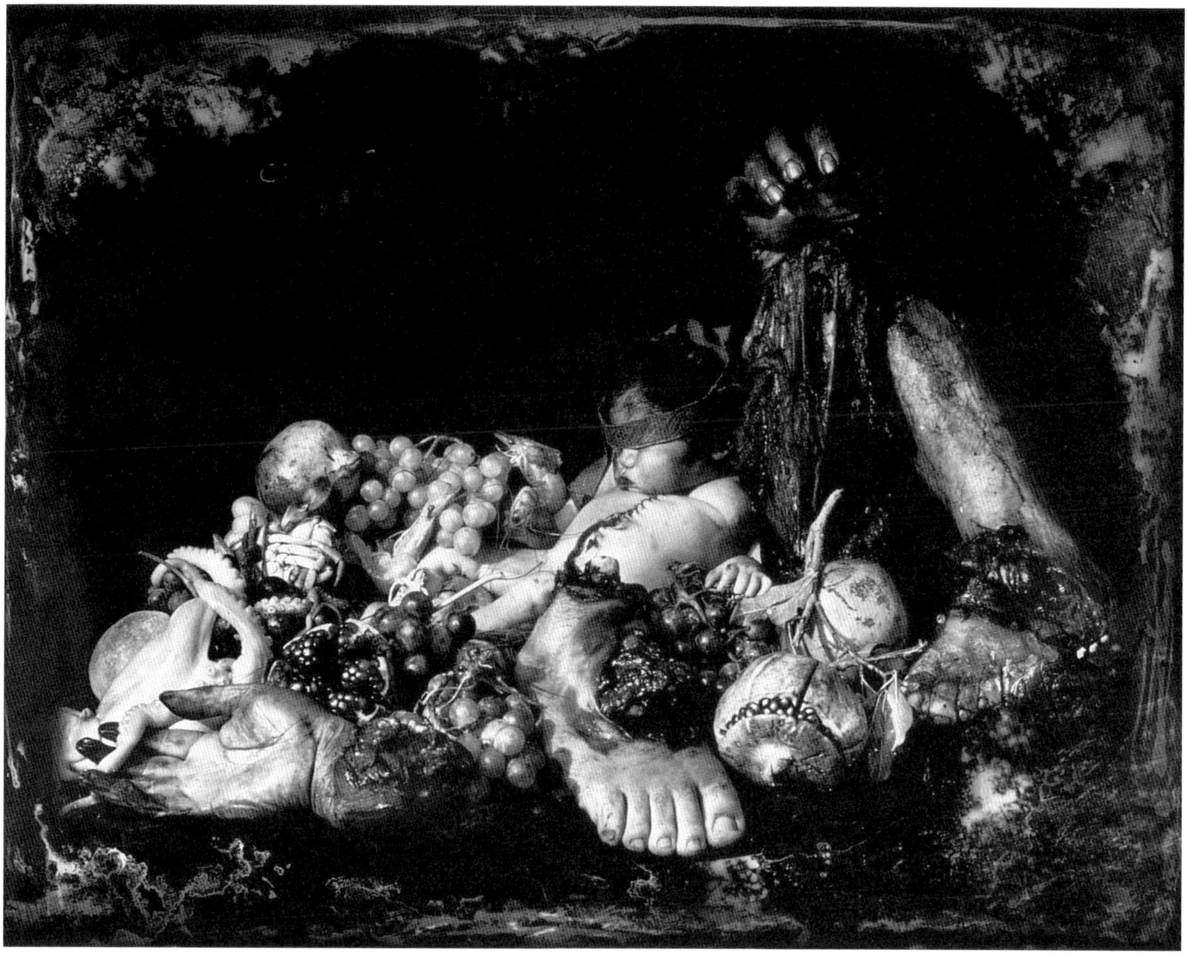

Joel-Peter Witkin Feast of Fools, Mexico 1990 *toned, silver-gelatin print (courtesy of Pace-MacGill Gallery)*

DONIGAN CUMMING *Canada*
Harry's Diary

Tramway

25 ALBERT DRIVE
GLASGOW

UK PREMIERE

6 OCTOBER – 12 NOVEMBER

In 1987 Donigan Cumming came into possession of an archive of autobiographical writing, the letters and diaries of a friend who had recently died at the age of 50. His name was Harry Strong. The material covered two periods of personal crisis, both centred on romantic relationships. Harry and Donigan Cumming had been friends since 1970. During one of these episodes they even lived as neighbours – but both of these events occurred without the artist's knowledge.

Before Harry's death all Donigan Cumming had were a few snapshots of him and his apartment. His letters and diaries gave a better understanding of his life. His relationships had failed for very ordinary reasons, but his manner of dealing with them, his examination of the facts, led him to futile repetition. He seemed completely encircled by disappointment and perceived betrayal.

Harry's Diary is composed of photographs, a 'wallpaper' of text and a soundtrack. There are three male voices on the soundtrack – a man reading from the diaries, the artist's comments in response and a man singing. The female voice and the woman who appears in most of the photographs is Nettie Harris, a former journalist and actress who died in 1993 at the age of eighty one. She poses with six models.

In its romanticism and in its redundancy, Harry's Diary was originally conceived as a counterpoint to an extended portrait of Nettie Harris which the artist had been making for a number of years. These photographs of Nettie Harris drew from the repertoire of her experiences, both real and imagined. She never knew Harry Strong.

Presented by Fotofeis in collaboration with Tramway

CONSEIL DES ARTS ET DES LETTRES DU QUÉBEC

Québec

AIR CANADA

CANADIAN HIGH COMMISSION

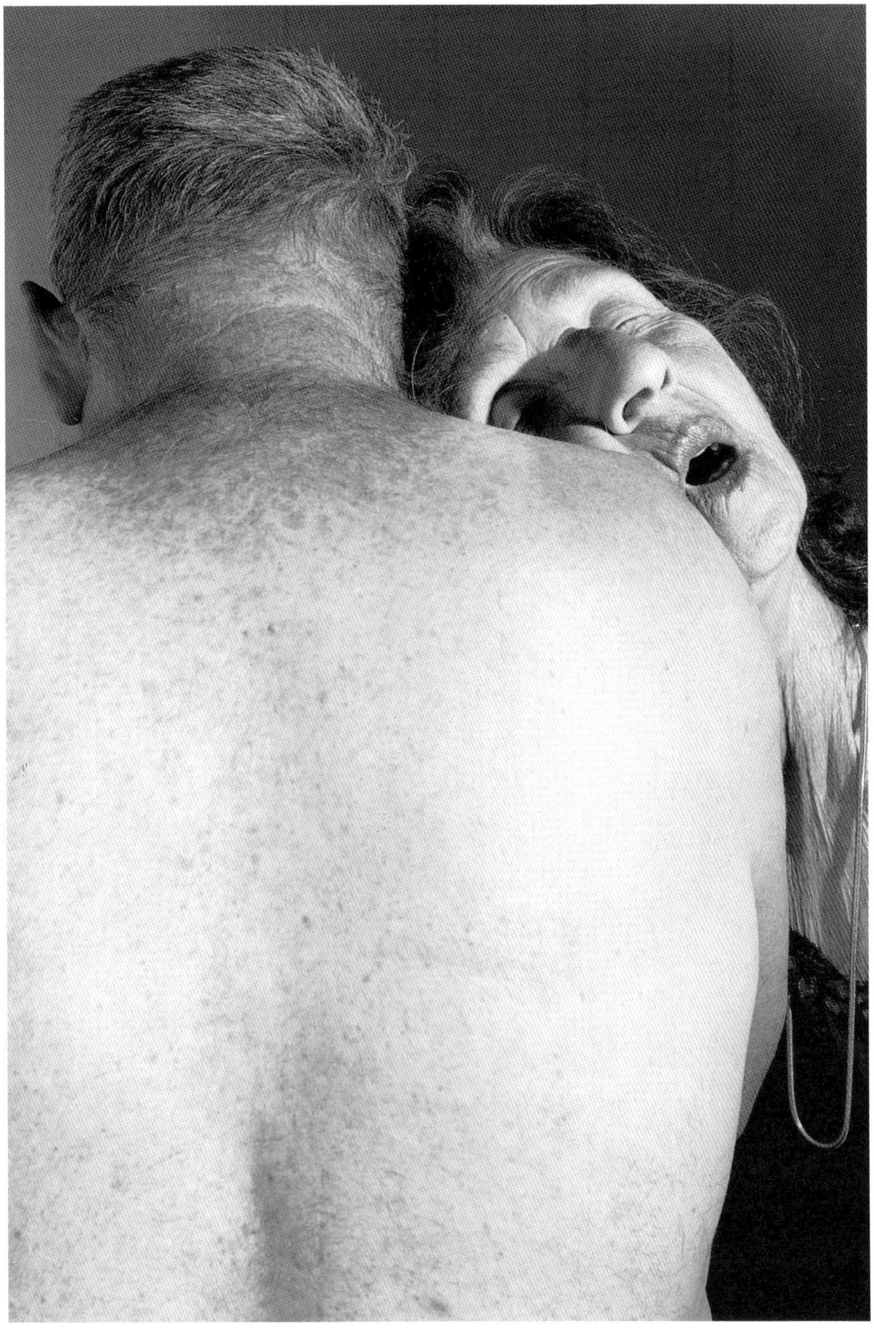

Donigan Cumming © *from* Harry's Diary 1992 *silver-gelatin print*

COLIN GRAY *Scotland*
The Parents

Maclaurin Art Gallery

ROZELLE PARK
AYR

PREMIERE

5 OCTOBER – 4 NOVEMBER

This exhibition is the fruit of a fifteen-year project documenting the artist's own parents, reflecting upon domestic ritual, the ageing body and the denial of old age. Presented in three sections, each made at a different point in its development the project has a compelling psychological truthfulness.

The opening section consists of narrative, staged scenarios – highly coloured works which spring from the artist's fantasies about his mother and father. In them, his parents are active collaborators in constructing the mood and meanings of the scenes. These images have a relaxed, playful quality resonant with the new-found freedom of early retirement.

In an abrupt change of mood and scale, the second section makes poignant comparisons between the worn-out carpets, furniture and utensils in the family home and the surface detail of his parents' ageing bodies. The large colour prints which expose a hidden world of translucent skin, broken capillaries and liver marks are filled with a sense of the strangeness, the 'otherness' of the body.

The final works continue this interrogation to look inside the bodies and possessions of his mother and father using the medical technologies of Magnetic Resonance Imaging (MRI), Computerized Tomography (CT scan) and X-ray. It is as though in embracing these objective, scientific modes of examination, the artist is emotionally distancing himself in preparation for his inevitable loss. This is heightened by the mode of presentation for, illuminated from behind, these have a sombre, ecclesiastical quality, like stained glass windows.

Over the course of the project, Colin Gray's increasingly intimate work with the ageing couple treads a compelling but uneasy line between the personal and the objective. From the high camp, colour-saturated burlesque of the opening images, to the sombre monochrome and almost brutally objective light-boxes, the artist faces up to the disconcerting shift of dependence that affects each generation in time, and through this touches on the profound if unsensational facts of human mortality.

A Fotofeis touring exhibition

THE SCOTTISH ARTS COUNCIL

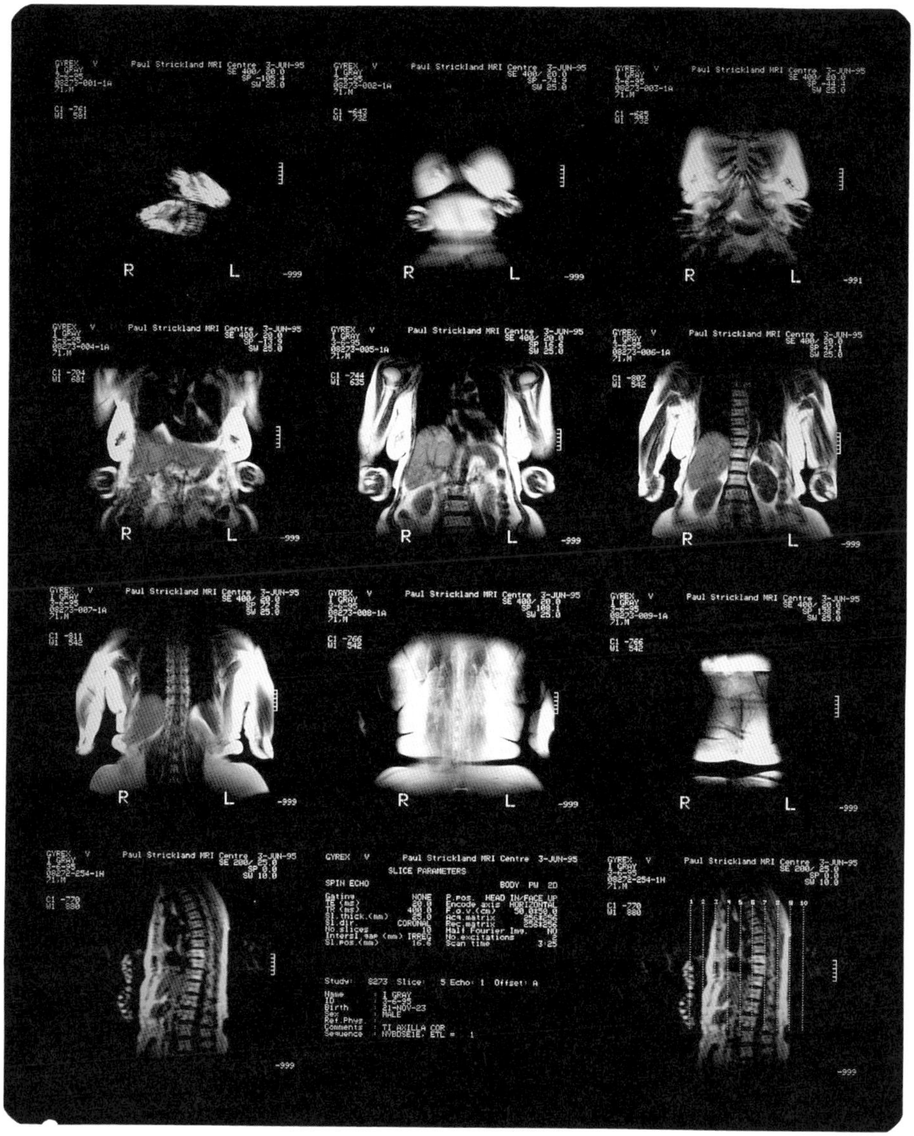

Colin Gray untitled 1995 *magnetic resonance image*

BLACK BUTTERFLY
Images of Death from Mexico

Aberdeen Art Gallery

SCHOOLHILL
ABERDEEN

PREMIERE

7 OCTOBER – 5 NOVEMBER

When a Mexican dies a black butterfly is said to have crossed the threshold of their house and a black bow of mourning is tied over the doorway. Pre-Columbian beliefs still prevalent in Mexico, adhere to the notion that the dead are always with us. Looked at from this perspective, the early photographic images of dead relatives (especially young children) take on a particular meaning. They are not only kept in remembrance, but because these people are considered to be still a part of the family. Thus it is that pictures, even of a relative long dead and perhaps never known, sit on the mantlepiece or altar of the home and are taken on the candle-lit processions to the cemetery to assist at the celebrations of the Day of the Dead.

This familiarity with death has another dimension – that of the omnipresence of death as the 'familiar friend' or 'fellow traveller'. The monumental photographic documentation of the Mexican Revolution bears witness to death in its most immediate extremes of violence: the death of warriors who lie destroyed and bleeding in the midst of their comrades. Alongside this one can consider the radical satires of the contemporary cartoonist Posada, which show us death in every social class, from the most affected bourgeois lady to the most vindictive mercenary.

Death can even be tamed through fiesta, when it is a figure who pokes fun at the ridiculous, or itself becomes an object of ridicule. The Day of the Dead is a banquet of sugar skulls, jelly skeletons and special cakes. Yet Death's festival has been given a more sinister aspect in the work of several more recent photographers, including Manuel Alvarez Bravo, Gerardo Suter and Eniac Martinez. Their work stresses less its folkloric surface than its more allusive and ambiguous undercurrents. This ambiguity is nowhere better exploited than in the masquerades depicted by Graciela Iturbide. In her depictions of Janus, angels and Death itself, the figures are neither quite male nor female: neither human nor ethereal. This exhibition explores the often intensely personal images of death in its many guises found in Mexico, and coincides with celebrations of the Day of the Dead at the beginning of November.

Presented by Aberdeen Art Gallery in collaboration with Fotofeis

Curated by Amanda Hopkinson

VISITING ARTS

b2 EXHIBITIONS

Embassy of Mexico

Relaciones Exteriores, Mexico D.F.

Centro de la Imágen, Mexico D.F.

Subsidised by City of Aberdeen

THE SCOTTISH ARTS COUNCIL

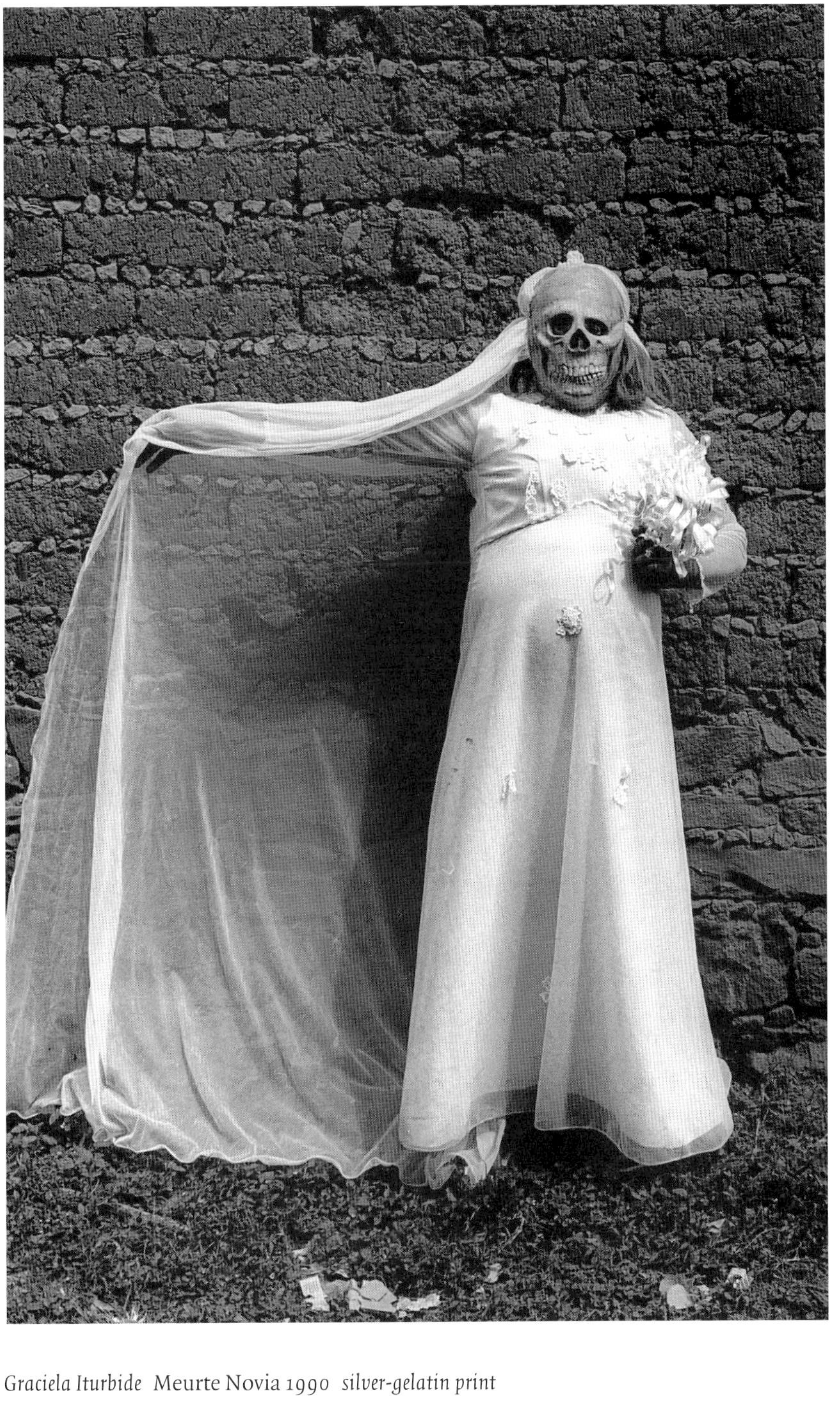

Graciela Iturbide Meurte Novia 1990 *silver-gelatin print*

Reminiscences

Aberdeen Art Gallery

SCHOOLHILL
ABERDEEN

PREMIERE

7 OCTOBER – 5 NOVEMBER

DÖRTE ESSFELDT
Germany

PAUL DEN HOLLANDER
Netherlands

THOMAS LENDEN
Germany

FRANS VAN LENT
Netherlands

GERT-JAN VAN ROOIJ
Netherlands

Curated by Mirelle Thijsen

Subsidised by City of Aberdeen

THE SCOTTISH ARTS COUNCIL

Reminiscences brings together recent installations by five artists from the Netherlands and Germany. Much like archaeologists and natural scientists, these artists attempt to visualize the remains of life and death, cultural artifacts and genealogical trees. They all seem attracted by the silent isolated forms of human civilisation. In their photoworks they express a strong affinity with icons of organic decay. In the work presented they show us reminiscences of mortality. Here, they accentuate the evocative power of primitive forms. These artists are concerned with the permanent tension between rationality and systematic order, on the one hand, and spontaneity and chaos on the other.

The artists photograph solid and delicate objects as sculptures against a void. These static and fragile objects are often presented in monumental scale. They are photographed frontally, texture and matter is accentuated, their function is ignored. It is their vibrant, mythical qualities that count. The viewer is entranced by the aura of the 'object' photographed, by the affirmation of its existence.

Roses, armour and skin are the motifs of Dörte Eßfeldt's work, which are given an emblematic value: skin is vulnerable, armour protects the body and the rose is an ancient symbol of beauty. Paul den Hollander's extensive project *Hortus Siccus* (1990–93) is a systematic presentation of details of herbariums (collections established in the 19th century), whilst Thomas Lenden examines the traces of natural processes of evolution, individual ageing and spontaneous mutation. His work in *Reminiscences* is based on the morphology of different types of octopus. Frans van Lent's series of monumental cibachromes deal with death, decay and the underworld; and Gert-Jan Van Rooij's compositions construct visual enigmas from organic and manufactured elements, suggesting the conflict between civilization and natural chaos.
Based on a text by Mirelle Thijsen

Presented by Aberdeen Art Gallery in collaboration with Fotofeis

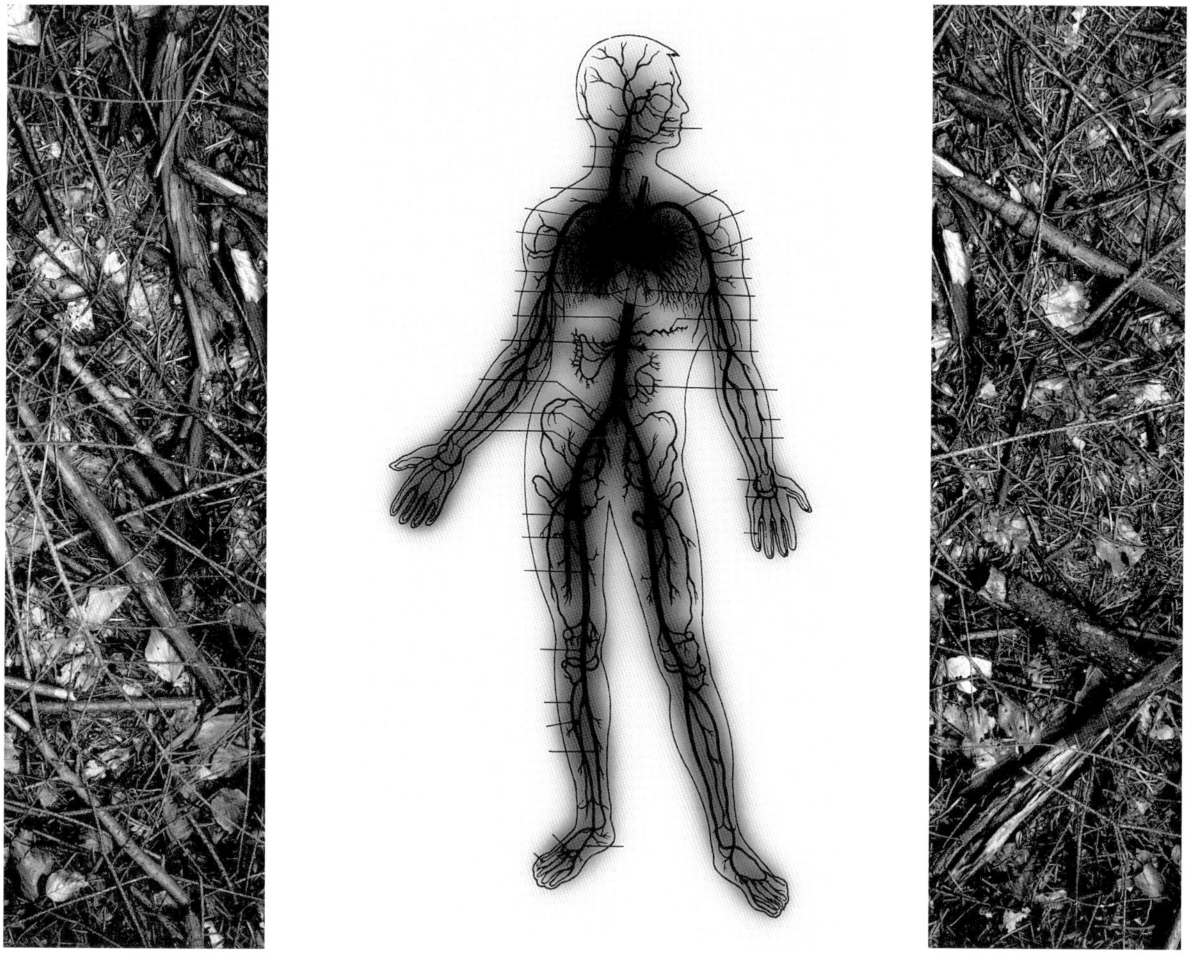

Gert Jan van Rooij Groundplan 1993–4 *mixed media*

ANDREA FISHER UK
Recounting

Portfolio Gallery

43 CANDLEMAKER ROW
EDINBURGH

PREMIERE

7 OCTOBER – 11 NOVEMBER

In this exhibition, commissioned by Portfolio Gallery for showing during Fotofeis, Andrea Fisher uses sensual and tactile imagery, sequencing and repetition to explore memory – both historical and personal. In these works, shared codes leave an inescapable imprint on even our most private moments of recall. Attempts to recount significant moments, public and private, are visually drawn into an apparent coherence, implying their continuity; yet that coherence fractures, leaving these two registers of experience irreducibly distinct.

Intimate images of hands are brought into proximity with found images of physical injury and death, but fail to meet. Images of a hand at rest in the privacy implied by a surface of white sheets are numbered, and seen in the process of being classified into piles on a crisp white clinical table. The image of a white sheet, drawn across the photographic frame, leaves a highly sensuous surface which nonetheless remains almost completely blank.

Yet in the midst of this intimacy, both acute and vacant, erotic and morbid, the shared conventions of digitised dates and times are imprinted into the very fabric of the images. There is a close-up of a dead woman, her hand still holding her purse, her hairband tossed into the street by her fall; although another equally ordinary hairband is displayed in a nearby vitrine, it remains irreducibly autonomous, leaving a silence at the centre of our attempts to recount.

Andrea Fisher has exhibited widely in Europe and the United States. *Impossible Relations* was shown at Gimpel Fils, London, in 1994. She lectures at Goldsmiths College, London and the Jan Van Eyck Academy, Maastricht, Netherlands.

Leeds Photo Litho

Jackson-Wilson Printers

Commissioned by Portfolio Gallery, Edinburgh

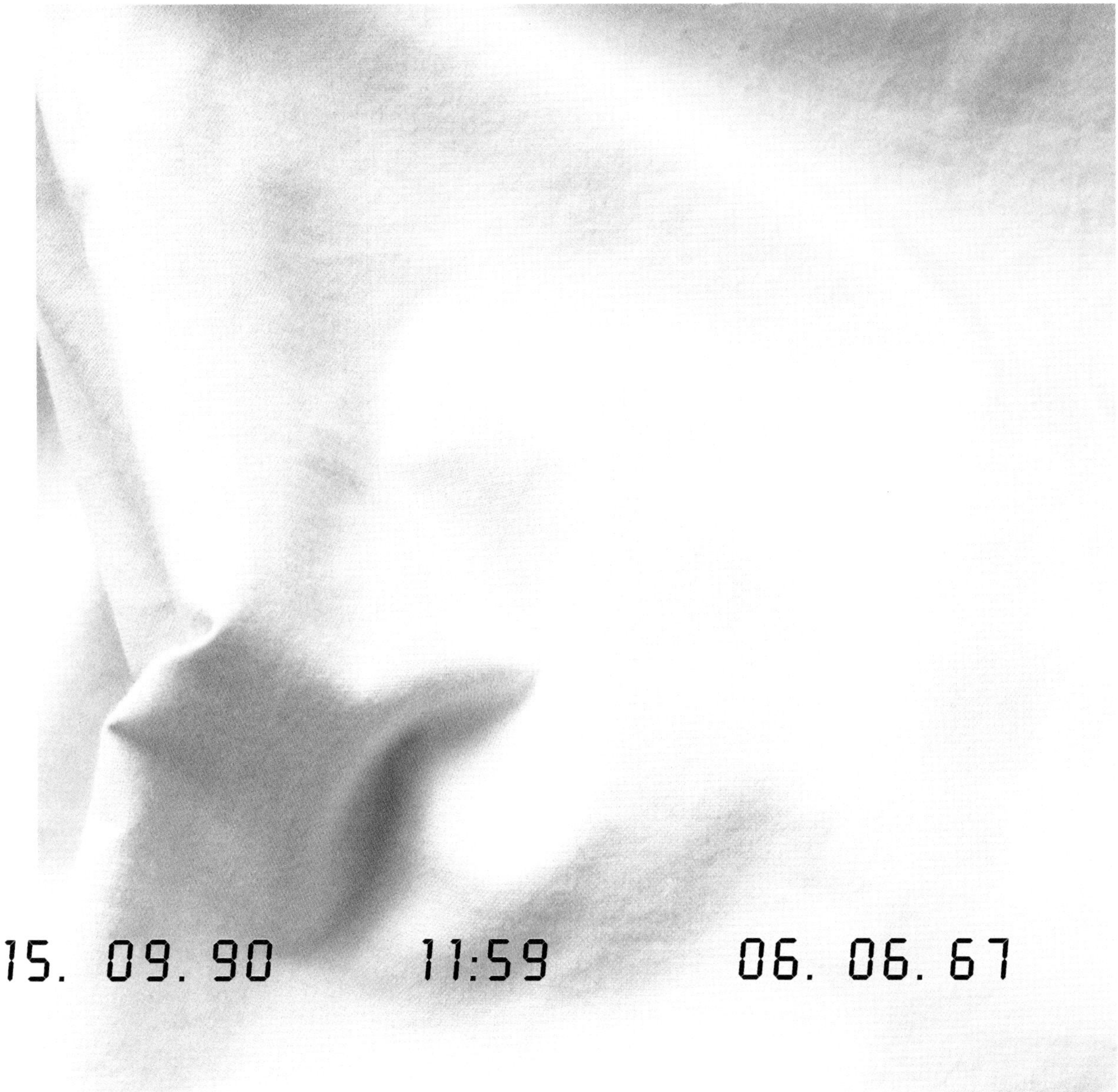

Andrea Fisher Recounting 1995 *silver-gelatin print with text (courtesy of Portfolio Gallery)*

LUCINDA DEVLIN USA

The Omega Suites

Aberdeen Art Gallery

SCHOOLHILL
ABERDEEN

EUROPEAN PREMIERE

4 OCTOBER – 5 NOVEMBER

b2 EXHIBITIONS

Subsidised by City of Aberdeen

THE SCOTTISH ARTS COUNCIL

In 1994, just before he retired, United States Supreme Court Justice Harry Blackmun reversed his long held opinion on the death penalty. He declared that "From this day forward I shall no longer tinker with the machinery of death". He was speaking symbolically of his role in the judicial process which affects how the death penalty is carried out in the United States. *The Omega Suites* comprise a more concrete view of the 'machinery of death'.

In 1991 Lucinda Devlin began a project to photograph the death chambers extant in the United States. What she found was both fascinating and horrifying. Since 1976 over two hundred and seventy people have been systematically executed behind closed doors under capital punishment laws, with the blessing of 70% of the American public. *The Omega Suites* show the death chambers behind those doors where the will of the people is carried out. These rooms, constructed for the specific function of killing human beings, raise important ethical and moral issues.

In centring on the killing apparatus, *The Omega Suites* coolly reflects back in full and frightening force the calculated methodologies of legal killing, leaving the viewer to speculate on what this implies about a society.

Presented by Aberdeen Art Gallery in collaboration with Fotofeis

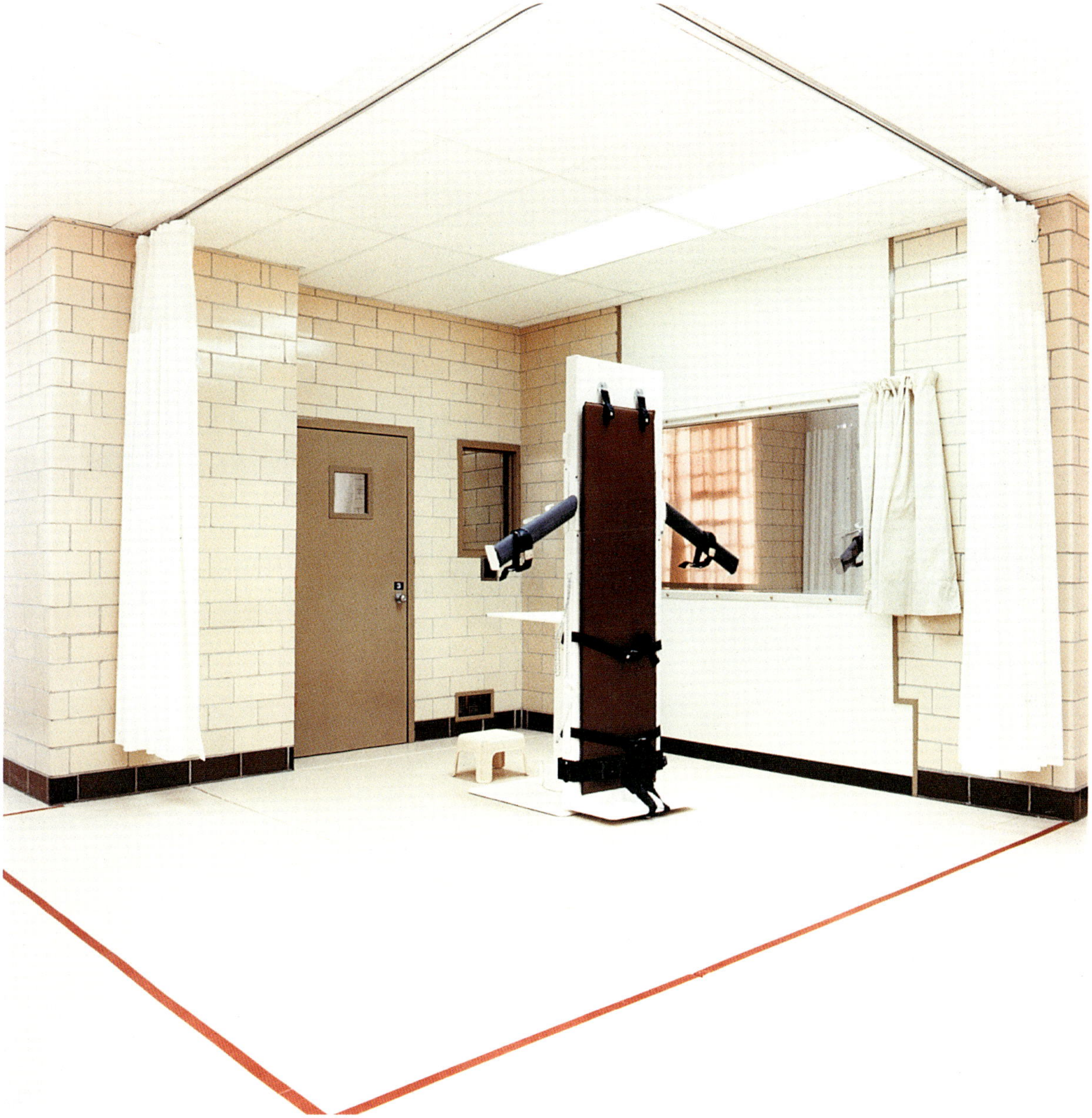

Lucinda Devlin Lethal injection chamber, Territorial Correction Facility, Cañon City, Colorado 1991 *colour print*

GRACE QUINTANILLA *Mexico* and LUCIA STUART *Scotland*

Ten Mexican Retablos

The Practice Gallery

50 VIRGINIA STREET
GLASGOW

PREMIERE

7 OCTOBER – 2 NOVEMBER

These ten computer manipulated, photographic prints each illustrate a true story of a miraculous escape from death. The work is based on the traditional Mexican retablo, a small, naive painting made on tin or wood which depicts a near-fatal incident and functions as an offering to the saint responsible for the individual's deliverance. They have the cultural layering of a robust and evolving popular artform. In an equally pragmatic synthesis of old and new, the artists use computer manipulation to create witty, narrative images of near-death situations.

An artist-run project presented in association with Fotofeis

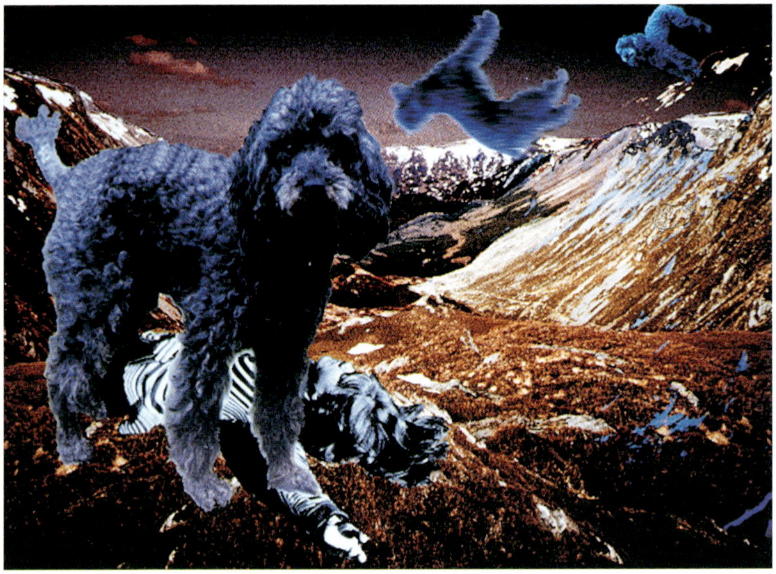

Grace Quintanilla and Lucia Stuart Suicide poodle crushes hill-walker 1995
computer manipulated colour print

GARRY FABIAN MILLER *England*

Observances

Pier Arts Centre

VICTORIA STREET
STROMNESS
ORKNEY

EUROPEAN PREMIERE

30 SEPTEMBER – 28 OCTOBER

Observances is Garry Fabian Miller's first exhibition in the UK for three years. It brings together a group of new photographs which continue the artist's preoccupation with light and spirituality. The abundant white light present in so much of the earlier work has been removed, to be replaced by dark fields, while a diffused white light activates the picture surfaces, bringing depth and apparent volume. Qualities of his earlier work are, however, still present, including the symbolic and emotional power of light and form. For the past ten years Garry Fabian Miller has been considering the true potential of photographic processes, in particular the direct relationship of light to photographic paper. More recently he has worked with other materials, notably oil and water, held within glass containers, through which light is directed.

Presented by the Pier Arts Centre

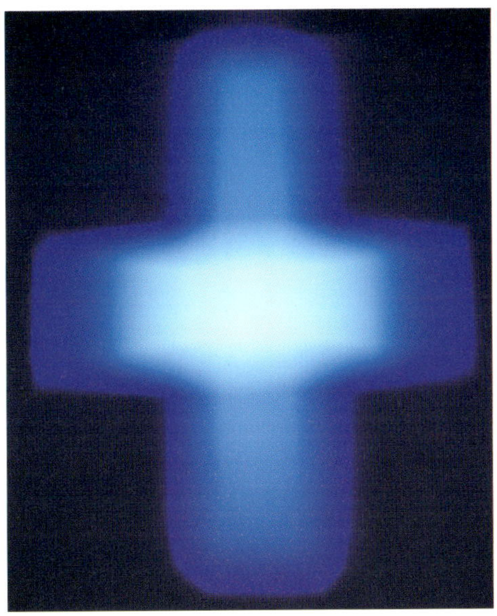

Garry Fabian Miller Good Friday 1994 *light-water cibachrome*

ROSE FARRELL and GEORGE PARKIN *Australia*
Black Room

Seagate Gallery

36–40 SEAGATE
DUNDEE

EUROPEAN PREMIERE

5 OCTOBER – 4 NOVEMBER

Rose Farrell and George Parkin have worked collaboratively since 1985. This commitment was the outcome of years spent together during which their life and art had become increasingly inseparable, and during which a unique visual language had been developed. The fundamental theme of their work is to communicate the mysteries and subterranean meaning of lost knowledge.

Black Room pushes this strategy further by taking advantage of the large and decrepit studios of PS1 and The Clock-Tower in New York, where Farrell and Parkin worked during a residency in 1992–93. Following *A Passion for Maladies*, a series that explored the now largely redundant clinical practice of bandaging which functions to both protect and to hide, *Black Room* deals with the obsolete medical technique of treating physical deformity using cumbersome and obtrusive corrective apparatus. 18th and 19th century accounts and drawings show what now appear to be instruments of torture but were once the machines of healing. The various apparatus used extreme means – suspension, counterweights and traction to force the deformed figure into a perverse approximation of the normal.

Used as the trappings of a theatre of the grotesque, these contraptions allow Farrell and Parkin a way of speaking about mortality through the human values of vulnerability and endurance.

Based on a text by Merryn Gates, Curator, ANU Canberra School of Art Gallery

Presented by the Seagate Gallery in association with Fotofeis

ARTS21

Supported by the State
Government of Victoria from the
COMMUNITY SUPPORT FUND

Australia Council for the Arts

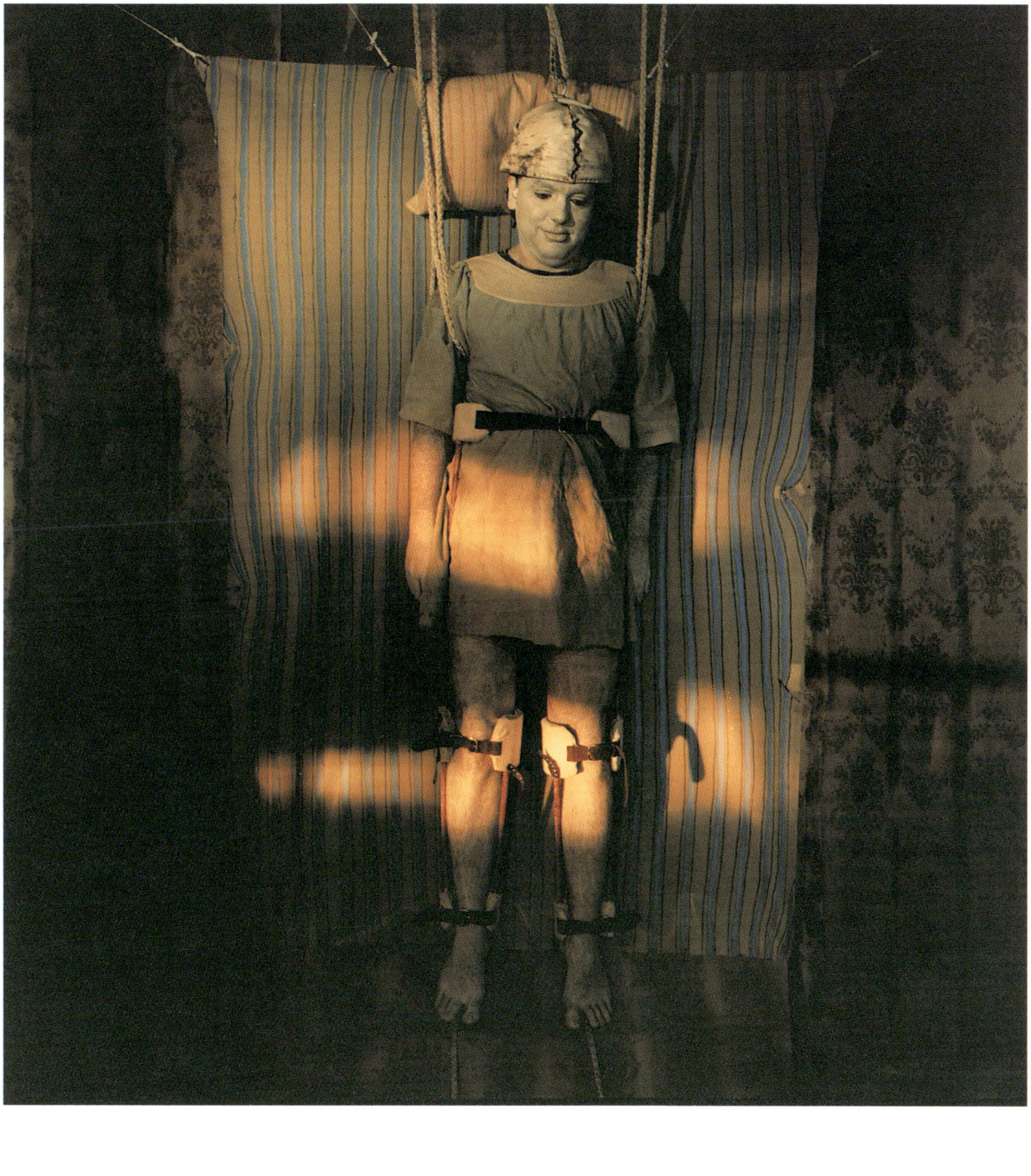

Farrell & Parkin untitled image #6 – triptych detail (central panel) 1992/93 *type C print*

FERNANDO ARIAS GAVIRIA *Colombia*, ROBERT FLACK *Canada*, BILL JACOBSON USA, STEPHEN ANDREWS *Canada*

Spirit & Loss

Kings Court

99–101 KING STREET
GLASGOW

PREMIERE

6 OCTOBER – 5 NOVEMBER

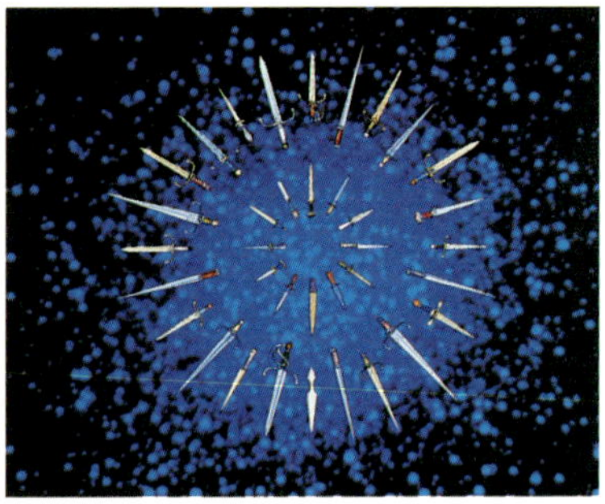

Robert Flack from Love Mind 1990
colour print and graphics

Many of the early exhibitions around the subject of AIDS and HIV addressed the anger, fear and political outrage felt by artists in the face of the epidemic and an unsympathetic establishment. *Spirit and Loss*, in contrast, involves work by four artists who deal with two interlacing concerns: the spiritual self and grieving for departed friends. While their work relates directly to the devastation caused by AIDS and HIV, the artists also seek to place the catastrophe within the more general cultural and emotional paradoxes which surround late 20th century attitudes to mortality.

Stephen Andrews paintings have a complex relationship to their original photographic source, 'in memoriam' portraits published in classified sections of the gay press of people who have died of AIDS. These are then faxed, the pixilated image providing the ground for a meticulous painted copy which is covered by wax. The images fade in time, making the work a many-layered contemplation of the invisible web of transmission and the vulnerability of the individual. Fernando Arias Gaviria's installation features a large image of a naked body placed on the floor. Illuminated by ultra-violet light, this dark and ethereal image of desire and memory floats in the darkness. Disengaged from time and space, it is recalled to reality by the livid red of blood specimens on glass slides from an HIV laboratory which are placed upon it.

Robert Flack's psychedelic installation, part eastern temple, part kitsch boudoir, weaves a rich tapestry of sexual energy. Faced with the failure of modern science to cure AIDS and the plethora of terminal diseases which still plague the late 20th century, he explores the holistic doctrines of Kundalini mysticism, which seeks to transcend the physical self and release a cosmic energy latent within. Bill Jacobson's *Interim Portraits* are black and white negatives, printed onto colour photographic paper, suggesting the tones both of flesh and of early photographs. These elusive, fragile images speak of personal and collective loss, and the fading of memory.

Presented by Fotofeis

Funded by THE ARTS COUNCIL OF ENGLAND

RAILTRACK PROPERTY

Glasgow City Council

AIR CANADA

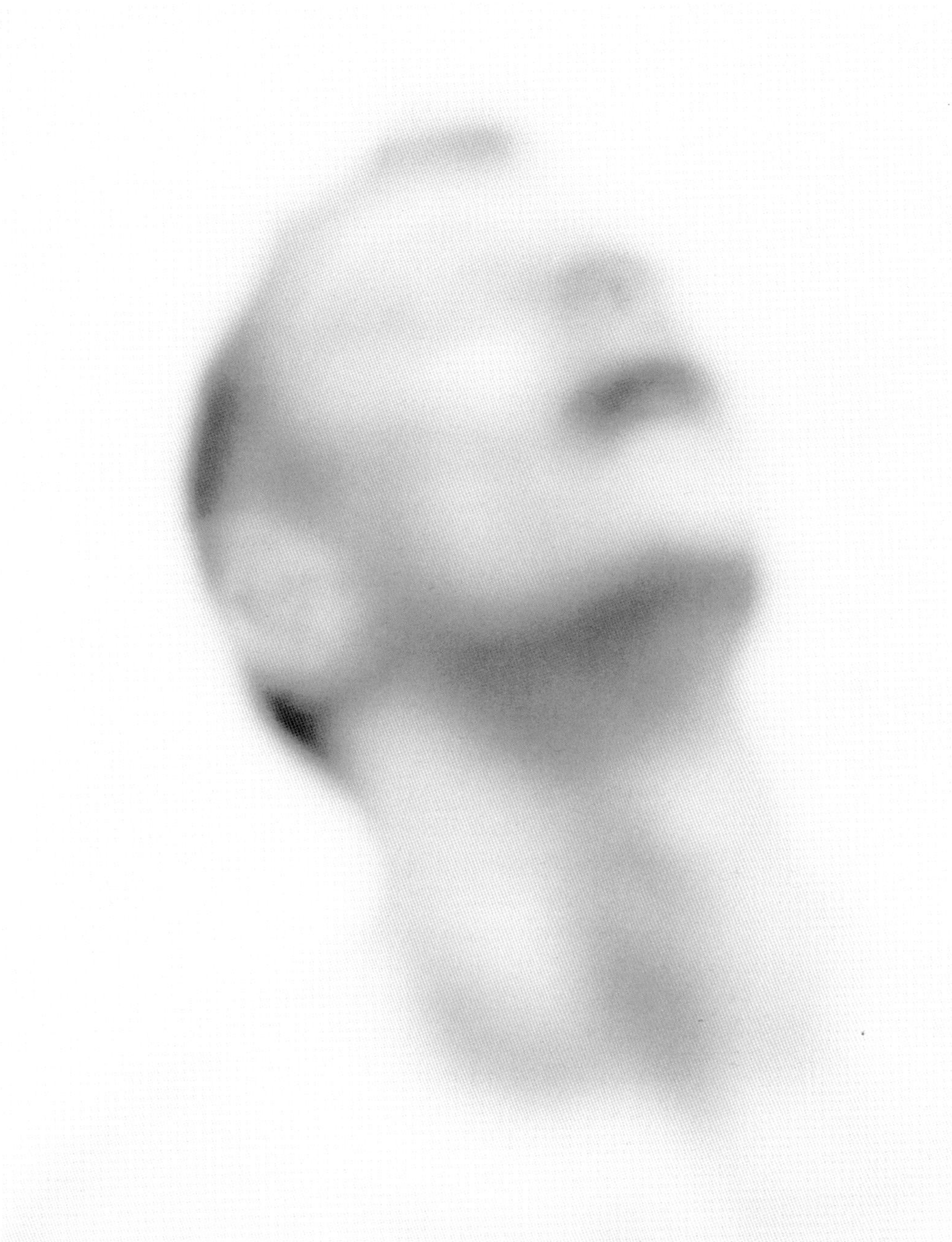

Bill Jacobson *Interim Portrait #378* 1992 *chromogenic print (courtesy of Julie Saul Gallery)*

ANDERS KJÆRGAARD *Denmark*

Collection

The Danish Cultural Institute

CARLSBERG HOUSE
3 DOUNE TERRACE
EDINBURGH

UK PREMIERE

5 OCTOBER – 3 NOVEMBER

Collection is a series of photographs of dead flies found by Anders Kjærgaard in the art galleries and museums of London and Berlin. The pictures are large, mounted on heavy sheets of galvanized steel and have a monumental, almost industrial presence. The flies are enlarged to about the same size as a small child and look just as substantial and vulnerable as they lie, crashed on the marble floors. Under each photograph is a reference number, the name of a museum and the date of the find: all neatly catalogued.

Yet this is not an entirely scientific project, or unemotional record. The descriptive detail of the images is reminiscent of the manner in which an old master might display and describe game on a tabletop. *Nature mort* takes on a very real meaning. These are sensual, sympathetic images. The flies serve as references to the places where they were found, the places where art is displayed.

Working on the principal that whatever one finds in art galleries exists within the context of art, the artist suggests that these flies have been overcome by art, indeed that they have themselves become art. They are tiny martyrs and their saintly remains are therefore also displayed – relics entombed in a glass cabinet at the centre of the exhibition.

Anders Kjærgaard's *Collection* is as comic as it is monumental; both aesthetic and satirical. He suggests that the status and veneration afforded to both religious and cultural artifacts is similar. Both require a willingness to believe, which is supported by the symbolic nature of the space in which the artifacts are presented. But he also leaves one with a disturbingly anthropomorphic view of a despised and disregarded insect.

Presented by the Danish Cultural Institute in association with Fotofeis

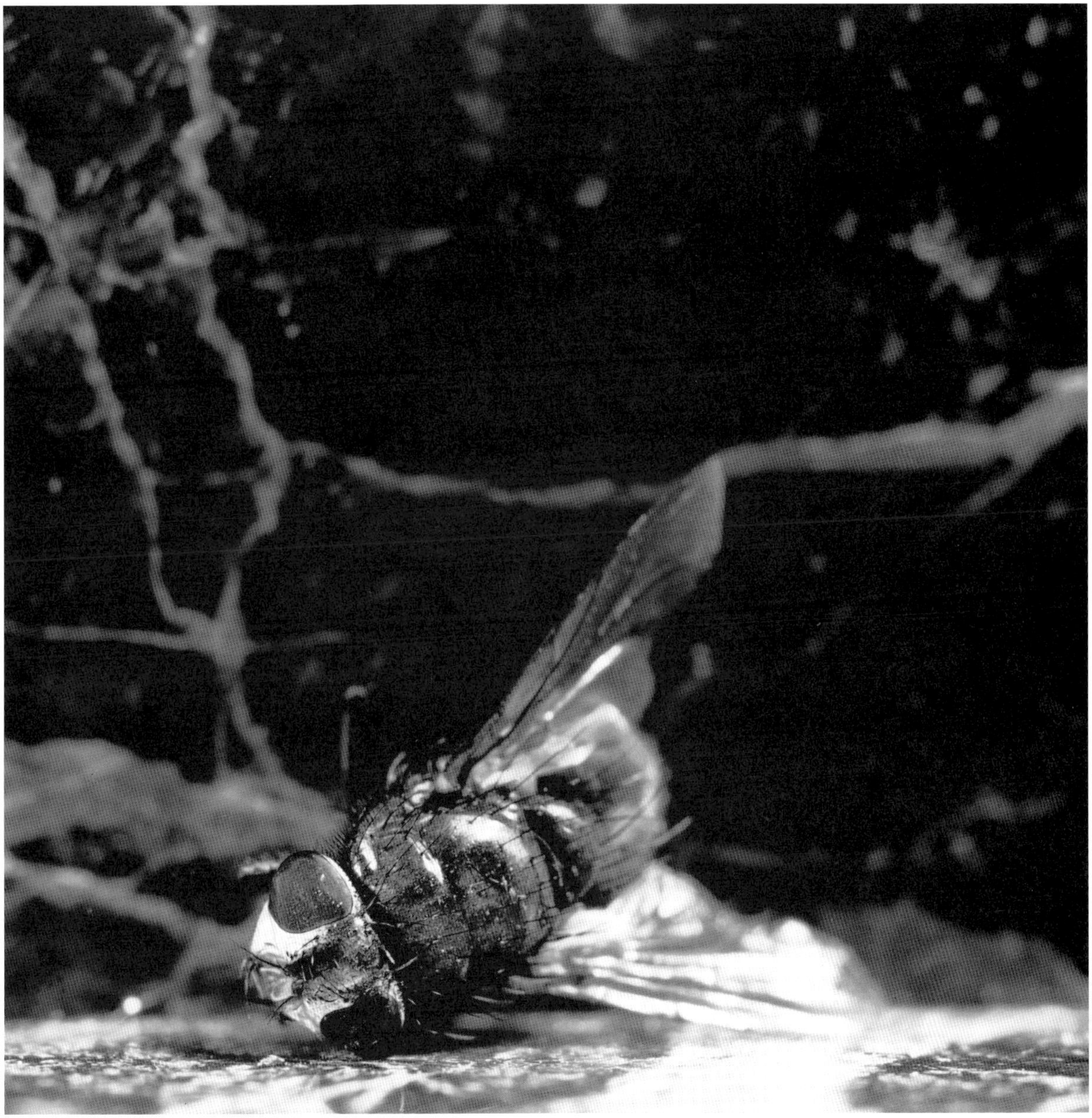

no. 10. museum of the moving image, london 09/05/1992

MICAH LEXIER *Canada*

A Portrait of David

Advertising sites across Scotland

EUROPEAN PREMIERE

OCTOBER – NOVEMBER

On Friday 26 November, 1993 an advertisement appeared in the *Winnipeg Free Press* asking, "Is your name David?". Over 400 Davids responded. Micah Lexier, who placed the ad, selected the first respondent of each age from one to seventy-five who were then photographed by the Winnipeg Art Gallery photographer, Sheila Spence. Each David posed individually, positioned with feet aligned to a tape mark, right hand covering left, and neutral facial expression.

The work used Lexier's own age and life expectancy as its conceptual foundation. According to the *Canadian Global Almanac*, the average Canadian male of thirty-three (Lexier's age at the time) can expect to live a further forty-two years. Each image thus suggests a point in Lexier's own life-span; situating himself as referent. In surveying the general, *A Portrait of David* suggests the specific and sets up a pivotal tension between the subjective and the objective, between self and others.

In this way the work functions as quasi-scientific experiment: age – the controlled variable; size, shape, race, class – the uncontrolled variables; photographic presentation – the constant. Each David's image resembles the others just enough to convey the work's conceptual motivations. The movement from age one to seventy-five allows one to marvel at the physical transformations and infinite diversity of the human form.

Based on a text by Lisa Gabrielle Mark

For Fotofeis '95 this work will be presented as an edition of three posters each containing twenty-five Davids, mapping three periods in the average male life-span. The posters will be shown in Adshel sites at bus stops around Scotland.

Presented by Fotofeis

Adshel

CANADIAN
HIGH COMMISSION

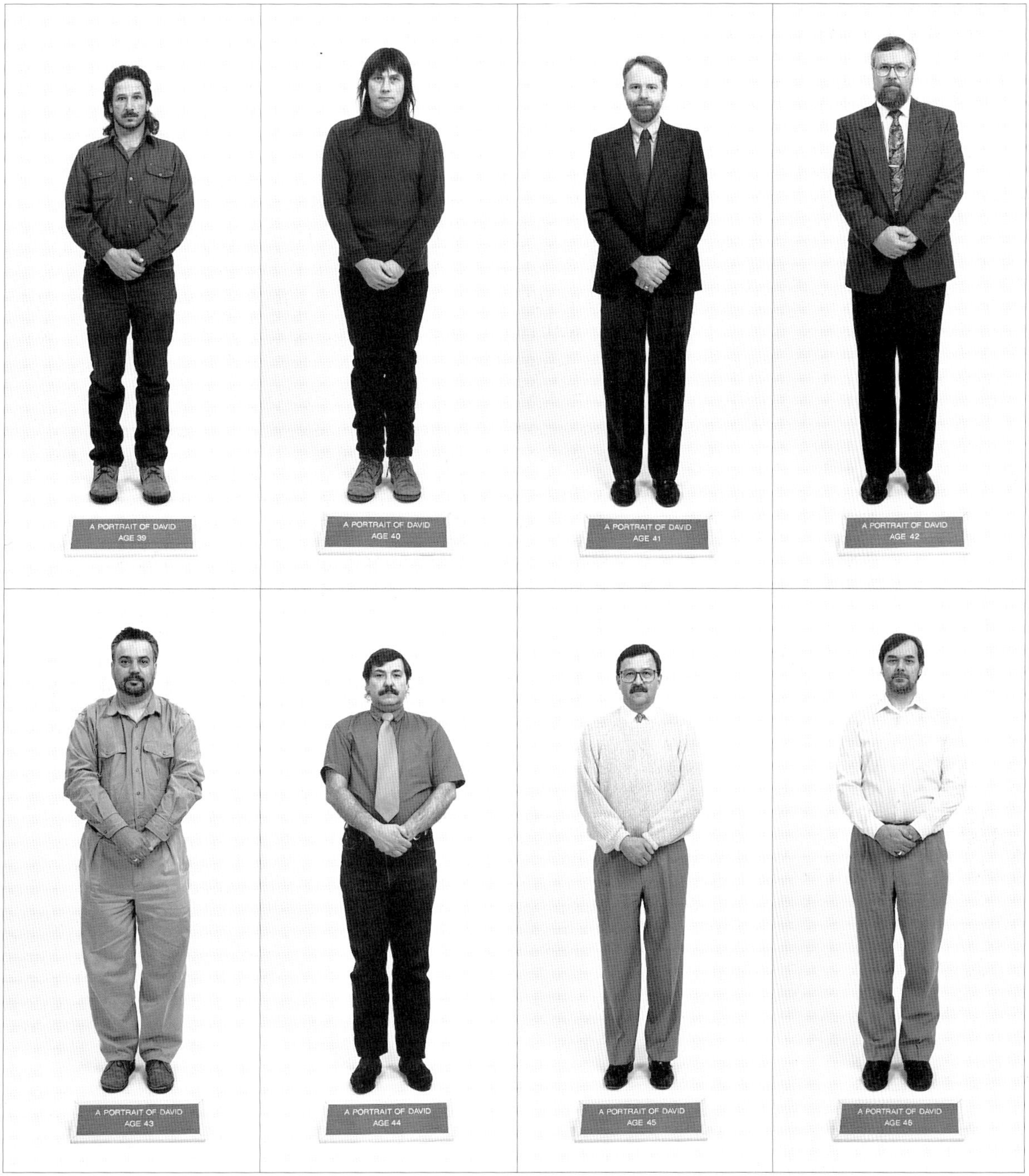

Micah Lexier *from* Portrait of David 1993 *silver-gelatin prints*

Ann Mandelbaum USA

Aberdeen Art Gallery

SCHOOLHILL
ABERDEEN

UK PREMIERE

4 OCTOBER – 5 NOVEMBER

The sensibility reflected in this body of work is variously creepy, lewd, comic and sensuous – sometimes all at once. The majority of Ann Mandelbaum's images involve orifices or the simulation thereof: cupped hands, the eye and ear in a few cases, but mostly mouths, seen in close-up, holding and apparently disgorging assorted organic objects. These include a horse-chestnut, green tomatoes, an eggshell, a dried peach half. There is a Rabelaisian quality to the deliberate conflation of the two ends of the digestive system; like the great French satirist she insistently reminds us of our ingestive and excretory functions as a way of grounding us in an awareness of our physical selves. Yet she does so with humour and genuine affection.

There is an aleatory aspect to Ann Mandelbaum's technique, which involves exposing the partially developed image to light and whose results are impossible to predict or control. She has managed to tame it, however, so that there is a flattened, oddly hermetic feel to her prints describing their subjects in rich, pewter tonalities. This intensifies one's awareness of the print as a thoughtful, patiently crafted object. The mood is consistently quiet and the understatement furthers the unnerving, sometimes grotesque nature of the imagery.

Based on a text by A. D. Coleman

Subsidised by City of Aberdeen

THE SCOTTISH ARTS COUNCIL

Presented by Aberdeen Art Gallery in collaboration with Fotofeis

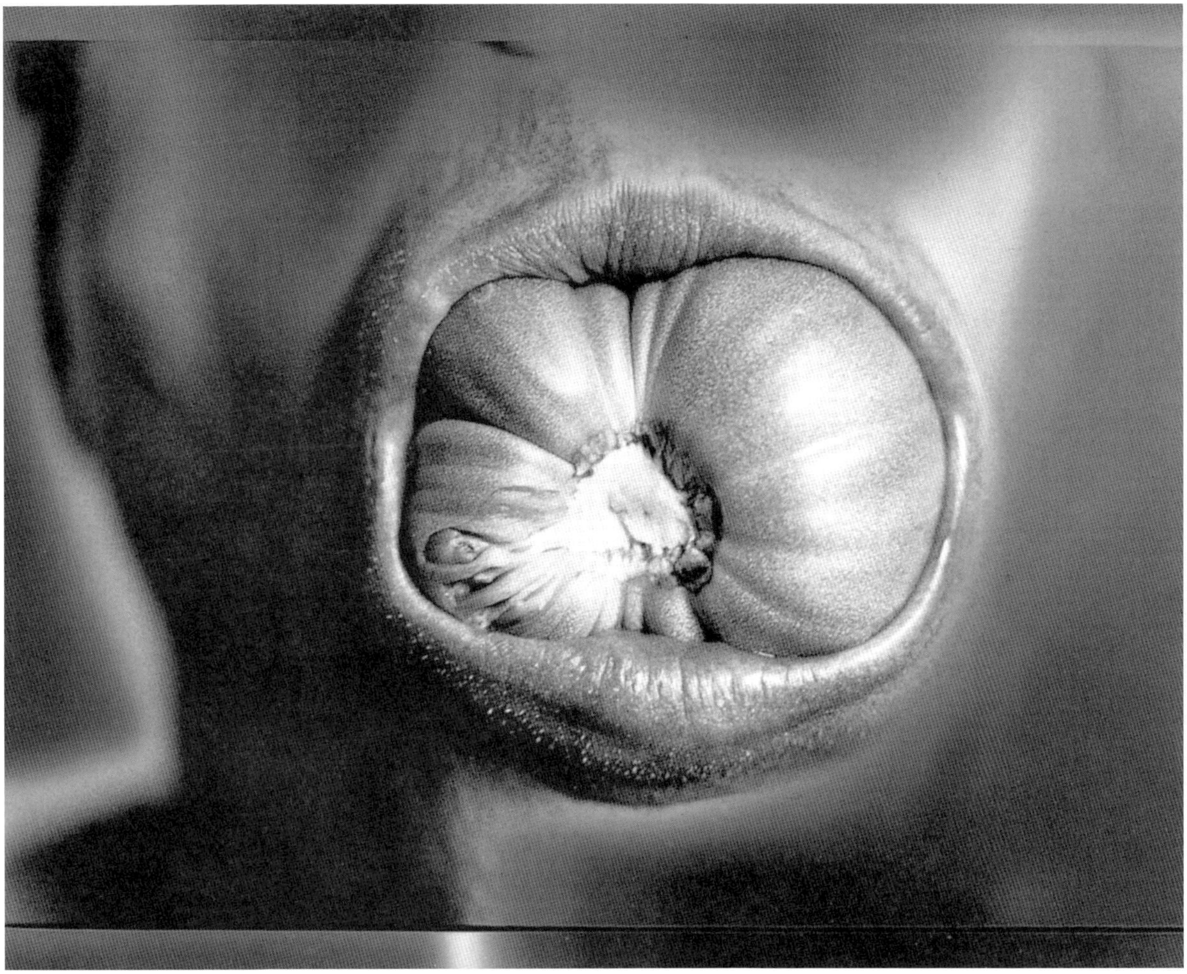

Ann Mandelbaum Untitled 1993 *silver-gelatin print*

TIM DALY *England*

All Weather Icons

Crawford Arts Centre

93 NORTH STREET
ST ANDREWS

PREMIERE

29 SEPTEMBER – 5 NOVEMBER

Nescot

All Weather Icons is a photographic documentary celebrating the visual properties of Roman Catholic statuary and imagery found at shrines and grottoes in Ireland. The pictures highlight the humour and poignancy manifest in the construction, decoration and positioning of these statues and religious tableaux.

Crucifixions, Saints and Calvary groups are found across Ireland, some at spectacular locations, marking out the far-flung territory of the Roman Catholic Church: wild mountain passes, rocky outcrops near the sea, and the roads that wind into remote villages all have their highly idiosyncratic figures.

Built by and for local people to withstand the harsh climate, their construction is simple and resourceful. Made of concrete, fibreglass and pebble-dash: material from builders' yards is more in evidence than that of a sculptor's studio.

Many are carefully painted: the heavenly aspect of the Virgin in 'Marian' blue, the mortal flesh tones and garments of kneeling devotees or the sallow complexion of a dying Christ. Some are adorned with real rosaries and halos of electric light bulbs. The decoration and embellishments are far removed from the precious, gilded votive statuary of Spain or Italy. Rather, they are in keeping with Irish folk art, the hand-lettered sign above the bar, shop-front ornamentation and the brightly painted figures to be found in many Irish gardens.

Presented by Crawford Arts Centre in association with Fotofeis

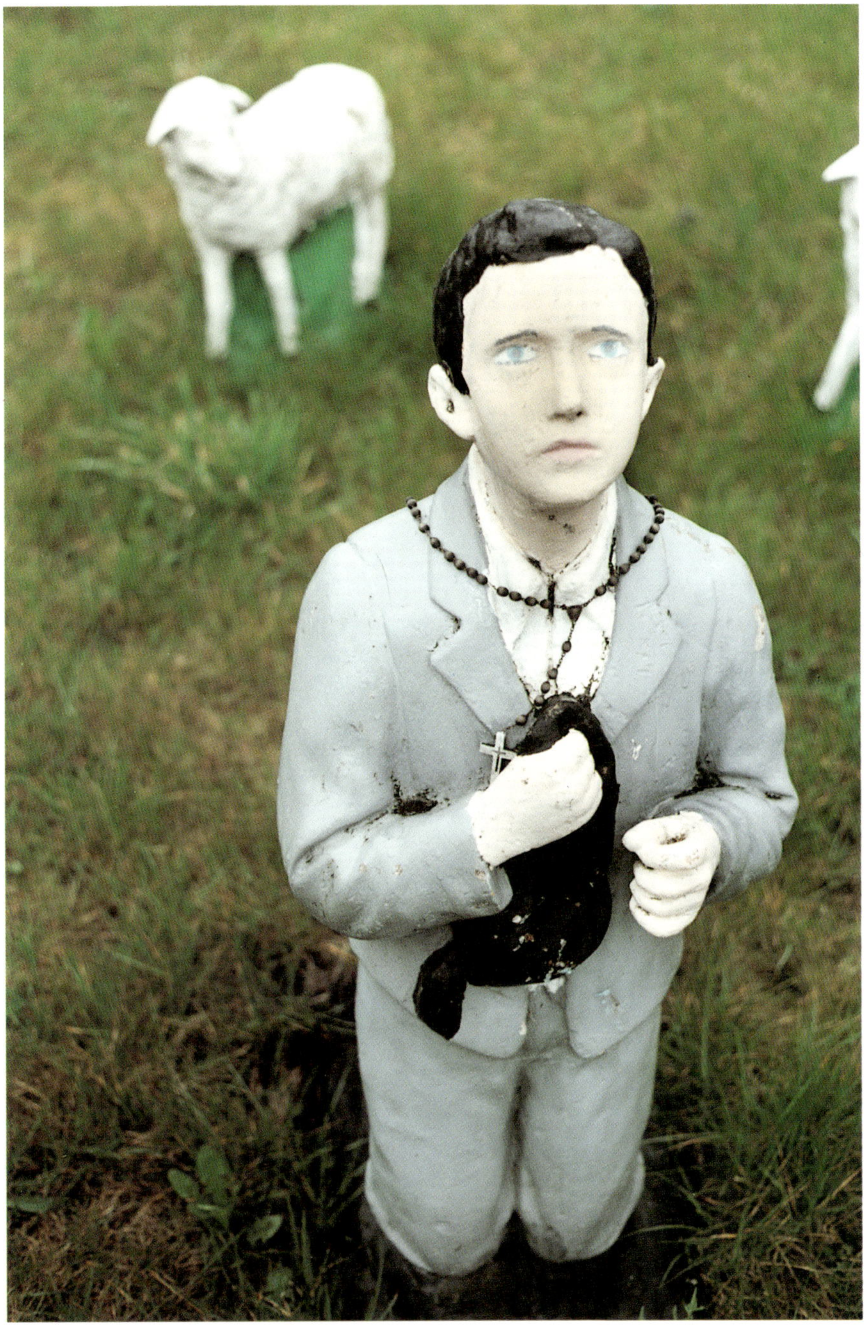

Tim Daly Traffic Island Statue, Cork City 1994 *colour print*

DAVID STEPHENSON *Australia*
Transfigurations

Paisley Museum and Art Gallery

HIGH STREET
PAISLEY

PREMIERE

5 OCTOBER – 4 NOVEMBER

Made in winter in northern Italy, two striking aspects come together in David Stephenson's *Transfigurations*. In the funerary images we see a few of many hundreds of photographs which he made of a particular form of memorial – photographic portraits of the dead screened onto marble and incorporated into headstones and crypts. Many of these images represent the deceased while still vibrantly alive, but what we witness is the inevitable erosion of these images as the elements corrode the surface of the marble.

The domes demonstrate quite the opposite. In these architectural monuments, the cupolas and their decorative schemes, so often cast into deep gloom by years of candle smoke and neglect, are brought to light. Long exposures counteract the dimness of these lofty spaces, and we are made conscious of their symbolism. They are representations of heaven.

Some cupolas are lit by lanterns, windows set in the curved walls below the dome. Others are lit by an oculus, a window which pierces the cupola itself. The oculus was meant to present an all-too-fleeting glimpse of infinity, of a paradise out of time, a sublime, awe-inspiring space beyond. In a curious way, the invention of photography created a representation of life which carried beyond death, by means of a new 'oculus', the camera. With the funerary photographs we are made aware, in the most remorseless fashion, of a life before death. Indeed, in the last 150 years another kind of 'afterlife' seems to have emerged, one peopled by millions upon millions of images of the living. Yet, as the funerary monuments bear witness, these images will in time 'die' and it is this inexorable reality which is represented so emphatically by David Stephenson in this exhibition.

Based on a text by Jonathan Holmes

Presented by Paisley Museum and Art Gallery in association with Fotofeis

University of Tasmania

Australia Council for the Arts

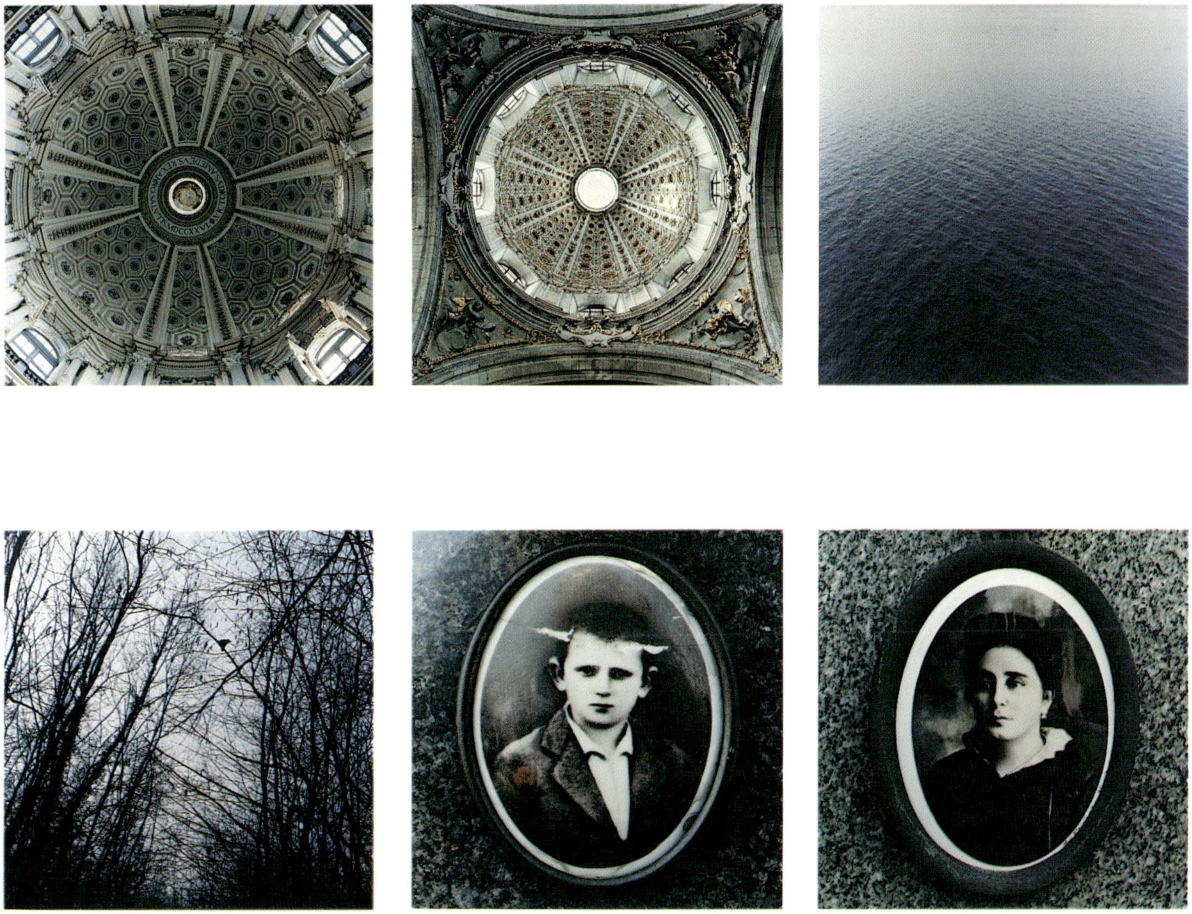

David Stephenson *from* Transfigurations 1993 *colour prints*

STEVEN MACLAURIN *England*

They Saw My Age and Not Myself

Motherwell Library

HAMILTON ROAD
MOTHERWELL

PREMIERE

5 OCTOBER – 3 NOVEMBER

Music by Ark Angel

Steven MacLaurin untitled 1995
floor mounted colour print

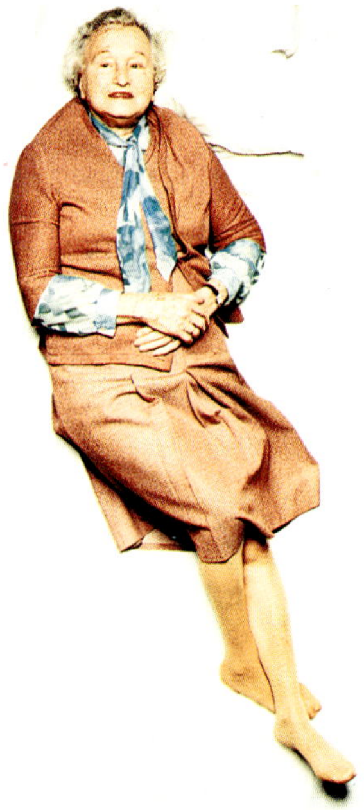

I thought getting old was going to be frightening, I thought life was like a wheel getting slower and slower, but it isn't. Getting older in itself is no threat. You just get better, richer, more varied, more faceted. Life has fed you enough vital material that you feel full all the time. It's society's attitude we need to change.

from *Older Than Time*, Allegra Taylor

In most countries the old are revered and respected for their wisdom, but in Britain people who have retired are then quickly excluded from full participation in society. They are the invisible generation. One third of all elderly people in Britain live in poverty.

They Saw My Age and Not Myself consists of large colour photographs of elderly people displayed on the ground, reaffirming their subjects' vulnerability and separation. Above each individual a continually changing sequence of projected images plays across a screen. The images here are taken from their photograph albums and each follows a familiar pattern, but each has its own unique disclosure of a social and personal history.

Presented by Motherwell Leisure in association with Fotofeis

SHEILA MACDONALD, JOHN PEARSON and ANGUS MONK *Scotland*
Caochladh

Museum Sgoil Lionacleit

LINICLATE
ISLE OF BENBECULA

PREMIERE

5 OCTOBER – 2 DECEMBER

Death – the end of this life or the door to the next? In Gaelic one can say, not that someone has died, but that she or he has 'changed'.

Caochladh (Changing) explores mortality and immortality through the distinctive culture of the Western Isles of Scotland. Sheila MacDonald uses underwater photography to explore the imagery of traditional laments, composed by women and sung to men who have perished at sea. John Pearson suggests a new life for dead, discarded objects from the local environment by imagining how they would be interpreted by someone from another place and time. Angus Monk contrasts the permanence of the land and continuity of the family with both the brevity of childhood and the changes overtaking traditional life on the islands.

Presented by Museum Sgoil Lionacleit

Comhairle nan Eilean

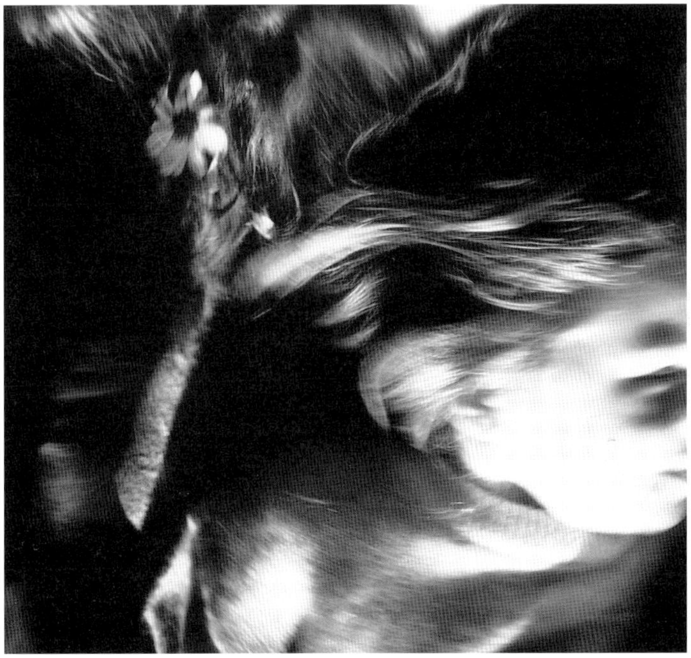

Sheila MacDonald untitled 1995 *silver-gelatin print*

DAVID NEWMAN *Wales*
Sanctum II

Marischal Museum

MARISCHAL COLLEGE
UNIVERSITY OF ABERDEEN
BROAD STREET
ABERDEEN

PREMIERE

10 OCTOBER – 3 NOVEMBER

Sanctum II concentrates on the equivocal beauty and fragility of the human condition. It explores the nature and role of disease (and our dis-ease with the mutability of human flesh) which is fundamental to our understanding of our own ephemerality and thus our true nature.

The installation consists of two large museum filing cabinets, each with many drawers, each drawer filled with hundreds of reference cards. The cabinets stand alone in a darkened, perfumed room, the scent based on the artist's earliest olfactory memory. The cards catalogue the artifacts within an imaginary collection, created by the photographic fusion of images documenting the extremes of human fear and aspiration – the eternal, perfecting surface of classical statuary and the dark, visceral secrets of the medical reference book.

David Newman's methodology is one of abandonment rather than control. His recent works have all involved him directly in either physical or psychological stress, which he admits have at times been terrifying to him. In embracing such intensity he seeks to reach a fresh insight into those most profound challenges to a positivistic view of life: suffering and the inevitability of death. He confronts the extreme forms of human physicality, which normally remain sanitised and euphemized in daily life.

In facing the fact of pain and suffering, David Newman seeks a fundamental truth: "that disease and creativity are intertwined and work against one another to propagate beauty". There is hope in the knowledge that despite it all, life goes on. And that is our future.

The Arts Council of Wales
Cyngor Celfyddydau Cymru

Presented by the Marischal Museum, Aberdeen
in collaboration with Fotofeis

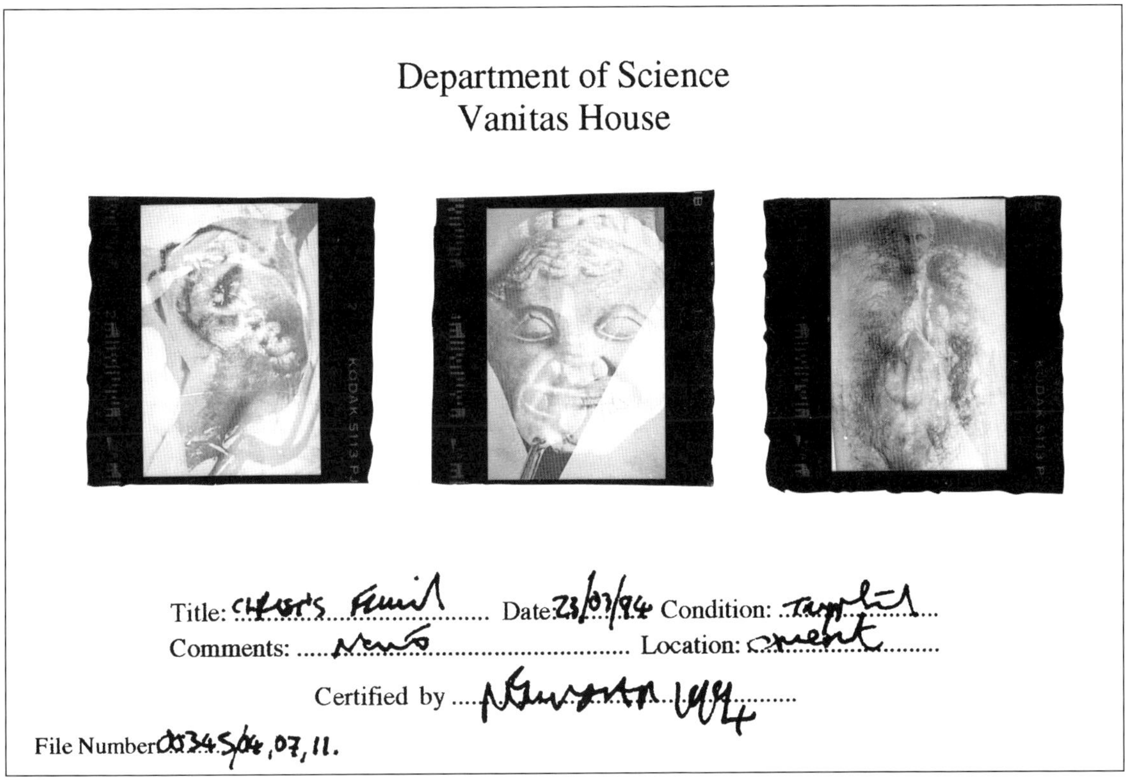
Department of Science
Vanitas House

Title: .... Date: 23/03/94 Condition: ....
Comments: .... Location: ....
Certified by ....
File Number 00345/04,07,11.

David Newman *index card from* Sanctum II 1995 *silver-gelatin prints and text on card*

ALLEN FRAME USA and LEON KOURY USA

Buddy & Frank

The Lemon Tree

5 WEST NORTH STREET
ABERDEEN

EUROPEAN PREMIERE

5 OCTOBER – 5 NOVEMBER

Buddy & Frank consists of two series of portraits depicting two young men in their twenties, taken by their older boyfriends over the course of a decade. Buddy is a young Polish dancer coming of age in New Jersey in the 1950's. Frank is a Cuban artist going through his twenties in New York City thirty years later. They are depicted in a range of moods and situations. Each diptych has its theme and motif – the lover at home, the lover on holiday, the lover with the family, at the beach, by the pool, with friends, nude.

Although Buddy and Frank never knew each other, the photographers themselves came from the same town in Mississippi and were close friends, though in age forty years apart. Buddy's photographer boyfriend was Leon Koury, a figurative sculptor who intended the photographs as studies for his sculpture rather than as formal portraits. Allen Frame discovered the photographs of Buddy in 1991. He was astonished at the similarity between his own depiction of Frank through the 1980's and Leon's earlier vision of Buddy. In placing the two bodies of work together, Allen Frame highlights the sense of inevitability behind those parallel depictions. The juxtaposition intensifies what is intimate and specific in the images, whilst creating a conceptual framework for wider philosophical reflection.

Art Matters Inc

Presented by The Lemon Tree in collaboration with Fotofeis

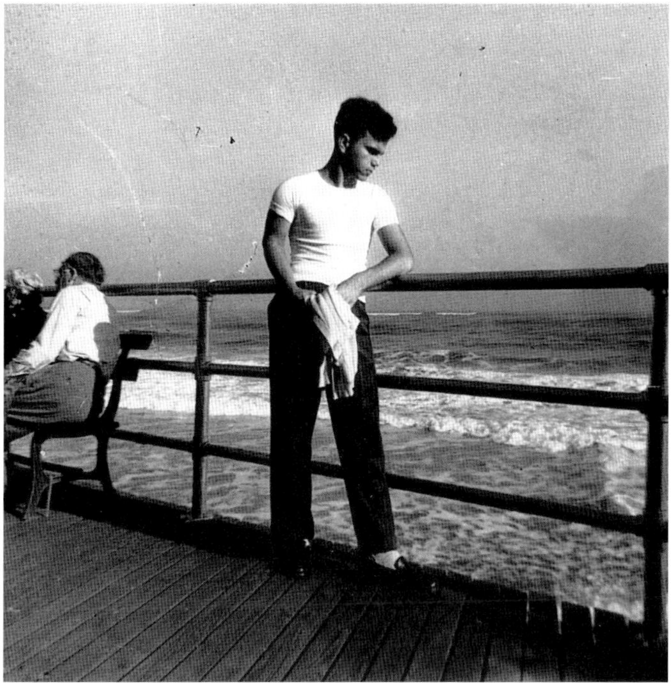

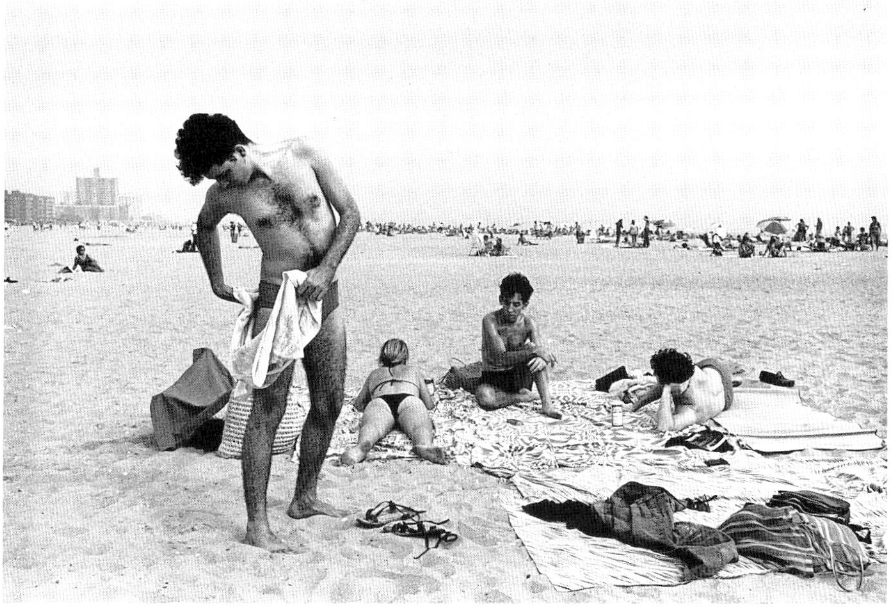

above *Leon Koury* Buddy at the beach c1953 *silver-gelatin print* below *Allen Frame* Frank at the beach 1984 *silver-gelatin print*

Luis Paredes *El Salvador / Denmark*

The Traverse

10 CAMBRIDGE STREET
EDINBURGH

UK PREMIERE

2 OCTOBER – 28 OCTOBER

One of the many striking qualities of Luis Paredes' work is the way in which he has used the nature of photography to create a metaphor for perception itself, denoting time and transformation within a single frame. His objective is not so much to create a feeling of nostalgia as a sense that time corrupts all memories and distorts all images until the only thing left is their elusive essence. Unlike many other photographers of Latin American origin, Luis Paredes does not suggest an access to knowledge only available to a culture of primitive but noble people. His work asserts a fundamentally individual vision flowing from within, rather than shaped or accommodating the cultural or political environment.
Based on a text by Pablo Swezey, Guatemala

Presented by Fotofeis

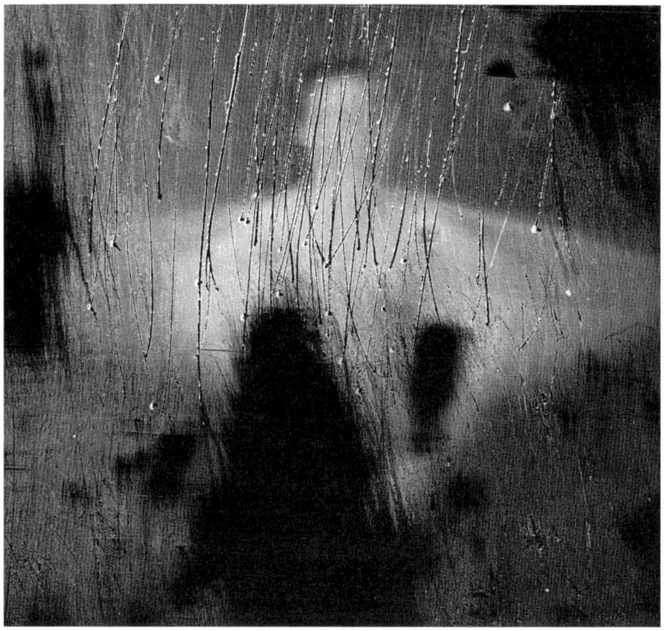

Luis Paredes Moth 1994 *toned and distressed silver-gelatin print*

SILVIA REICHENBACH *Italy*

Il Resto E' Silenzio (The Rest is Silence)

Istituto Italiano di Cultura

82 NICOLSON STREET
EDINBURGH

UK PREMIERE

12 OCTOBER – 18 NOVEMBER

Presented by the Istituto Italiano di Cultura, Edinburgh

Since the invention of photography, self-portraiture has exerted an almost magical fascination upon photographers. As both photographer and subject, Silvia Reichenbach moves constantly between the positions of artist and subject, oscillating between being viewer and viewed. Looking into the camera, her face is frozen into a gaze of ambivalent invitation that gives itself and holds back with equal energy. Her work is intensely introspective and penetrating, and has its origin in the uncertainties of self-interrogation and the ambiguities of the answers she finds.

In the construction of the image, nothing is left to chance. Each nuance is caught, to animate the appearance of the re-created subject. When she faces her camera, the artist confronts an absence both literal and metaphorical, to which she then gives material form and real presence. But does the ardent face in the photograph promise a journey into the artist's interior world or does it in fact deny that very possibility?

Based on a text by Yoav Dagon, former Director, Herzlia Museum, Israel

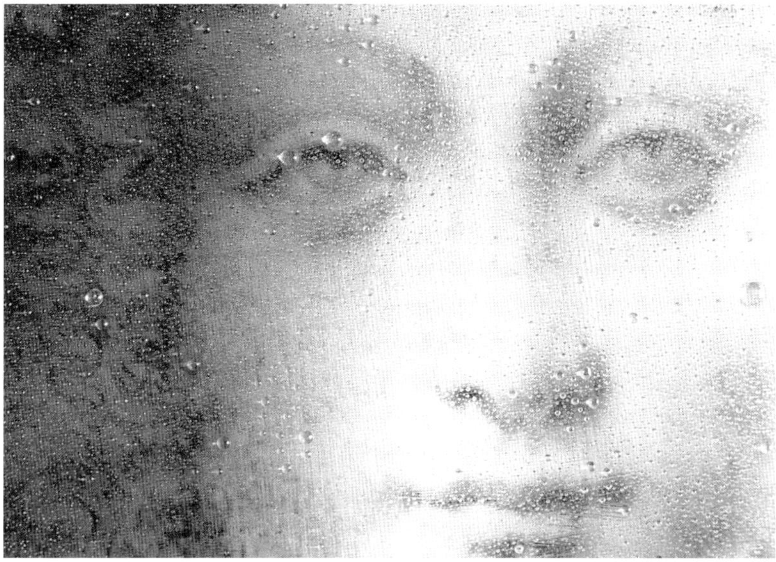

Silvia Reichenbach from the series The Rebirth 1993 *silver-gelatin print*

GHOSTS IN THE MACHINE
Conan Doyle and Spirit Photography

Aberdeen Art Gallery

SCHOOLHILL
ABERDEEN

PREMIERE

27 SEPTEMBER – 5 NOVEMBER

An Akehurst Bureau touring exhibition from the Richard Lancelyn Green Collection, presented by Aberdeen Art Gallery in collaboration with Fotofeis

Spirit Photography, which had been in vogue in the mid-19th century, was waning in popularity when Arthur Conan Doyle first became interested in the subject. Initially, the creator of Sherlock Holmes sought to explore the subject from a neutral and scientific standpoint, but he was to become one of its most energetic and celebrated defenders.

Following the Great War the idea enjoyed a revival when grieving relatives often willingly believed that the shadowy 'extras' that appeared on photographic plates were indeed loved ones slain in battle.

This exhibition, drawn in part from spirit photographs collected by Arthur Conan Doyle himself, tells the story of the defence and final unmasking of the work of the Circle of Crewe (William Hope and his accomplice, Mrs Buxton) and the enterprising if talentless Mrs Deane, a cleaning lady who specialised in manifesting the dead *en masse* each Armistice Day and who was not above circulating the images in advance of the event to hit a newspaper deadline.

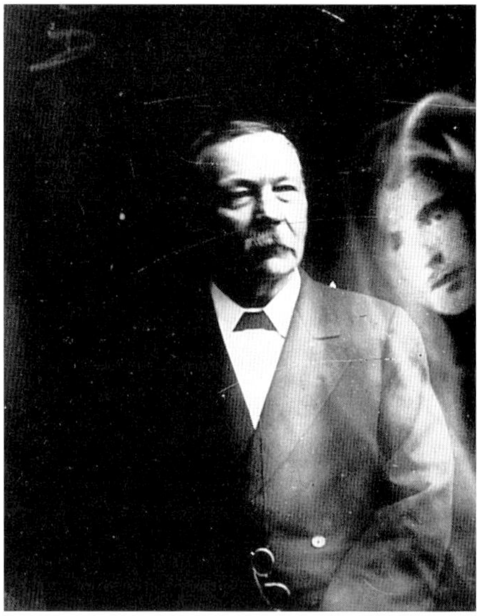

Unknown Arthur Conan Doyle with 'extra' said to be his son *no date silver-gelatin print (courtesy of The Richard Lancelyn Green Collection)*

Subsidised by City of Aberdeen

THE SCOTTISH ARTS COUNCIL

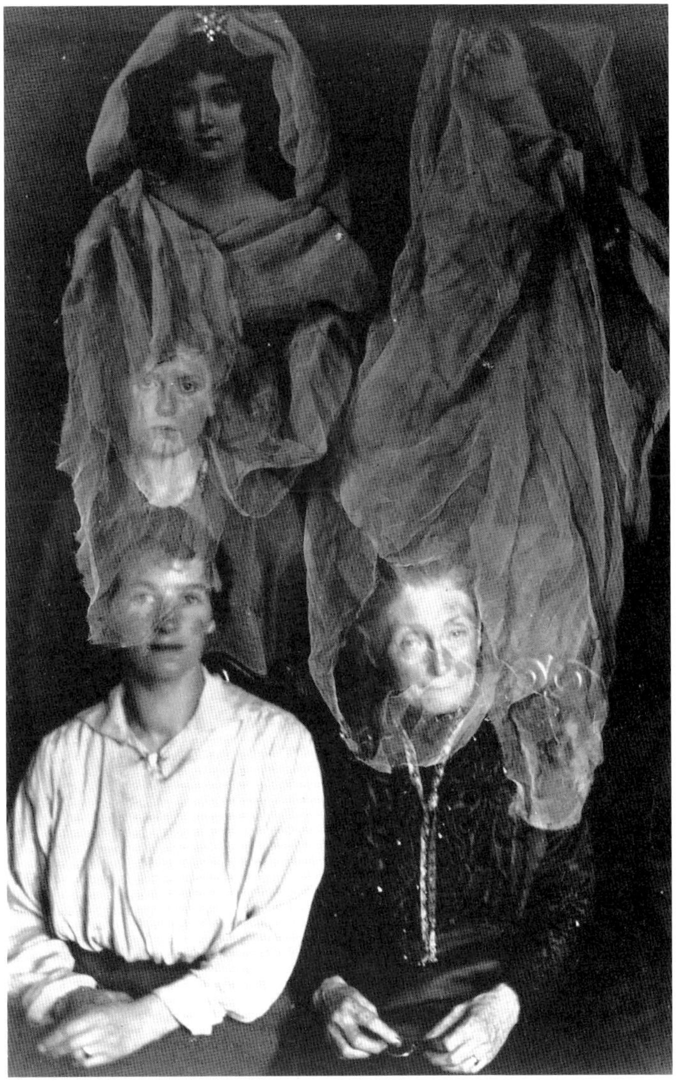

Ada Emma Deane Mrs Deane and her daughter (at back) with 'Indian spirit guide' 1921
silver-gelatin print (courtesy of The Richard Lancelyn Green Collection)

Migration

MY PASSPORT WITH MY PHOTOGRAPH

PAVEL BÜCHLER

The flows and counterflows of migration crisscross the cultural map of the post-colonial world. A web of influences and interdependences, diversities and differences is beginning to obliterate the boundaries of Culture laid down with conceited self-indulgence not so long ago. Navigation in and across these currents is becoming more than ever before a matter of negotiating relativities: there are no fixed spatial axioms, only the uncertain points of origins and destinations; not locations, only *dis*locations. The old bearings of East/West, derived from the geography of conquest, or the more recent North/South co-ordinates, reflecting the reality of multinationalist economic orientations, can no longer be relied upon when we are confronted with the unsettling meanderings of cultures in transit. Now, does the techno-political scheme of a three-tier hierarchical world offer more than an abstract image (painted by numbers) when it comes to charting the complexity of cultural dynamics driven by migration? For while the world remains asymmetrically divided along the lines of technological and logistical supremacy, it is often the local cultural divisions that determine the strength and direction of the flow. Migration begins at home, so to say.

Least of all can we make any sense of either the global patterns or the local detail of migration if we perceive the world as a patchwork of national cultures, held together by the boundaries of states. Such cartography defines culture as a system of interlocking frames which separate the individual and collective identities of the 'nationals', and represents migration as a problem of transference, compatibility and adaptation.

How do we draw a map which would guide us through a terrain stretching between 'here' and 'there' in which we strive to locate 'our' culture so that we may know who we are?

Who are (or *where are*, or *what is*) 'we' in these declining years of the Century of the Refugee? What used to seem so simple has become most difficult – to *imagine* ourselves.

Recently, a friend pointed out to me a curious semantic diffraction in my use of the pronouns 'we' and 'they' as though they were interchangeable. The conversation was about Czechoslovakia (a country which no longer exists), where I come from and where he studied, and about Scotland (a country which is not a state), where he was born and where I now live. I was talking about the liberal drinking laws *they* enjoy in Prague, comparing them unfavourably to those *we* have in Glasgow; I was musing about the beer *we* brew in Bohemia and complaining (as Czechs do) about how *they*, here in Scotland, don't know how to look after it. When in 1979 half of *our* ice hockey team fled to Toronto and played against *us* on *their* side in Vienna, *they*, my compatriots, didn't know who to cheer for ...

We also talked about my passport. It is mine and it is not: it is in my pocket, it has my name on it, yet the note on its last page cautions me that it 'remains the property of Her Majesty's Government'. As it 'may be withdrawn at any time', it is clearly not mine at all – at least for as long as I live. When I die, my passport 'should be submitted for cancellation' and then, the last sentence states reassuringly, 'it will be returned on request'. It is a nice thought: born Czech, having arrived in Britain with a one-way travel document which described me as a 'person of undetermined nationality', and having lived here on a borrowed identity perhaps for the rest of my life, I will depart from this world with a passport truly of my own! The question of my belonging forever resolved.

But until then, there is at least *my photograph*. It is a picture of me, it was taken by me (strictly speaking – using a railway station photo-booth), I paid for it. It exists (for argument's sake) in two copies: I have one in my passport, 'they' have the other in their files. Like identical twins disunited by destiny, the two share an identity of separation. In the eyes of those for whom the photograph was taken ('they', immigration officers, border guards and such like), the picture is less an image of 'me' than a double of 'their' copy of it. The very proof of my identity is in my separation from my photograph: I am what I am through what 'they' hold.

This is why they invented passport photographs in the first place: to *give* me an identity as they *take* my picture (why 'they', the Paris police, took the first ones – those of the dead Communards). They noticed that there is always a bond between a photograph and a time and place, that through photographs our lives are tied to locations – if not in the 'real' world, then at least in the nomadic world of images. It is true that our identities based on such 'territorial claims' are no less ambiguous than those that can be constructed in language (where a 'we' is nothing but a range of possibilities legislated by language). After all, photographs too are mere abstractions, subject to classification, the conditions of use, the laws of optics and the conventions of communication. But it is also true that, somehow, in every photograph we retain possession of what is no longer ours: not just a past but a certain history.

Photographs, like maps, accompany our movements. But unlike maps, which are projections of future journeys, photographs are traces of returns. They are intersections of past and current passages, 're-presentations'. Mobilising the claims we have on 'our' photographs, holding onto them, could help us to begin reconstructing a perspective for a different kind of mapping. A mapping which acknowledges that 'departures' and 'arrivals' are not separated by geographic distances but connected by a life-span; that 'home' is not where journeys begin or end but what they pass through; that 'here' and 'there', 'us' and 'them', are not opposites but polarities; that 'our' culture is not a given denomination but a name we give to our interaction with others; and perhaps also that 'Tutsi' or 'Tuzla' are not just recent entries in the dictionary of diaspora but part of what we must imagine as 'ourselves'.

As with some photographs, the images we may create through re-tracing our steps as we move on may be blurred or unfocused but they will help us to build the larger images that we really need: visions of another society, another way of living, the kind of images, mental maps, with which migrations begin – they call them 'hope'.

Pavel Büchler is an artist. He is Head of the School of Fine Art at Glasgow School of Art

THE BITTER YEARS 1939–1947
Through the Eyes of Czech Photographers

Talbot Rice Gallery

UNIVERSITY OF EDINBURGH
OLD COLLEGE
SOUTH BRIDGE
EDINBURGH

UK PREMIERE

9 OCTOBER – 4 NOVEMBER

VÁCLAV CHOCHOLA

KAREL LUDWIG

JINDŘICH MARCO

LADISLAV SITENSKY

SVATOPLUK SOVA

ZDENĚK TMEJ

Curated by Vladimir Birgus in cooperation with Blanka Chocholová

Ministry of Culture of the Czech Republic

Following the 50th anniversary of the end of hostilities, this exhibition brings together six highly subjective testimonies of World War II in central Europe. It shows us, not the generals and marshals, but the effects of the War on ordinary people, people not so different from ourselves, whose lives were radically changed by a war that was not of their making.

The work of six leading Czech photographers of that generation are brought together for the first time in this exhibition. They were not merely observers, privileged war-zone journalists who could return to the safety of home after the dramatic shot had been recorded. They were direct, if unwilling, participants in the events they depicted. Zdeněk Tmej risked all in secretly recording his life amongst the young Czech men (specifically those born in 1920 and 1921) who were deported to Germany to work for the victory of the Third Reich. Published just after the War, they have not been shown for fifty years. Ladislav Sitensky photographed other young Czech men who helped British pilots win the Battle of Britain. Photographs by Václav Chochola and Karel Ludwig portray the nameless heroines and heroes of the Prague uprising and the spontaneous joy and enthusiasm which marked the celebrations at the end of the War. Svatopluk Sova's previously unpublished shots show the darker side of post-war retribution: the shearing of female collaborators and the execution of the former deputy mayor of Prague. This execution, in September 1945, was watched by tens of thousands of spectators including mothers with small children. Dealing with the more mundane, but no less moving realities of daily life, Jindřich Marco's photographs depict post-war chaos and slow return to normal life amidst the ruins of Berlin.

Presented by Fotofeis in conjunction with The Ministry of Culture of the Czech Republic, Prague House of Photography and Silesian University, Opava

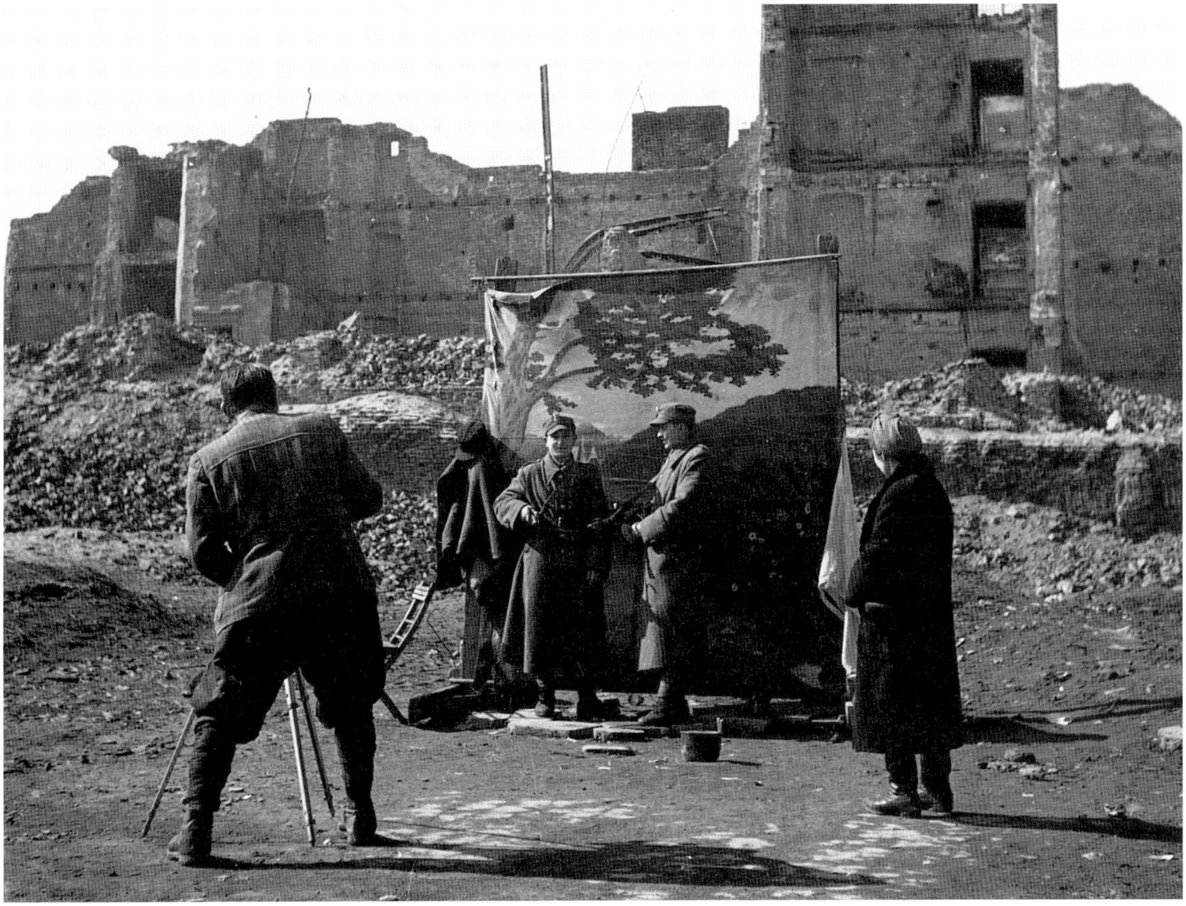

Jindřich Marco Photographer in the centre of Warsaw 1947 *silver-gelatin print*

GILLIAN STEEL *Scotland*

Move

The Customs House

CUSTOMSHOUSE QUAY
GREENOCK

PREMIERE

9 OCTOBER – 12 OCTOBER

THE SCOTTISH ARTS COUNCIL

RENFREWSHIRE ENTERPRISE

Move is a series of film projections in three areas around and within the Customs House in Greenock situated on a quay from which many thousands of people took their leave from Scotland. Each projection explores the experiences of those who have left their homeland forever, especially those who emigrated to the colonies in the New Worlds, such as Canada and Australia. They focus in turn on the journeys, sense of belonging and survival strategies of those who have emigrated.

Much of *Move* was generated during a period of research and development spent in Sydney and thus many of the images focus on the history of that particular colony. The cultural symbols of the immigrant colonizers bring to mind not only those who have moved in, but those who were moved on in the process.

The work conflates different periods of time so that a picture of a Fifties emigrant is seen juxtaposed with a drawing of an Australian aborigine; gold prospectors of the 1880s alongside details of contemporary migrants. By denying a focus on any one particular era the work suggests connections between the past and what is happening around us now.

An artist-run project

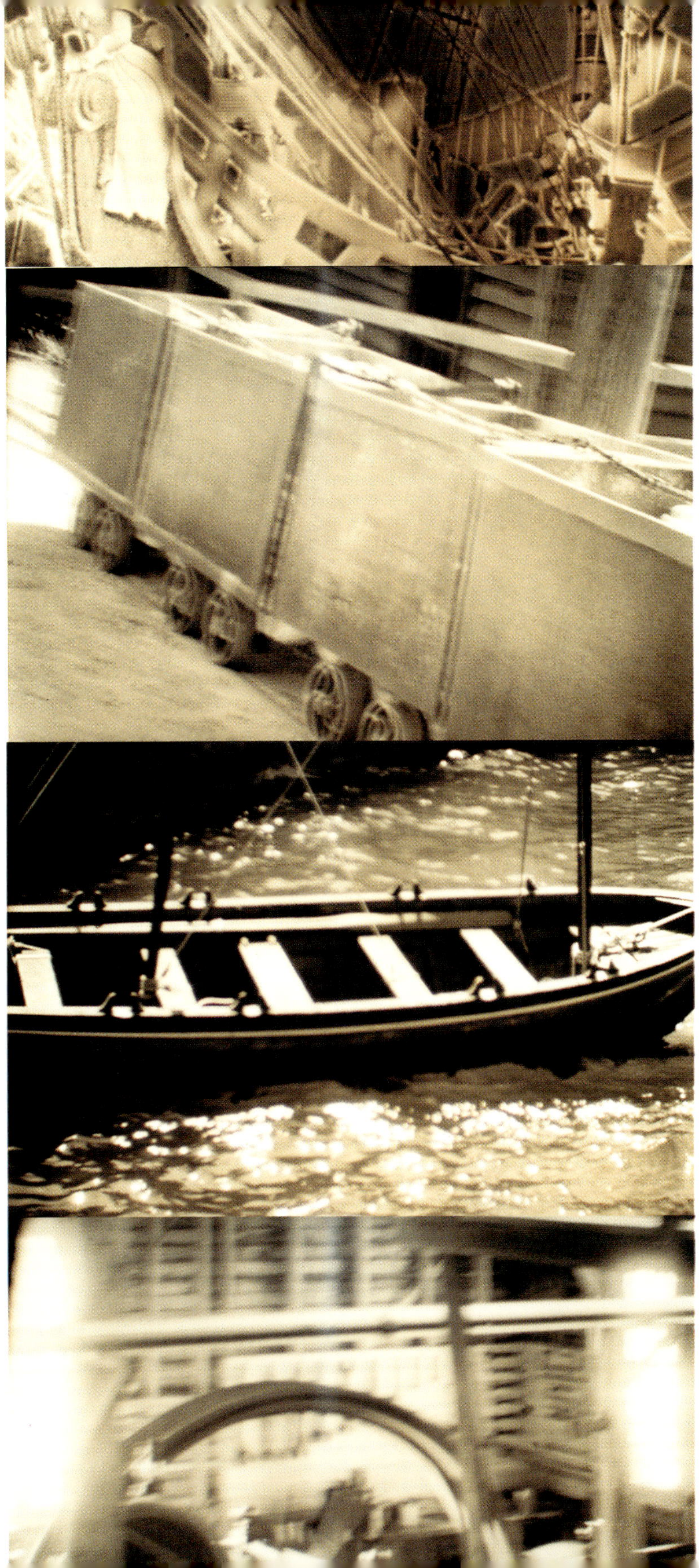

Gillian Steel stills from Move 1995
from film loops

SHARYN YUEN *Canada*

John Chinaman *and* Full Circle

An Lanntair

TOWN HALL
SOUTH BEACH
STORNOWAY
ISLE OF LEWIS

EUROPEAN PREMIERE

7 OCTOBER – 28 OCTOBER

Sharyn Yuen is a Canadian-born Chinese living in Vancouver. She makes paper directly from plant fibres and uses it as the material on which to print photographic images which are drawn from her own family album and from the broader history of Chinese immigrants to western Canada. As a second generation Canadian Chinese, unable to speak the language of her ancestors and living in one of the fastest growing cities in the world, her work revolves around questions of displaced identity.

In *John Chinaman* she considers a history of racial discrimination experienced by her father growing up in British Columbia in the early part of the century. Chinese immigration had been taxed from the latter part of the 19th century, leading to a complete ban in 1923 which lasted until after World War II. The Chinese who were in Canada at this time lived in isolation, both from the local Canadian community and from their families back in China. This installation is an arrangement of white jackets constructed from hand-made paper and printed with photographs of the period. Both the colour white and paper are associated with death in Chinese culture, and the jackets are of the type traditionally worn by Chinese workers. Each jacket, lit from within, glows alone in the darkness, bearing a photographic memory of the past.

The motivation for the other work, *Full Circle*, was a desire by Sharyn Yuen to build a picture of herself through the images of her antecedents. She selected portraits of her female forbears and enlarged them onto slabs of hand-made paper. Touching sometimes on the similarities, but more often on the differences between her life in contemporary Vancouver and that of her older female relatives, the artist pays homage to her past – quite literally in fact, as small offerings are placed before each image.

The Canada Council
Conseil des Arts du Canada

Presented by An Lanntair in association with Fotofeis

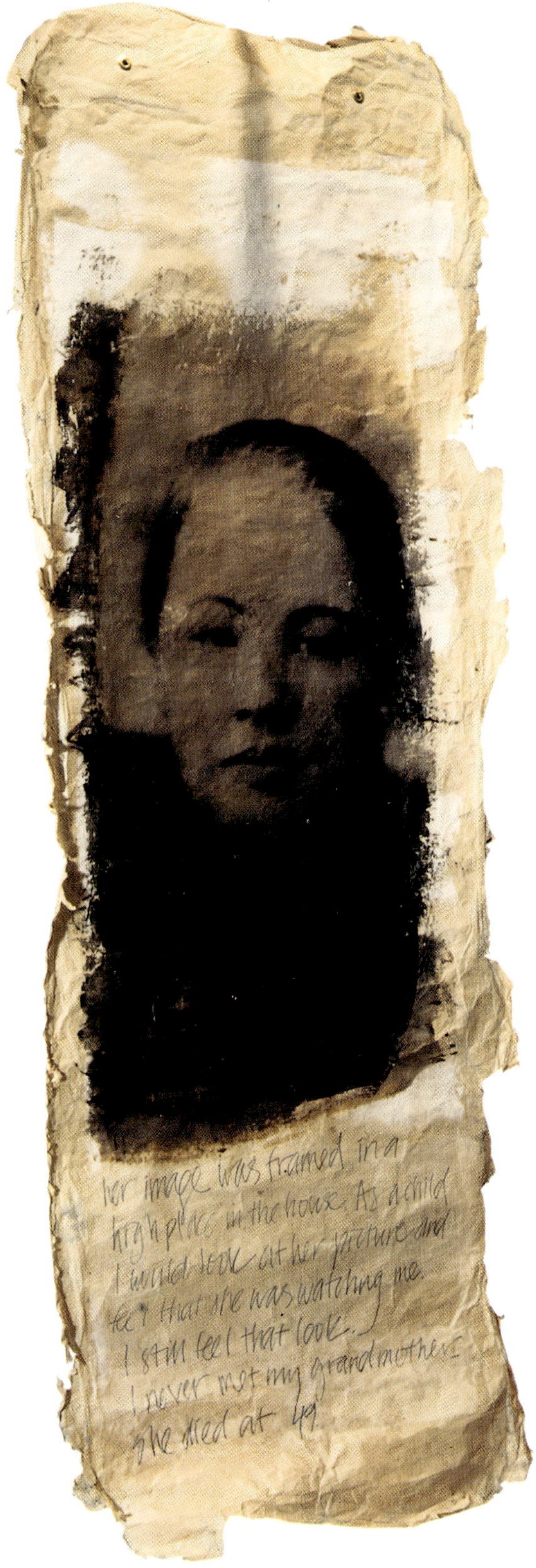

Sharyn Yuen *from* Full Circle 1991
photographic emulsion with text on hand-made paper

ALLAN SEKULA USA
Fish Story

Tramway

25 ALBERT DRIVE
GLASGOW

UK PREMIERE

6 OCTOBER – 12 NOVEMBER

Growing up in a harbour town predisposes one to retain quaint ideas about matter and thought. I'm speaking only for myself here, although I suspect that a certain stubborn and pessimistic insistence on the primacy of material forces is part of a common culture of harbour residents. This crude materialism is underwritten by disaster. Ships explode, leak, sink, collide. Accidents happen every day. Gravity is recognised as a force. By contrast, airline companies encourage the omnipotence of thought. This is the reason why the commissioner of airports of the city of Los Angeles is paid much more than the commissioner of harbours. The airport commissioner has to think very hard, day and night, to keep all the planes in the air. ALLAN SEKULA

Allan Sekula is one of the leading photographers and critics to emerge from the radical cultural politics of the late Seventies in the United States. As an artist, writer and teacher, he has been influential in developing a critique of photography based on its social, political and historical content.

Fish Story, a monumental six-year project, presents global capitalism in cultural and geographic terms. Harbours around the world, from Los

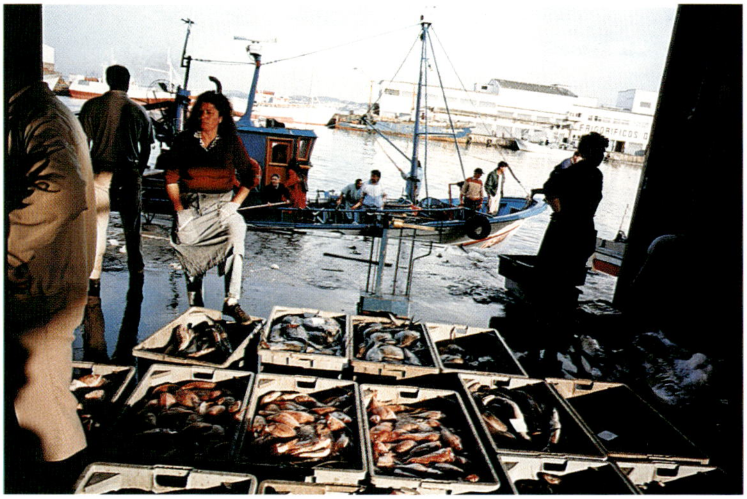

Allan Sekula *from* Fish Story *colour transparency*

Angeles to Glasgow, and Rotterdam to Ulsan, Korea, are recorded in photographs and texts to create a picture of international trade and the changes that the macro-economic order has wrought on all port cities. Ports have evolved from romantic sites of arrival and departure, where the produce of the world could be seen, heard and smelt, into cargo processing facilities where anonymous containers are shifted from one place to another.

The photographs themselves are presented as documentary narrative, often emphasising the incidental and chance discovery. The captions, detailed and layered, serve to undermine the idea that the photograph can tell the whole truth. Here, the text introduces a different reading and traces a network of hidden relationships not visible in the images.

Presented by Tramway as part of a European tour of Rotterdam, Stockholm, Glasgow and Calais

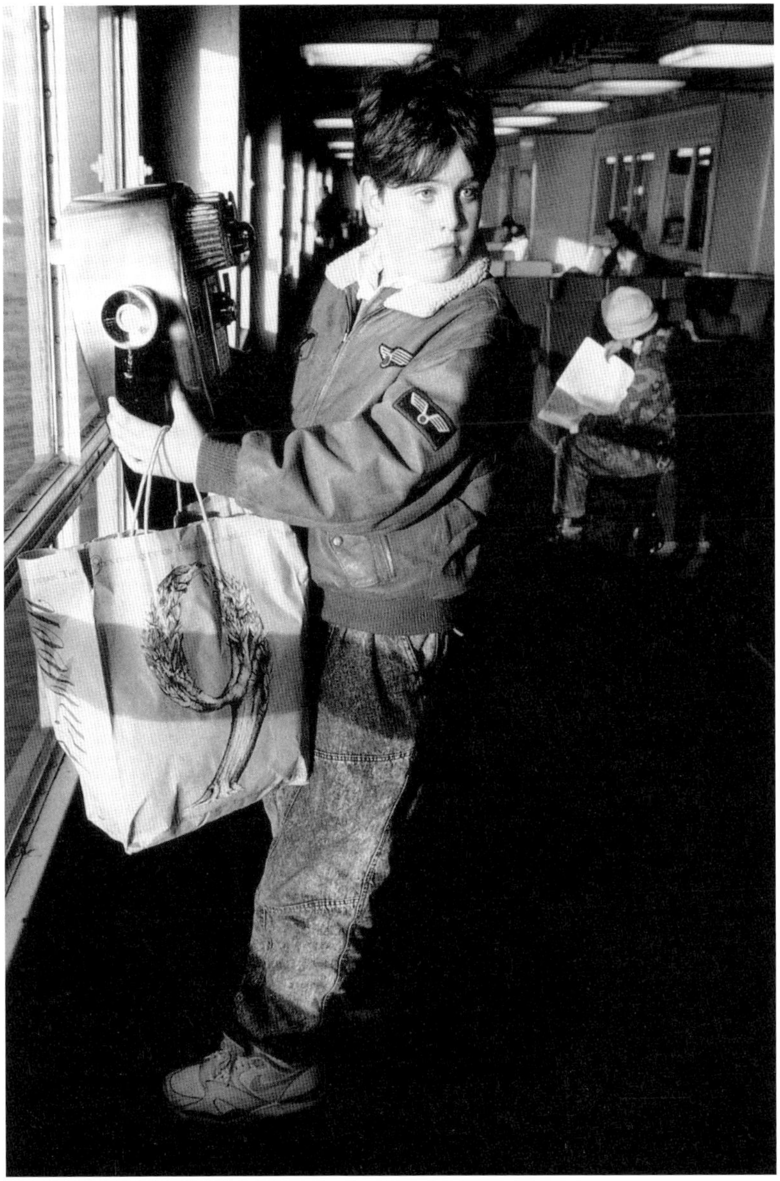

Allan Sekula Boy looking at his mother, Staten Island ferry, New York Harbour 1990 *(original in colour)*

MAUD SULTER *Scotland*

Alba

Centre for Contemporary Arts

350 SAUCHIEHALL STREET
GLASGOW

PREMIERE

23 SEPTEMBER – 28 OCTOBER

Maud Sulter's new work *Alba* is an enigmatic, late 20th century faerie tale. Celebrating the continuum of contact between Africa and Europe, *Alba* takes as its source historical evidence of the presence of black people at the Scottish Court in the 15th century. The artist weaves an elegant, melancholic narrative of symbiosis and passion, pleasure and loss, and the redemptive power of love.

This new body of work was commissioned by the Centre for Contemporary Arts (CCA) for *Fotofeis '95*, and will take the form of an installation made from a series of components – large scale emblematic photoworks in black and white, antique sculptural African objects, plinths of tobacco, small photographic portraits in colour, poetic texts and a haunting soundtrack performed on traditional West African *mmenson* horns, which call down ancestral spirits. The soundtrack is the artist's first collaboration with Nano Danso Abiam and the Ghanian-based Pan African Orchestra. Alongside *Alba*, CCA will present Maud Sulter's recent video and photography project *Plantation* – an intimate, personal and powerful work.

Maud Sulter was born in Glasgow in 1960 of Scots and Ghanian parentage. An artist, writer and cultural historian, her previous publications include: poetry – *As A Black Woman*, Akira Press (1985) and *Zabat: Poetics of a Family Tree*, UFP (1990); art history – *Echo: Works by Women Artists 1890–1940*, Tate Gallery Publications (1991); and audio – *Hysteria*, a compact disc in collaboration with Ghanian Miles Ofusu-Danso.

Maud Sulter's first major body of work, the celebrated portrait series *Zabat*, is now in the collection of the Victoria & Albert Museum in London. Recently, she was selected as the official British representative at the Johannesburg Biennale in South Africa. *Alba* is her first solo show to originate in Scotland.

THE SCOTTISH ARTS COUNCIL

Commissioned by the Centre for Contemporary Arts

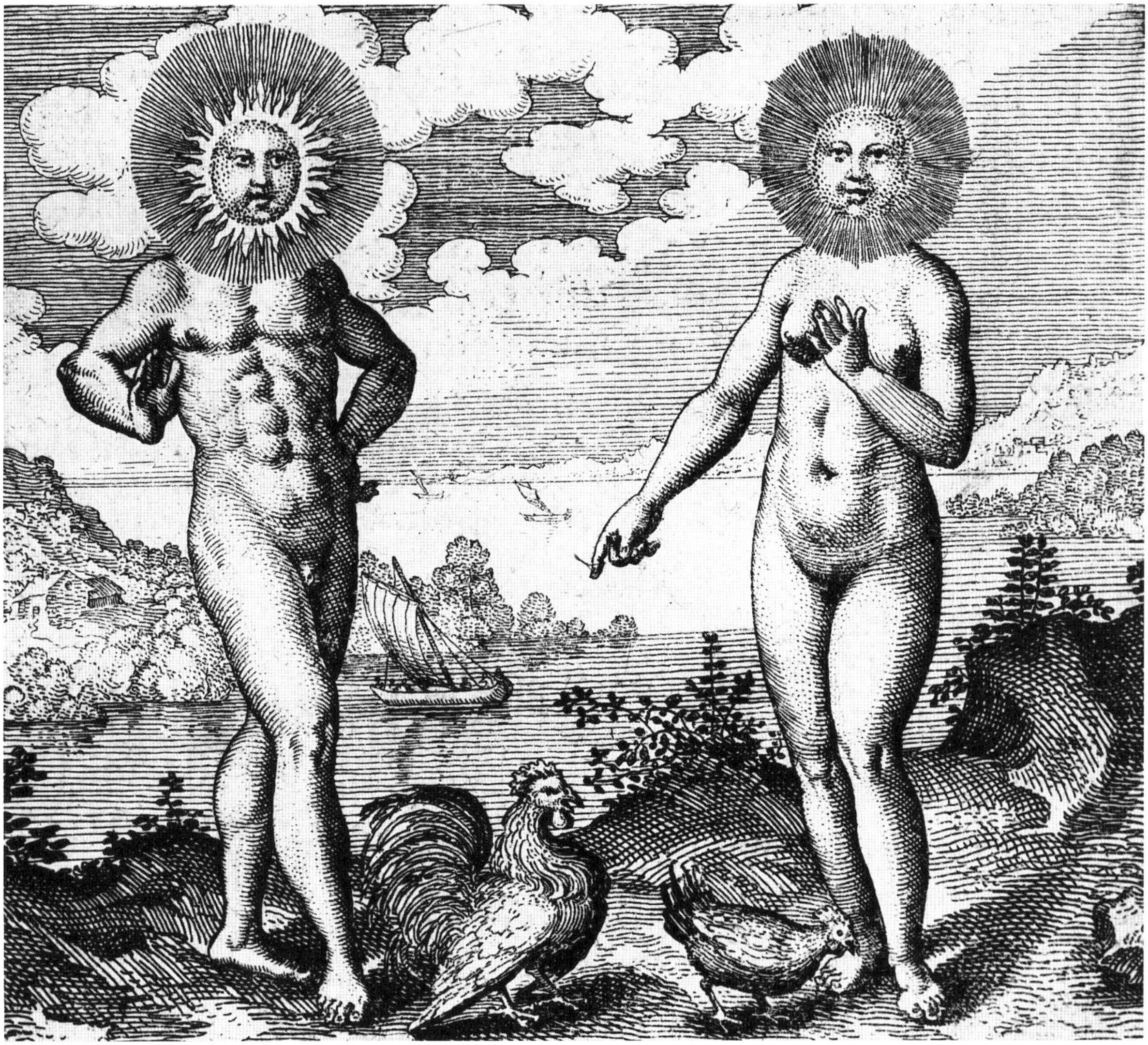

Maud Sulter The Sun Needs the Moon, as the Cock Needs the Hen, *from the* Alba *series* 1995

TINA MODOTTI *Italy / USA / Mexico*
Her Life and Photography

Inverleith House

WESTGATE
ROYAL BOTANIC GARDEN
ARBORETUM PLACE
EDINBURGH

UK PREMIERE

8 OCTOBER – 19 NOVEMBER

Edward Weston Tina, Mexico 1924 *silver-gelatin print (courtesy of Comitato Tina Modotti)*

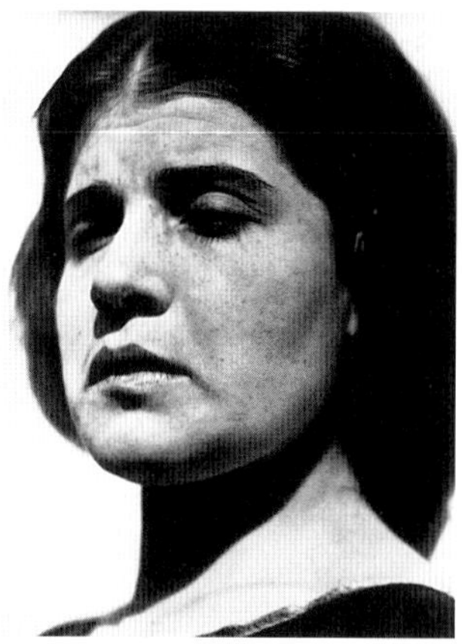

Istituto Italiano di Cultura, Edinburgh

QLG LINDSAYS WS SOLICITORS

I am forever struggling to mould my life according to my temperament and needs, in other words I put much art in my life ... TINA MODOTTI

Tina Modotti (1896–1942) was a spirited and independent woman who grew up in the turmoil of the early 20th century. In 1913, at the age of seventeen and trained as a dressmaker, she left her home in Friuli, a poor region in the North of Italy. She travelled to San Francisco and Los Angeles, where she worked as an actress in Hollywood. In 1923 she went to Mexico where she discovered a lively cultural and political atmosphere which suited her own convictions. She moved amid a circle of artists including the muralist Diego Rivera, and the painters Frida Kahlo and José Orozco, and, most significantly, she met Edward Weston who was to become both her teacher and lover.

For the next few years Tina Modotti created images of great beauty, life and social conscience. She engaged society through her camera. A gifted and visionary photographer, Tina Modotti believed photography should occupy 'a place in social production, to which we should all contribute'.

Tina Modotti became deeply involved in revolutionary politics, joining the Communist Party in 1927. She was deported from Mexico in 1929 and went first to Berlin and then to Moscow. Later she went to Spain to involve herself in the Civil War. In Europe she soon gave up photography to devote herself to politics and revolutionary struggle. Here, known simply as 'Maria', she stayed until the outbreak of World War II. She returned to Mexico with the intention of turning once more to photography, but died quite suddenly less than three years later.

Today, Tina Modotti's works are recognised as being among the great 20th century photographs, equal to and even surpassing those of her famous mentor, Edward Weston. Her work includes portraits of her artist friends; sensitive documentary images of Mexican Indian life; delicate still-lifes and more ideologically inspired arrangements of symbolic objects.

A exhibition created by Comitato Tina Modotti, presented by Fotofeis in collaboration with the Istituto Italiano di Cultura, Edinburgh

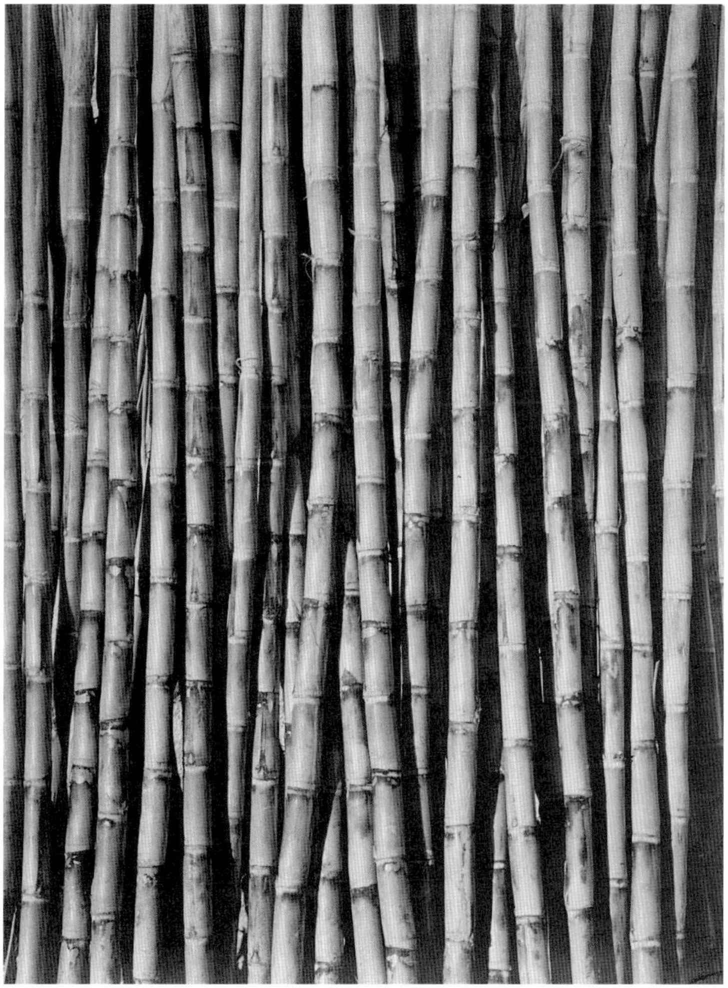

Tina Modotti Bamboo Canes 1924 *silver-gelatin print*

FRANK DARIUS *Germany*

Foreign Home: Portraits of Asylum-seekers in Germany

Street Level Gallery

26 KING STREET
GLASGOW

UK PREMIERE

7 OCTOBER – 11 NOVEMBER

In 1993 the Berlin photographer Frank Darius produced a series of portraits of the residents of a Red Cross hostel in Berlin. About three hundred refugees are housed in living quarters there within a fenced enclosure. All of them are currently in so-called 'Phase II' of the asylum process: in that waiting period between hope and despair, often lasting several years, while the validity of their application is checked and a decision finally reached.

That Frank Darius has avoided any hint of sensationalism in his pictures is a testament to his sensitive attitude towards his subjects. It is perhaps precisely this which makes these pictures special and gives them their particular resonance. Rather than make the distressing living conditions of the refugees the central theme of his work, he focuses our attention on the people themselves. He did not want to produce photographs which would be interpreted in the same way as Media information or as news – as an affirmation for something we think we already know. The important thing, he stresses, is learning really to see, opening our eyes to the possibility that we could be standing there ourselves.

Frank Darius won the Kodak Gold Award in the European Portrait Photographer of the Year Awards in 1994.

GOETHE-INSTITUT

Presented by Street Level Gallery in association with the Goethe-Institut Glasgow

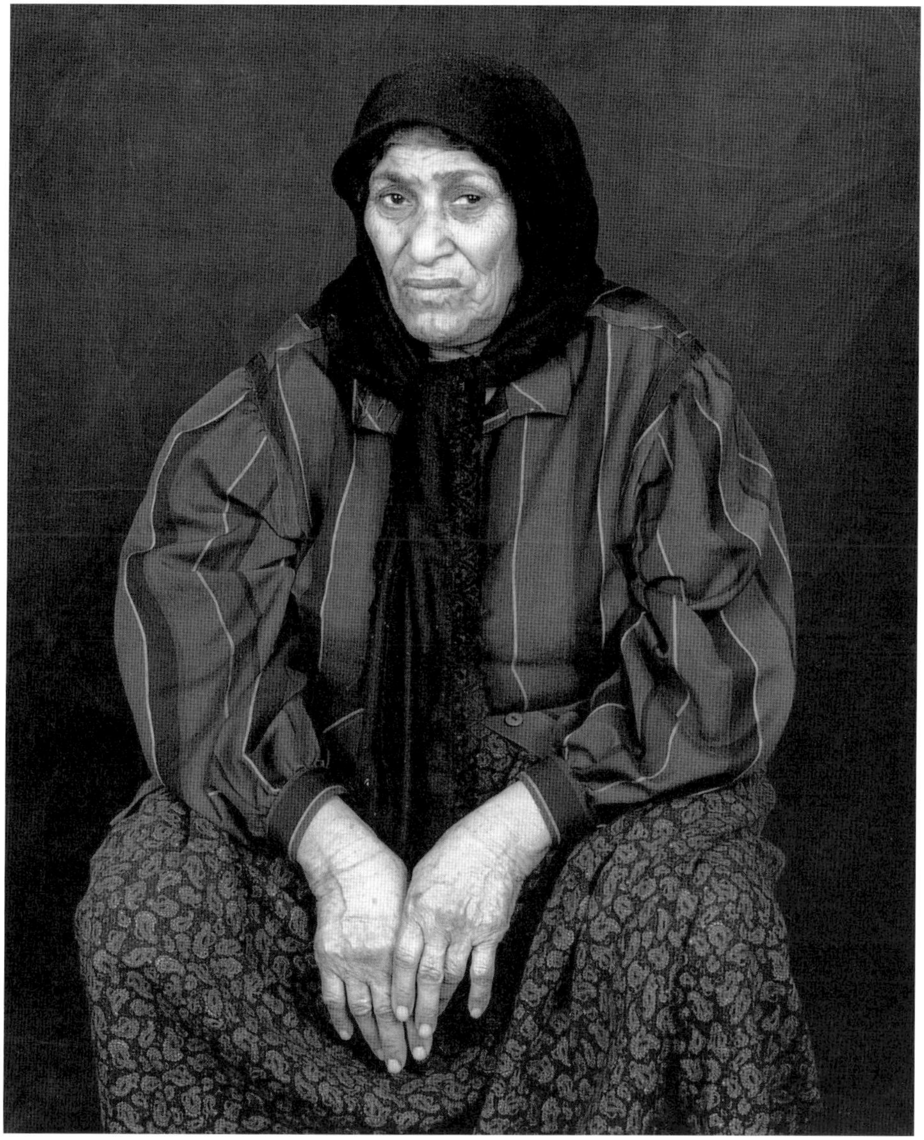

Frank Darius © untitled 1993 *silver-gelatin print*

SHAHEEN MERALI *England*

Paradigm Lost

Scottish Arts Council Travelling Gallery

TOURING
DUMFRIES & GALLOWAY
CAITHNESS
MOTHERWELL
ANGUS
THE WESTERN ISLES

PREMIERE

26 SEPTEMBER – 18 NOVEMBER

Paradigm Lost is a new work by multi-media artist Shaheen Merali. The title is a pun on Milton's *Paradise Lost*, an Elizabethan text that deals with expulsion and emigration. Shaheen Merali maintains that the process of settlement of a 'new' population into a 'native' community still remains painful.

The artist draws on his personal experience of being a victim of racial violence to create a dark installation which encompasses photography, video, light and sound. The installation includes a bookcase with the spines of the books turned inwards. This faces a computer manipulated image of a bookcase on which one can discern the face of Muktar Ahmed, who was disabled in a racial attack. By linking images of the consequences of racial violence with the books, the installation reminds us that racism and violence have historically sought 'justification' in ideological discourse.

A soundtrack – produced in collaboration with composer Philip Chambon and percussionist Billou Ghandi – incorporates elements of Nineties, semi-ambient mood music and Seventies Reggae and Punk. The whole installation is bathed in a seductive blue light creating a dreamlike space suggestive of the limitless power of the subconscious.

Commissioned by the Scottish Arts Council for the Travelling Gallery

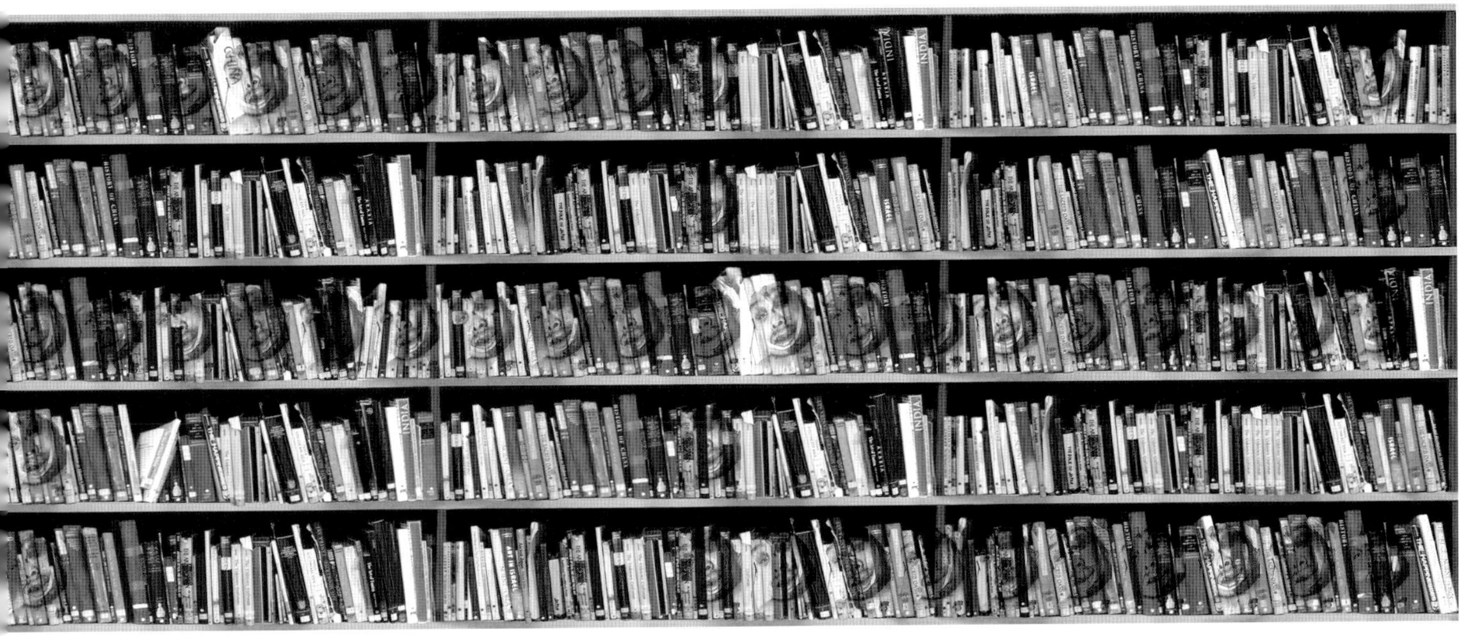

Shaheen Merali untitled [faces of Muktar Ahmed with bookcase] 1995 *computer manipulated image*

MICHEL BUHRER *Switzerland*

Transit – Refugees at the Doorstep of Europe

St Fergus Gallery

SINCLAIR TERRACE
WICK

PREMIERE

10 OCTOBER – 29 OCTOBER

Migrants seeking refuge in Europe face enormous difficulties. They can become trapped between borders, in airports and transit centres, often abused by middlemen and carriers. Psychologically, they are caught between 'before' and 'after', but their past is broken and the future is no longer in their hands.

In Europe, the refugees from Hungary, Czechoslovakia or Tibet were welcomed, as later were those from Chile. They were perceived as 'good' refugees fleeing from 'bad' regimes. Then came the Tamils, Kurds and Zairians, the Liberians, Albanians and Lettons. European laws on immigration began to change, making it increasingly difficult not only to get asylum, but to qualify to file a claim.

This series documents the moments and the places where the asylum seekers find themselves in a kind of judicial and geographical no-mans-land. Whether in transit centres or along borders; whether just arrived or just expelled, they are in the middle of nowhere.

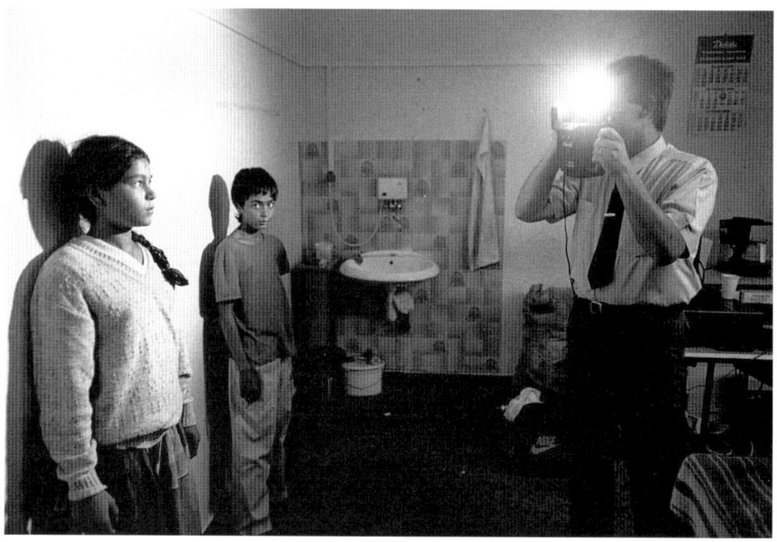

Michel Bührer Eisen Lüttenstadt, Germany, along the Polish border. A family of gypsies has just arrived. 14/07/92 *silver-gelatin print*

Presented by Highland Regional Council in association with Fotofeis

MANUEL FERROL *Spain*
Emigracion

St Fergus Gallery

SINCLAIR TERRACE
WICK

UK PREMIERE

10 OCTOBER – 29 OCTOBER

Emigration has been a constant fact in the history of the people of Galicia. As the writer Xose Manuel Beiras has suggested, since there was no entrepreneurial class to create jobs in industry, the only future working people had was starvation or exodus.

In the 19th century and the first half of the 20th, emigration to America reached epidemic proportions. It became almost inevitable that young people who reached working age left the country for Cuba, Argentina, Brazil and other South American countries. So much so that in some countries of Latin America all Spaniards are simply referred to as Galicians.

In 1956 Manuel Ferrol photographed the men and women who sailed to a future in Argentina. His pictures convey the tragic situation with great passion. The work also unwittingly echoes the American avant garde of the fifties through its unconventional style. The technical imperfections (blurring, shallow depth of field, tilting horizons) become expressive resources, in sharp contrast to the arid pictorialism of the salon, the predominant style of the time in Spain.

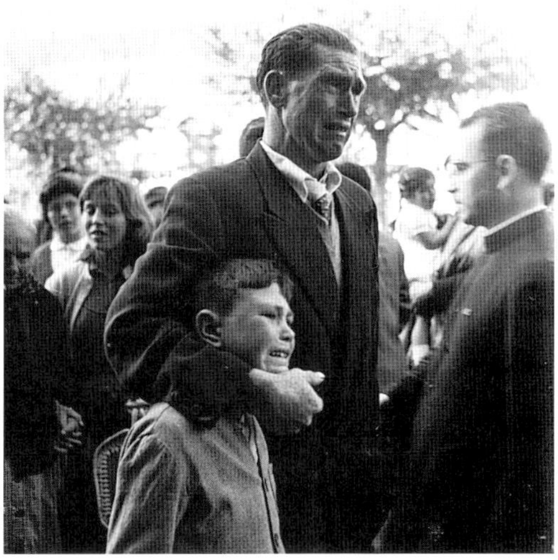

Manuel Ferrol untitled [father and son] 1956 *silver-gelatin print*

Curated by Manuel Sendon

Presented by
Highland Regional Council in association with Fotofeis

THELMA PEPPER *Canada*
Decades of Voices

Inverness Museum

CASTLE WYND
INVERNESS

EUROPEAN PREMIERE

5 OCTOBER – 4 NOVEMBER

I'm not going to promise to obey because I could never live up to that – so you can just take it out. I'm not going to obey anyone if I don't want to.

GRACE BOLTON on her marriage in Outlook, Saskatchewan, Canada in the 1930s

Thelma Pepper's exhibition, *Decades of Voices*, is a multi-facetted portrait of ten ordinary pioneer women from Saskatchewan, Canada, now all over 85 years of age. Through an extended personal and photographic involvement with residents of a senior citizens home in Saskatoon, Thelma Pepper developed a close relationship with these women who shared their thoughts, feelings and memories with her.

Photographic portraits, panoramas, text and a sound track come together to unfold a compelling story of personal relationships and simple survival in the prairies of early 20th century Saskatchewan. Each portrait reveals the personal strength, courage, compassion, determination and commitment of these women. Above all they possessed a genuine desire to help each other in the harsh environment in which they found themselves. The dramatic panoramas, so wide that they are presented as a series of prints laid side by side, show the inevitable isolation of subsistence farming with each homestead strategically placed at the centre of its own plot on the endless prairie plain. Other photographs focus on the details of the women's home environment and past events from their daily routines.

In the audio component of the installation the women reminisce about their earlier lives – the struggles, joys and disappointments – giving further insight into each individual's history and personality. The listener learns of the events that brought fulfilment or built self-confidence. The women give their opinions on the importance of spiritual and moral values in the face of hardship. They speak of their role in maintaining family solidarity and their commitment to a way of life that was important to them. They also recall a time when, as women, their opinions and capabilities were not highly regarded.

Saskatchewan Arts Board

The Canada Council
Conseil des Arts du Canada

Presented by Inverness Museum in collaboration with Fotofeis

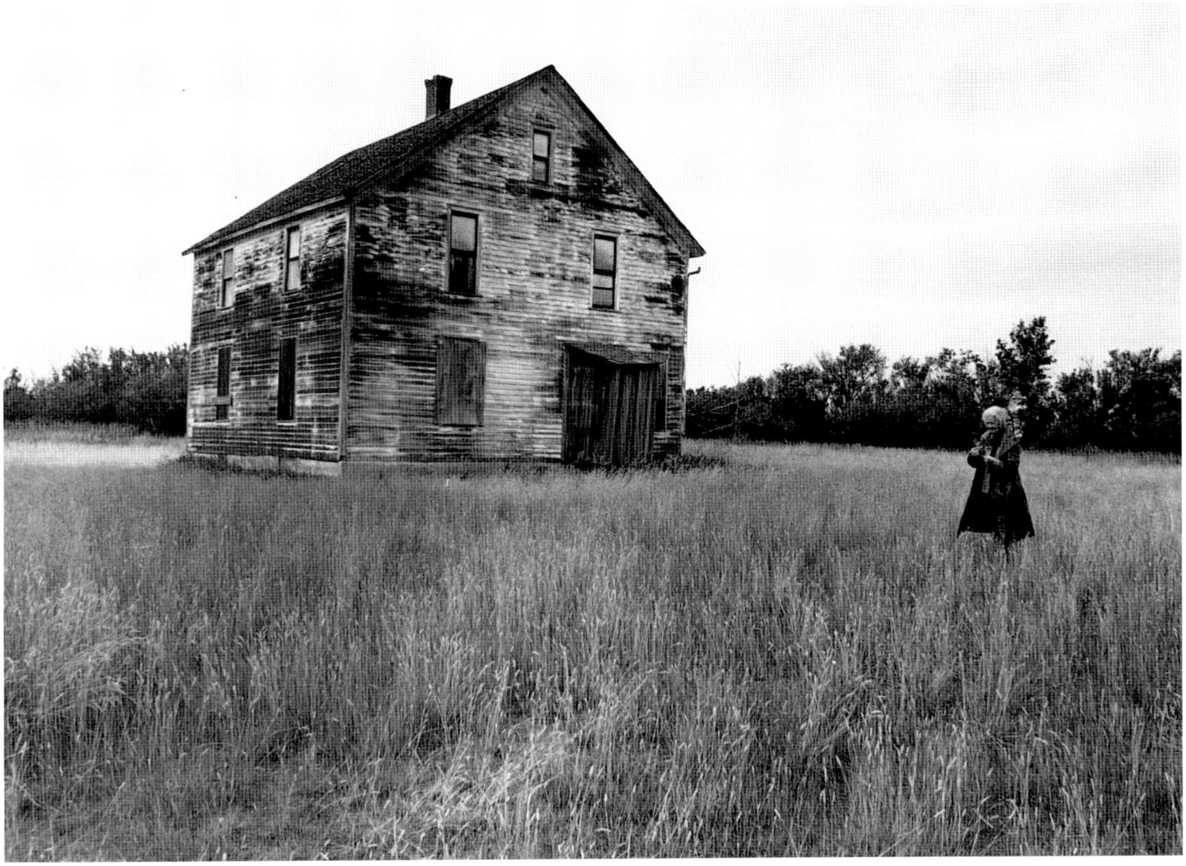

Thelma Pepper Memories Come Flooding Back 1989 *silver-gelatin print*

MARIA MIESENBERGER *Sweden*
Sverige / Schweden

Arbroath Library Gallery

HILL TERRACE
ARBROATH

7 OCTOBER – 28 OCTOBER

The photo-album is the prime chronicle of real and imaginary family life. The brief history of the family snapshot has shown that such trivial photographs, unsophisticated documents of family rites, are embellished with a precise aesthetic and a seemingly *a priori* image repertoire. Indeed the family snap does seem to harbour pivotal visual clues to childhood phenomenology and the psychology of self-formation. The snapshot which frames a memorable moment (making it memorable) out of one's past turns out to be a transitional object, a source of consolation, an instrument of recollection and a tool for overcoming – or suppressing – fear.

The images in Maria Miesenberger's *Sverige/Schweden* originate in family photographs from her own childhood in Austria and Sweden. The contents are standard vernacular: visits, a walk in the fields, a picnic, children playing in the grass, parents standing around talking, farewell ceremonies ... But Maria Miesenberger's re-articulation of these images transforms them to another order of communication. The people photographed are no longer recognizable as individuals. They are set afloat as dark shapes in the image. As the detail and nuances of the figures are obliterated, they become trap-doors in the pictorial surface, leaving us alone with our projections and associations. Like Rorschach tests aimed at the family, they evoke and narrate archetypal levels of human existence. Through minimal means a chain of associations is generated. Each photograph, surprisingly, is identifiable as a specific scene or event. *Sverige/Schweden* choreographs photographic traces of childhood and self, evoking, laying bare and questioning our birth into the social. Simultaneously sinister and sweet, they disclose and conceal, confront and evade their apparent content: the dreams and nightmares of childhood.

Based on a text by Jan-Erik Lundström

Embassy of Sweden

Presented by Angus District Museums in association with Fotofeis

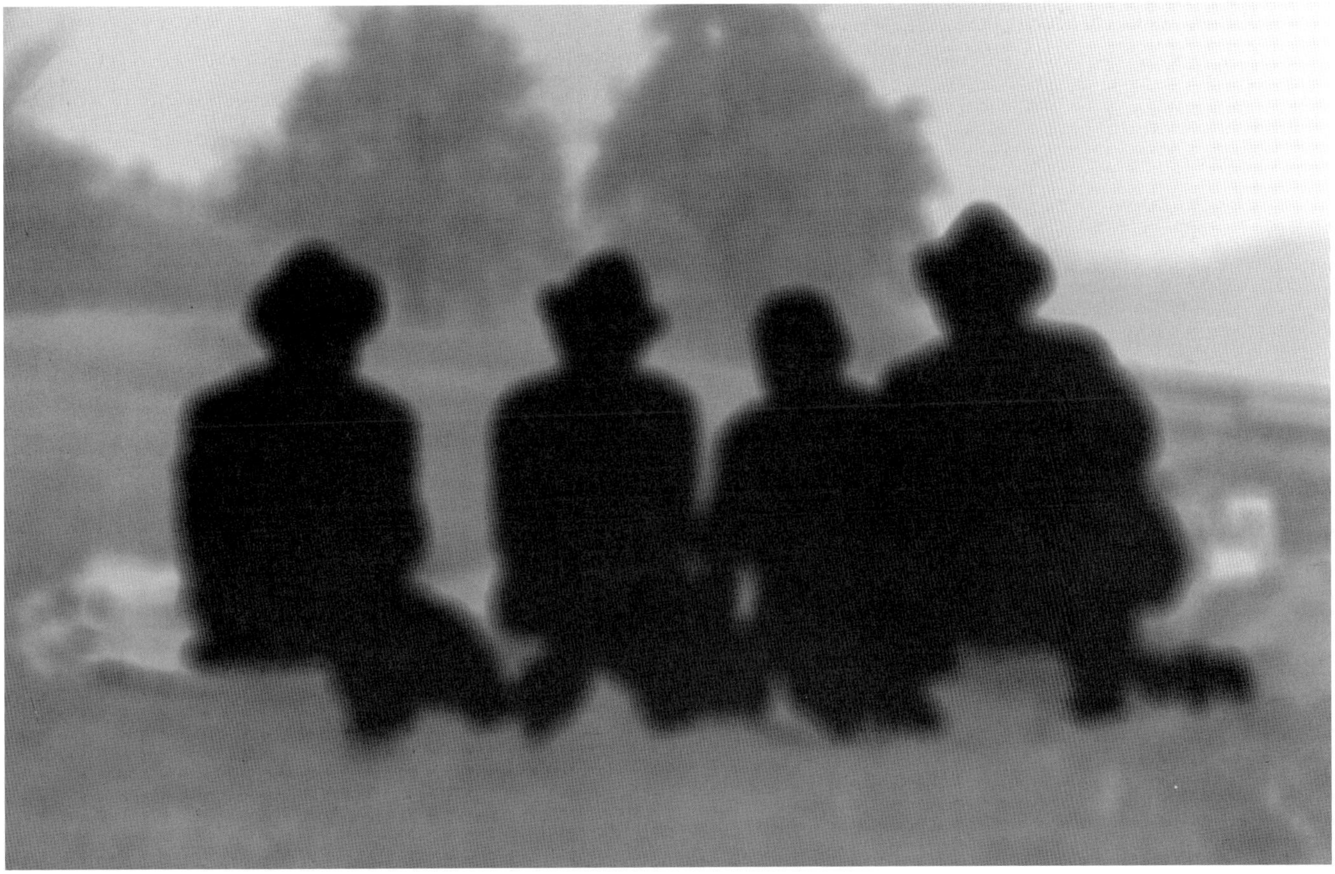

Maria Meisenberger untitled 1994 *silver-gelatin print*

ROSEMARY DONOVAN *Canada*

Ex Patria

Lillie Art Gallery

STATION ROAD
MILNGAVIE

PREMIERE

7 OCTOBER – 28 OCTOBER

This exhibition comprises forty portraits and is a study of expatriate Scots now living in Canada. Each has had to adjust and has succeeded in making a contribution to Canada's social and cultural fabric. Rosemary Donovan's quietly presented photographs seek to capture the essential qualities of her subjects by using her camera to suggest something of their individual stories.

Each photograph is accompanied by a brief statement from the individual concerned, describing their feelings about leaving Scotland to make a new life in Canada and their present sense of cultural identity. The stories describe their initial experiences as immigrants and their feelings today. In many cases they still suffer the migrant's dilemma of being torn between two countries, two identities.

Presented by the Lillie Art Gallery

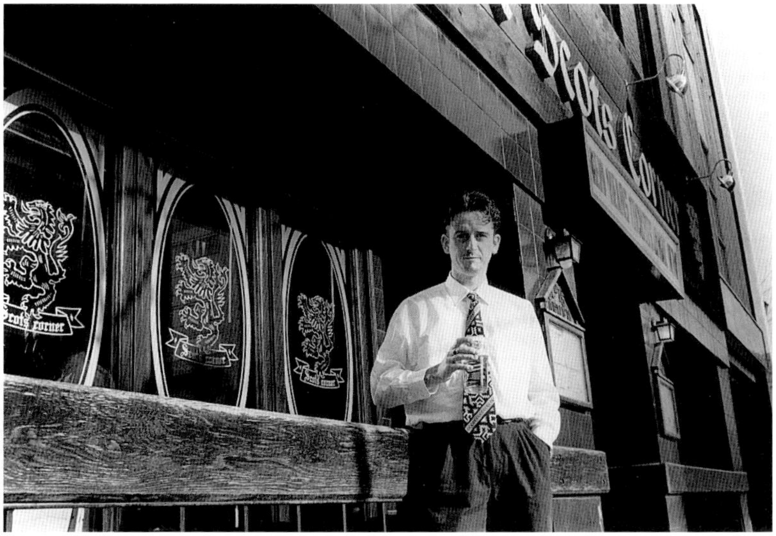

Rosemary Donovan Paul Byers 1994 *silver-gelatin print*

JAIME DAVID TISCHLER *Costa Rica*

Descent into Heaven

Unst Leisure Centre

BALTA SOUND
ISLE OF UNST
SHETLAND

UK PREMIERE

5 OCTOBER – 5 NOVEMBER

Descent Into Heaven is a visual reflection on the emigré's pervasive feeling of longing. Taken in Ojo de Agua (Costa Rica's most popular bathing resort since the Thirties), this series is part of an extensive photographic research conceived during many years of living abroad and nurtured by brief return visits, laden with the feeling of impending loss. Ojo de Agua is a place where ancient memories intertwine with the more recent nostalgia of the tourist who returns again and again. Jaime David Tischler exploits the dual capability of photography to both represent physical reality and simultaneously leave it floating in the ambiguous time of memory.

Presented by The Shetland Arts Trust in association with Fotofeis

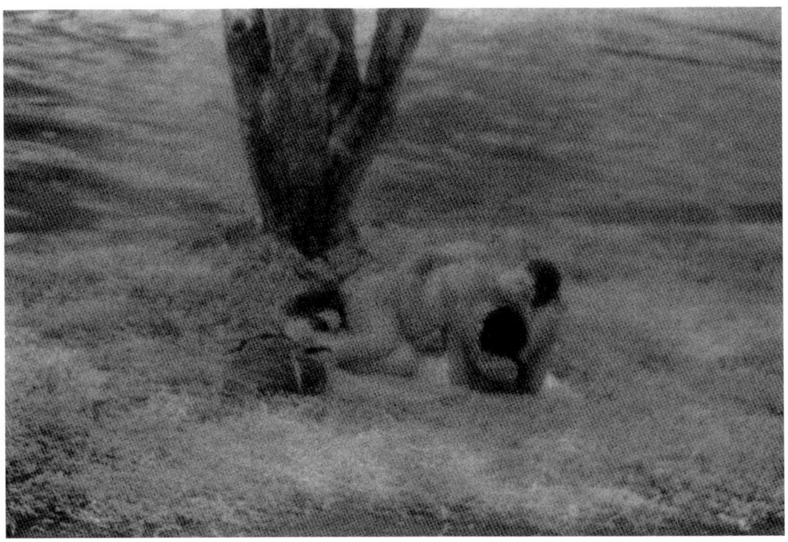

Jaime David Tischler untitled 1994 *toned silver gelatin print (from infra-red film)*

City

A PLACE THAT LOOKS LIKE HOME

VAL WILLIAMS

Cities became cities as we know them just as photography became a medium which was more than an inventor's dream. You could say that the two have grown up together. We become familiar with cityscapes even before we visit them and that familiarity comes primarily from photography. I went to New York for the first time just a few years ago, but the bright midday lights, the sharp shadows, the Chrysler building and the beach at Coney Island were already familiar. You can travel the world with photography without moving a step.

But our knowledge of the city through photography can make the actuality disappointing. Paris no longer looks like the city Eugene Atget photographed in the 19th century, or Cartier Bresson turned into the setting for an urban romance some decades later, but we go there in the hope that it might. Though the face of the city changes swiftly, we rarely stop to consider that perhaps London, Paris and New York never really looked as they did in photographs and more than time has created the illusion. The great cityscapes, the intimate bohemias and the underworlds which inhabit our imagination were merely someone else's well-crafted fiction.

In Britain, we have a singular relationship with urban life. Rather than living in our cities and walking to work, we live outside them, see them as a place of work or entertainment rather than as home. They are perceived as sites of danger, especially for women, even though most violence against women takes place in the home, quietly, behind the suburban nets. Photography has played its part in this demonography, for photographers are attracted to dark corners and sinister alleyways, they linger over rubbish and pounce on the derelict and the destitute.

I grew up in the city of Coventry, centre of the West Midlands industrial heartland, and one of Britain's oldest settlements. In World War II, Coventry's ancient core (and much else besides) was reduced to rubble by a massive German bombing raid. As a young woman, my mother stood on a hill in the neighbouring city of Leicester and watched Coventry burn and her recounting of that night formed one of the great narratives of my childhood. Coventry became famous for its ruination and when it was rebuilt, its corporate symbol was a phoenix rising from the ashes. Everyone came to photograph it after the raid, the mounds of shattered bricks, the broken buildings and the great gaunt walls of the wrecked cathedral stretching towards the sky. These photographs became a central part of the collective memory, as the new city rose from the ruins of the Fifties and Sixties.

Immured in this bright new bubble city, I became fascinated by that 'other' urban England which could be glimpsed in the photojournalistic essays which came to prominence in the Sixties. These places were beguiling and full of mystery, the street corner life of Roger Mayne's Southam Street in West London, Don McCullin's dour portrayal of Bradford, Leonard Freed's documentary of the sweatshops of Brick Lane in East London, and the compulsion has remained, to gaze at the tumbledown, the bereft and the forsaken. Again, the fulfilment of this desire has come through photography rather than travel – Sophie Ristelhueber's exploration of the wrecked buildings of Beirut, like giant dinosaurs stumbling towards the end of civilization, Wolfgang Bellwinkel's phantasmagorical still-lifes of Sarejevo's streets, Nick Waplington's documentation of the scrawled rubble of the Berlin Wall.

Everything comes full circle. The West Midlands has lost its prosperity and there are beggars on the streets of Coventry just as there are in other British towns. There is no need to look so hungrily for the 'other' when it is just around the corner and the optimism of the Sixties has faded away. I left a long time ago, and other memories, other images have taken the place of those childhood ones. But in the Eighties, photographers began to look beyond bohemia and rejected the romance of the inner city with its slums and its characters and began to gaze intently at the post-war cityscape. It all looked very familiar, and, oddly enough, it was yet another reflection of ruination, the frayed Sixties council estates, broken-down shopping malls, a jumble of road signs and miles of tarmac. Andreas Gursky's clear and clinical studies of the industrial belt of Western Germany, Thomas Ruff's Sixties apartment blocks, Thomas Struth's sweeping views of the skyline of East London – these are photographs of ruined places, destroyed by a potent mix of hope and greed, and the damage has no romance. But at last, in photography, I had finally found a place which looked like home.

The photographers and artists who have explored the notion of urban life in this current series of exhibitions prove how widely and variously visual artists use the motif of the city to express their individual concerns and fascinations. There could be no greater contrast than that between Beat Streuli's laconic documentary of modern urban life and Satish Sharma's collection of studio portraits from contemporary India. And Sharma's archive contrasts sharply with Dario Mitidieri's documentary of the street children of Bombay. Roger Palmer has looked at the furniture of street lighting in Glasgow, while John Duncan explores the topography of Northern Ireland. All of their views will be contested and compared and we as audience will gain insight or be at odds with the way that these photographers have interpreted the physical. But the city, observed, analyzed, praised or condemned, will rumble on its own extraordinary rhythms, heedless of our fantasies and desires, a site of renewal and re-interpretation.

Val Williams is a curator, writer and critic living in London

SEYDOU KEITA and MALICK SIDIBÉ
Photography from Mali

Fruitmarket Gallery

29 MARKET STREET
EDINBURGH

UK PREMIERE

20 SEPTEMBER – 21 OCTOBER

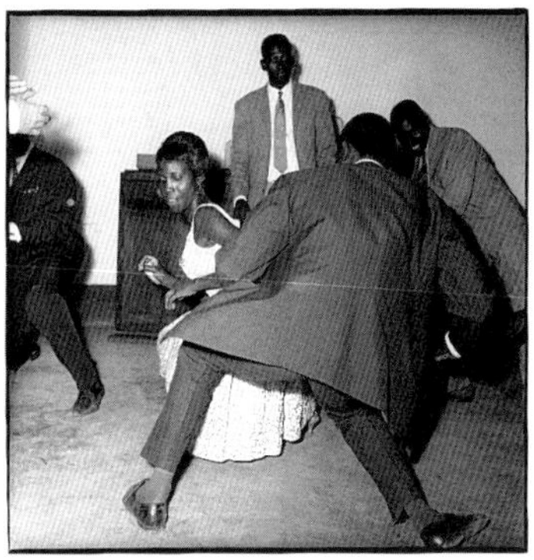

Malick Sidibé Danseur le Twist 1962 *silver-gelatin print (courtesy of Jean Pigozzi Collection © Malick Sidibé / CAAC)*

Curated by Hervé Chandès, Conservateur de la Fondation Cartier, and André Magnin, Independent Curator and Curator of the Contemporary African Art Collection

All photographs exhibited in the show are from the Jean Pigozzi Collection (CAAC), Geneva

From 1949 to his retirement in 1970 Seydou Keita photographed thousands of people in Bamako, the capital of Mali. Using a large-format camera and natural light, he photographed his subjects however they wished: alone, in couples, with their entire families. Often they appear with symbols of their professions – a sewing machine, a pen or a bottle of ink. During these years traditional culture was beginning to erode and the townspeople became influenced by European fashion. To provide for those who could not afford European modes of dress, Keita kept clothes in his studio: suits, ties, shirts, shoes and hats.

Women in particular were photographed in grand style, with the emphasis on their patterned robes and gold jewellery. "Their hands, their long slim fingers, their jewellery, were all terribly important", Seydou Keita remembers, "The women were very conscious of that. These were symbols of wealth, elegance, beauty."

Malick Sidibé also worked in Bamako from the 1950's. His chief interest was reportage and he travelled widely through Mali taking photographs of road-building, track-laying for the railway and construction sites. He also photographed christenings, first communions and weddings, but his preference was for "parties and young people", and increasingly he concentrated upon youth culture.

Films and music were the chief vehicles of European influence at this time, which was initially manifested through fashion and youth culture. A club culture had begun to grow up in Bamako, and Malick Sidibé went to these clubs to take spontaneous photographs of the young, stylish people, dancing and enjoying themselves. He also spent days photographing groups of young people swimming in the local river, dancing in the open air and having picnics. His photographs of the youth of Bamako capture their energy and optimism and the excitement of the time.
Based on a text by André Magnin

The exhibition was conceived by the Fondation Cartier pour l'Art Contemporain, Paris.

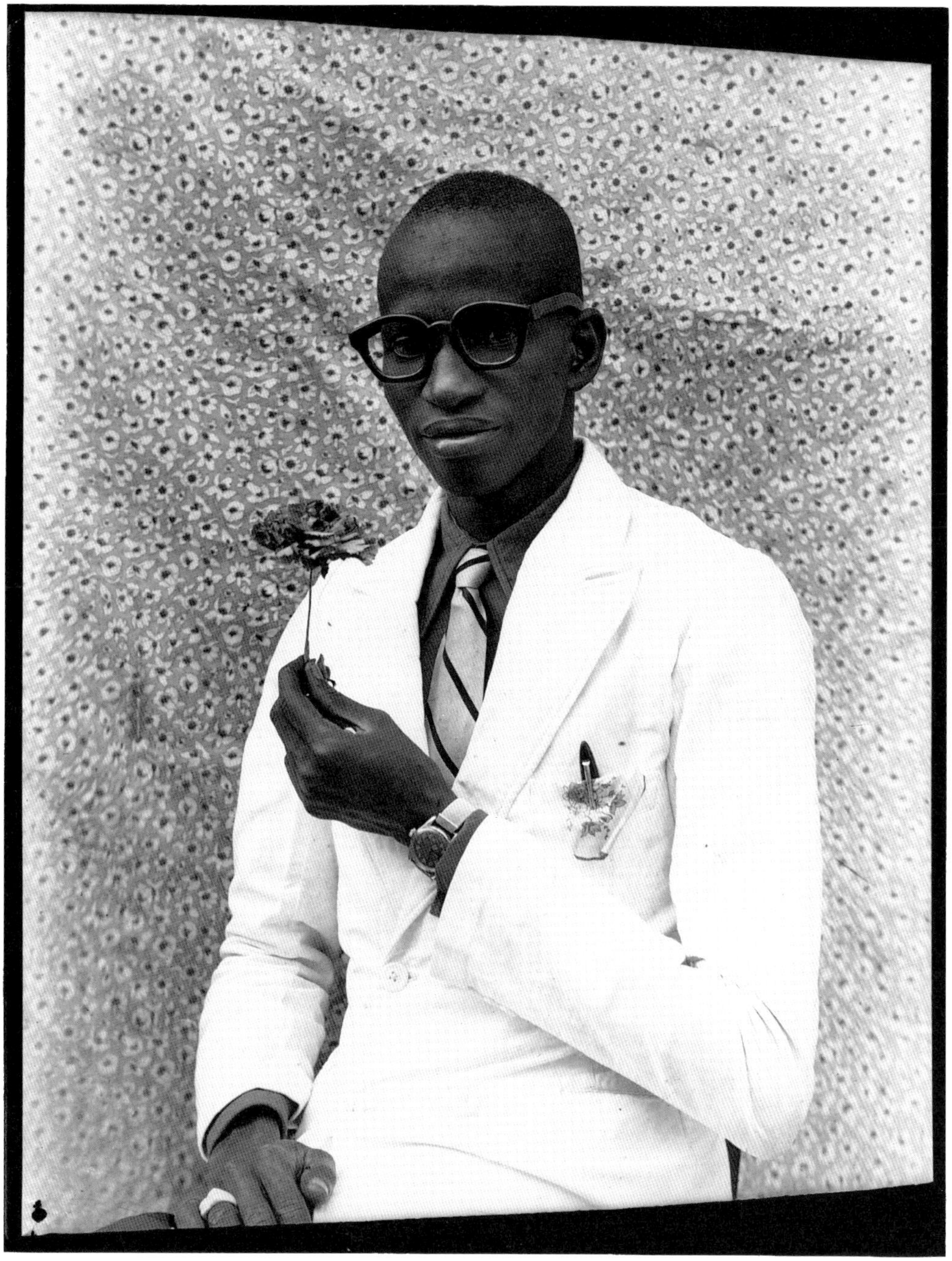

Seydou Keita untitled (Bamako) 1958 *silver-gelatin print* *(courtesy of Jean Pigozzi Collection © Seydou Keita / CAAC)*

On the Face of It

City Art Centre

2 MARKET STREET
EDINBURGH

PREMIERE

9 OCTOBER – 18 NOVEMBER

ROOT CARTWRIGHT
Scotland

GREGORY CREWDSON
USA

STÉPHAN GUÉNEAU
France/Scotland

ULRICH HORNDASH
Germany

JOHN KIPPIN
England

EDGAR LISSELL
Germany

GORDON MATTA-CLARK
USA

ALAIN PAIEMENT
Canada

Curated by Jane Warrilow and Amanda Farr

THE SCOTTISH **ARTS** COUNCIL

The term 'facade' brings with it associations both of architecture and pretence. A facade is literally a face, a front, a surface which mediates between public and private space. The facade projects the private into the public in one sense, in that it is an artifact of deliberate intention, a carrier of cultural and ideological values. But a facade also serves simultaneously to close and conceal and may even be deliberately constructed to disguise or dignify, like a neo-classical front on a department store.

The architectural facade helps orchestrate the quality of urban experience and what is true materially can also be true metaphorically, of persons and societies. A facade can as easily be a defence, an adopted *persona*, a set of values behind which another reality is at work. And in a culture ever more dominated and seduced by surface, appearance and image, the facade threatens to become the essential metaphor of contemporary living, a screen on which the appearance of real life is enacted.

On The Face Of It brings together the work of eight very different artists who share a common interest in exploring the concept of the facade in the urban and suburban environment. It includes such contrasting work as Stéphan Guéneau's slide projections of neon signs in Budapest; Alain Paiement's photo-construction of the Paris Bourse, which, quite literally, turn this international money-market inside out; the seminal work of Gordon Matta-Clark who opened up the hidden structures and spaces of abandoned buildings; Gregory Crewdson's mutant homes and gardens which subvert the comforting myths of American suburbia; John Kippin's exposure of the fictions and ironies of the British heritage industry; Root Cartwright's categorisation and typologies of buildings and materials; Ulrich Horndash's 'fantasy of ruins' which meditates on the collapse of political and social idealism vested in modernist architecture; and Edgar Lissel's chilling pin-hole camera images of Italian Fascist architecture. Each artist, ultimately, has been fascinated by the relationship of outward appearance and inner meaning.

Presented by the City Art Centre, Edinburgh in collaboration with Fotofeis

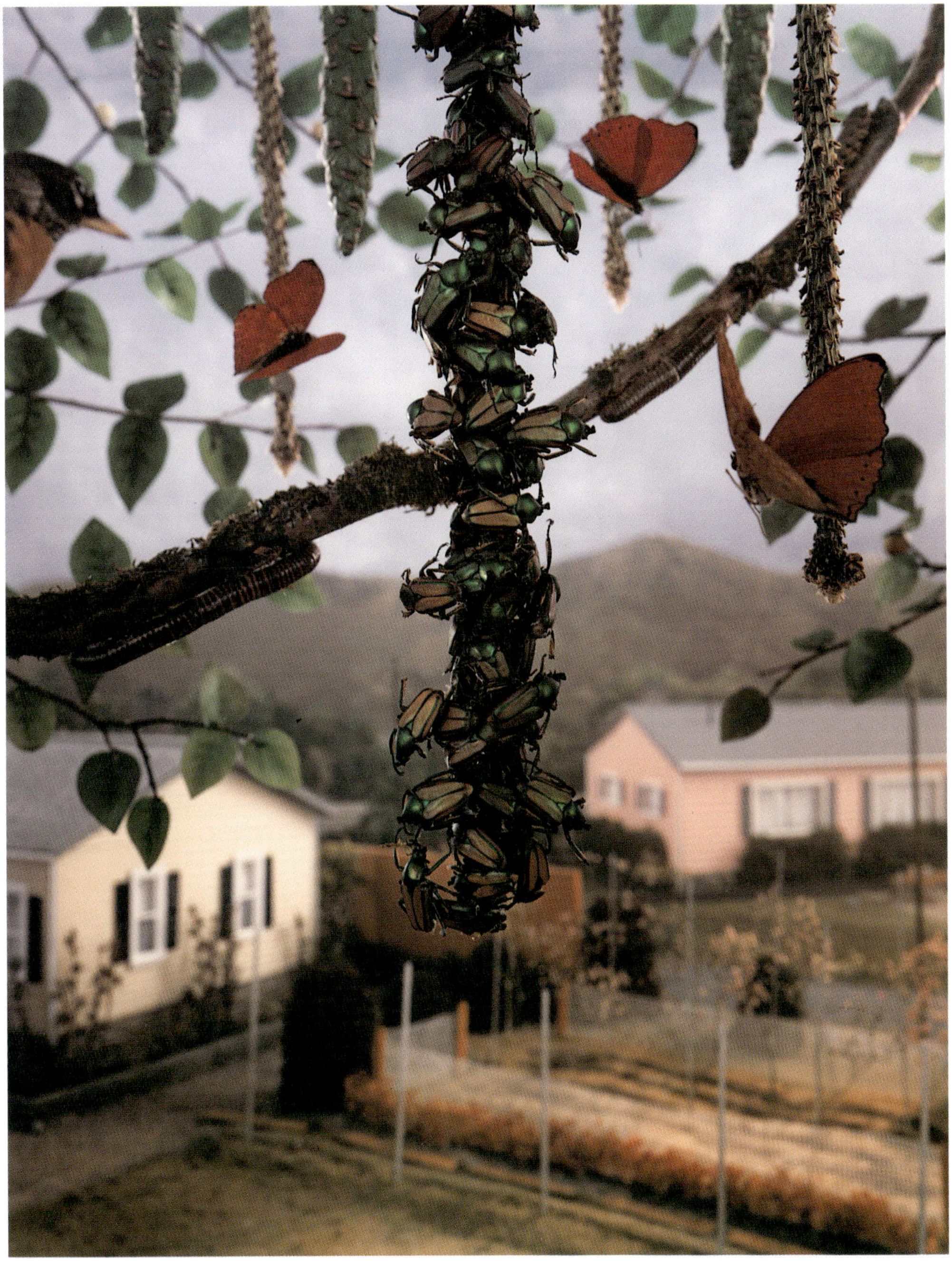

Gregory Crewdson untitled 1994 *type C print (courtesy of Luhring Augustine)*

BEAT STREULI *Switzerland*
Glasgow

20 WILSON STREET
GLASGOW

PREMIERE

Beat Streuli makes slide sequences of city life. This, his first made in Britain, has been shot in Glasgow. Using a motor-drive and long lens, he captures people unawares and through this builds a portrait of the city – transforming the chaos of urban life into a gently shifting surface of slowly dissolving images. Projected, they are cinematic in scale and texture. Moving invisibly through the city streets Beat Streuli's approach is similar to that of the photo-journalist, documenting the world dispassionately. In such ordinary and unprepossessing raw material, he finds an exotic choreography and sophisticated language of gesture employed in the daily negotiations of urban life.

Rather than images of the homogenised mass, the view is resolutely that of an observer as his camera records the micro-events linking and interconnecting. He teases apart the complex make-up of the crowd as it moves across the city slowly dissipating and dispersing. He tracks individuals, couples and small groups as they traverse crowded streets, march resolutely on business or as they idly window-shop. It is an uncommon view of the city, at odds with the notion of urban space as dark, subversive and potentially dangerous. Beat Streuli's vision reveals the colour, texture and rhythms of the city in daylight – a hiving, vibrant organism.

Commissioned by Fotofeis

CAPPA

Glasgow City Council

Pro Helvetia

VISITING ARTS

FUJI Professional

SSK LIMITED

dataton

B&S VISUAL TECHNOLOGIES LIMITED

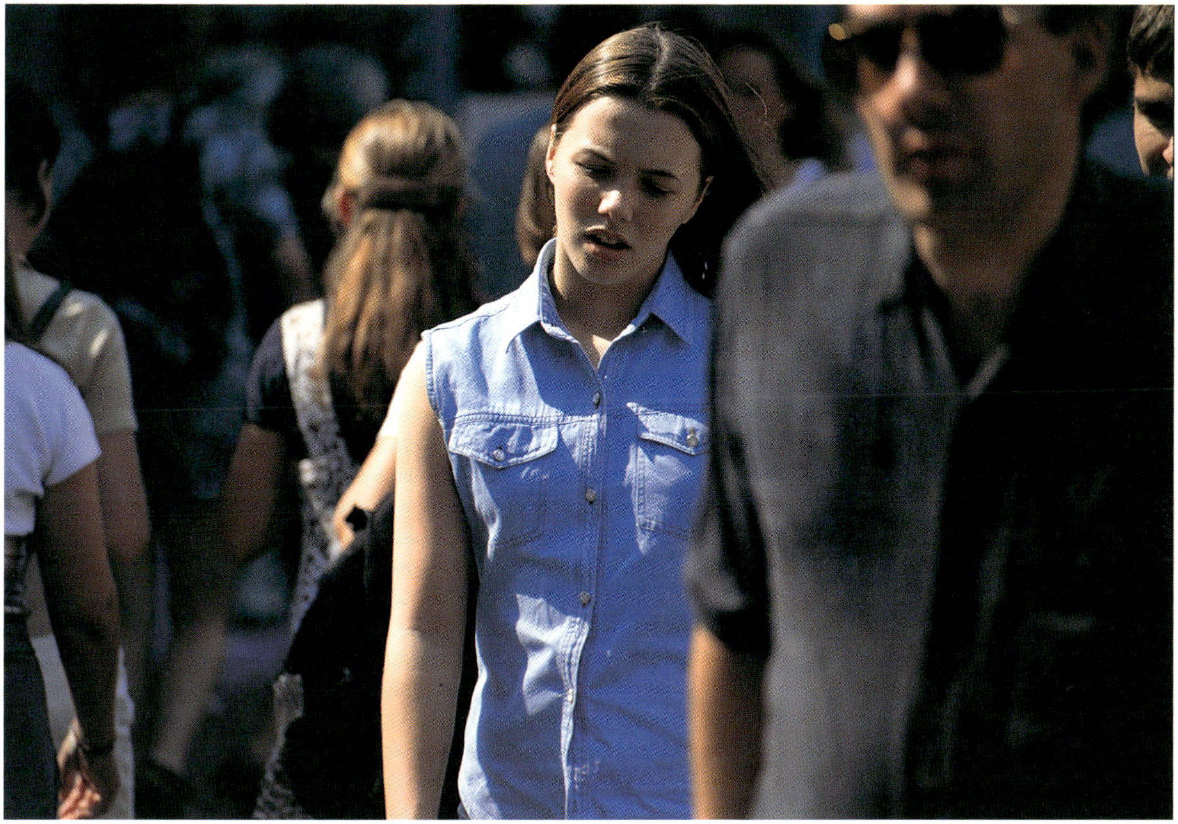

Beat Streuli untitled [from Glasgow sequence] 1995 *colour transparency*

FOTOFORUM SCHWARZBUNT *Germany*

1 to 6

Aberdeen Art Gallery

SCHOOLHILL
ABERDEEN

PREMIERE

7 OCTOBER – 5 NOVEMBER

KATHARINA BOSSE

JAKOB FEIGL

STEFAN SCHILLING

JÜRGEN SCHMIDT

FLORIAN SCHWINGE

HEIDI SPECKER

In this exhibition six young German photographers, members of the collective Fotoforum Schwarzbunt, each take a new and challenging approach to the topic of architectural photography – an artistic representation of another cultural form. Whilst the works in this group exhibition can be compared one to another, they should also be considered within the recent history of architectural photography.

Stefan Schilling's photographs record the reconstruction of the Alexanderplatz Station in the recently reunified Berlin, suggesting the disruption in the name of progress which accompanied the rapid demographic transition suffered in the name of progress. Jürgen Schmidt takes a more formal view of construction sites, transforming them into arrangements of pure form and colour.

In a similar approach, the reductive simplification of modern architecture is explored in Heidi Specker's computer manipulated images which take the ideal of reductive design to its logical conclusion as a series of fundamental underlying forms. While Heidi Specker addresses the exterior of modernist buildings, Katherina Bosse deconstructs the anonymous spaces of international interior design.

Jakob Feigl brings an oddly disconcerting view of architecture through his images of a toy city photographed from the perspective of a miniature citizen. The social aspects of rooms, buildings and urban environments are challenged in *Bricks*, the work of Florian Schwinge, in which he creates new social, functional and aesthetic arrangements.

The members of Fotoforum Schwarzbunt consciously set their work within the larger context of architectural photography – recognizing that they are not simply representing buildings, but commenting on the traditional formulae of architectural photography. With its focus on the function and aesthetics of the modernist ideal, the exhibition is in sharp contrast to the neo-classical environment of Aberdeen Art Gallery – creating a further, rich dialogue of ideas.

Curated by Thomas Seelig for Fotoforum Schwarzbunt

Subsidised by City of Aberdeen

THE SCOTTISH ARTS COUNCIL

Presented by Aberdeen Art Gallery in collaboration with Fotofeis

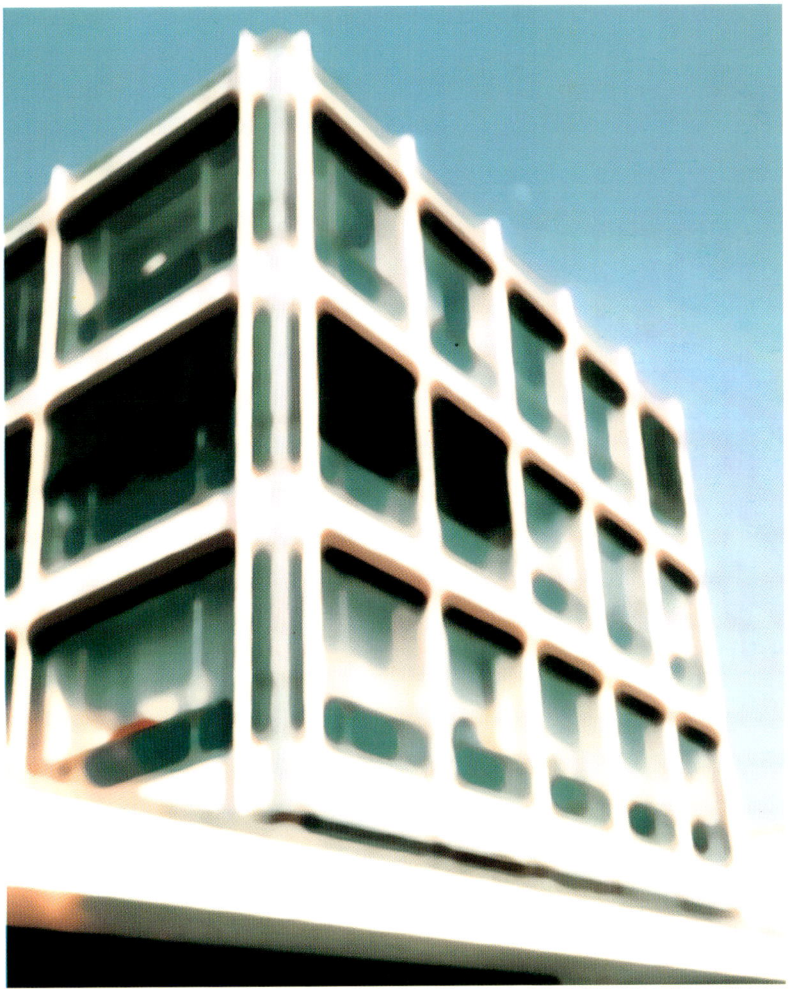

Heidi Specker untitled 1995 *colour print*

Art Club 2000 USA

Transmission Gallery

28 KING STREET
GLASGOW

PREMIERE

7 OCTOBER – 4 NOVEMBER

Art Club 2000 is a seven-person collaboration which came together at Cooper Union Art School in New York in the early Nineties, a central part of whose work has been the making of carefully constructed group photographs. These draw on imagery that is intrinsic to late 20th century consumer culture – the kind found on film posters, album covers, fashion spreads, or in lifestyle magazines. Part of a generation that has grown up both in love with and suspicious of the glamorous media images around them, they conspire to turn this part of our culture against itself.

In each photograph they assemble new identities, all seven members near identical, interchangeable. They play with locations, clothing, gestures and expressions which already have a history, a meaning in culture. Their pictures refer us back to other pictures, to the way in which contemporary consumer society uses images to package and market lifestyles and aspirations. They also point to what may be the eventual fate of art, to the fact that many of the experiments of the avant-garde have been absorbed so completely into popular culture that their origins no longer seem to matter.

As the name they have chosen acknowledges, the work of Art Club 2000 is very much a product of this decade – ironic, self-critical and dependent upon the systems that it accuses. Balancing compliance and critique, Art Club 2000 asks the viewer to question the conditions of the culture in which we live.

For *Fotofeis* '95, Transmission Gallery have commissioned Art Club 2000 to make new work in Glasgow.

Commissioned by Transmission Gallery in collaboration with Fotofeis

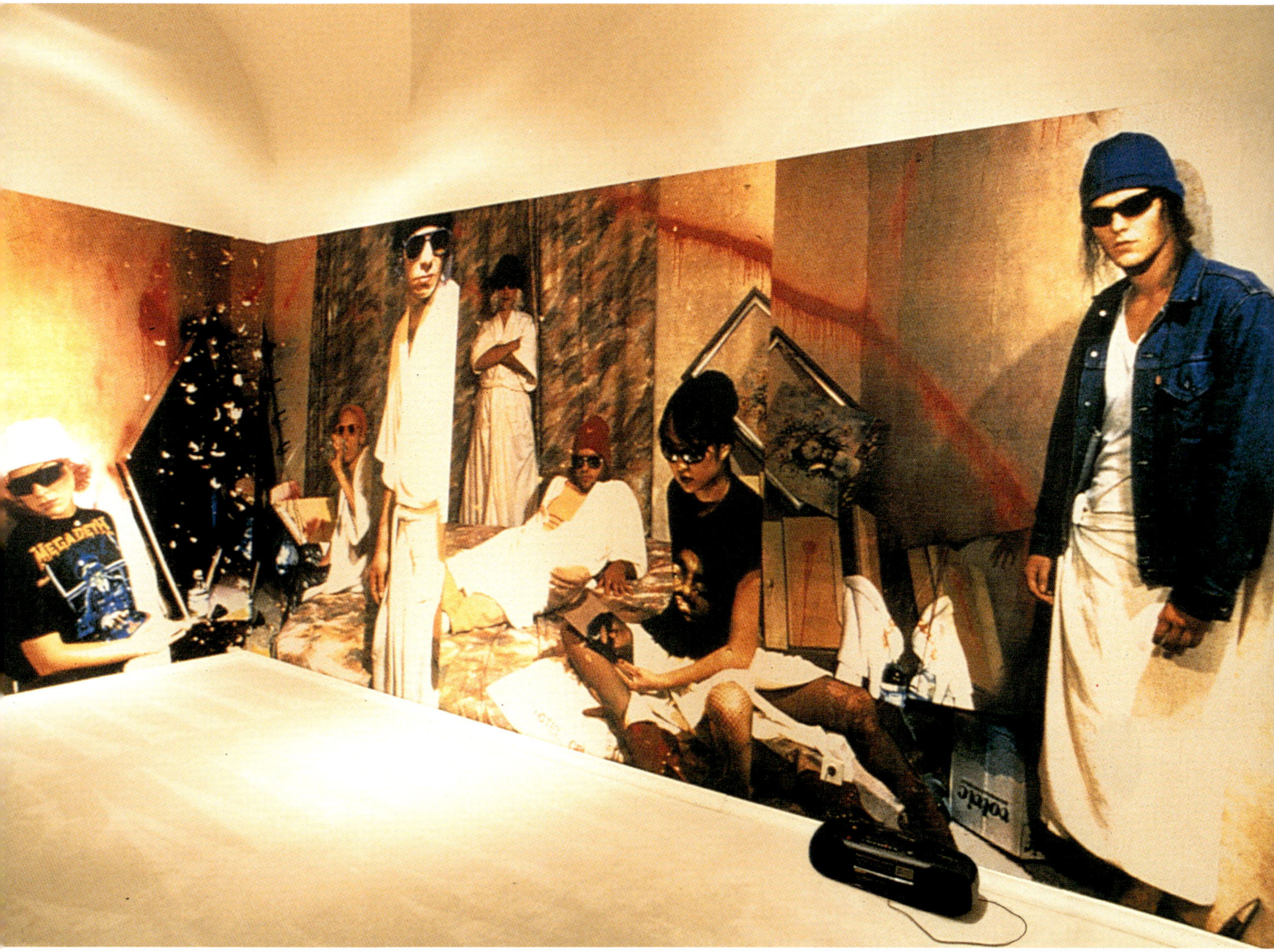

Art Club 2000 untitled 1994 *colour mural print (courtesy of Kunstverein Graz)*

MARK DENEYER, DANIEL DESMEDT, GILBERT FASKENAEKENS, CHRISTIAN MEYNEN, JACQUES VILET *Belgium*

04° 50° – The Brussels Photography Project

Barrack Street Museum

BARRACK STREET
DUNDEE

UK PREMIERE

16 SEPTEMBER – 4 NOVEMBER

Curated by Jean-Louis Godefroid, Contretype

THE SCOTTISH ARTS COUNCIL

Originating as a commission from the Region of Brussels, Belgium's five leading landscape photographers were asked to comment on their capital city and its environs. The photographers' remit was 'to give their considered reflection about what Brussels, its history and its probable future, meant to them'. The resulting works of art, thoughtful, individual and expressive, offer highly personal insights into the character and life of the city.

Jacques Vilet concentrated on Brussels' vegetable gardens. They are photographed as modern versions of the medieval *Hortus Conclusus* (walled garden), and emphasise the city's fragmentation. Gilbert Fastenaekens' work is presented in the form of five large books dealing with specific subjects: clouds; the great outdoors; urban landscape seen from above; building sites; and greenery. One image from each book is presented daily, providing a changing kaleidoscope of the eccentric character of the city. Christian Meynen's series of seventeen pictures forms a narrative sequence, giving the impression of an animated sequence. They illustrate his journey across the city from periphery to centre. Topographical and detached, his images express a cool, modern aesthetic. Daniel Desmedt investigated the places he knew well from his childhood. He focused on vegetation and lush undergrowth, shooting from a very low angle to recreate a child's feeling of adventure. Mark Deneyer went in search of 19th century parks and gardens as the areas which most moved him. His photographs have a classical quality with strong spiritual connotations.

Presented by Dundee Art Galleries and Museums in association with Fotofeis

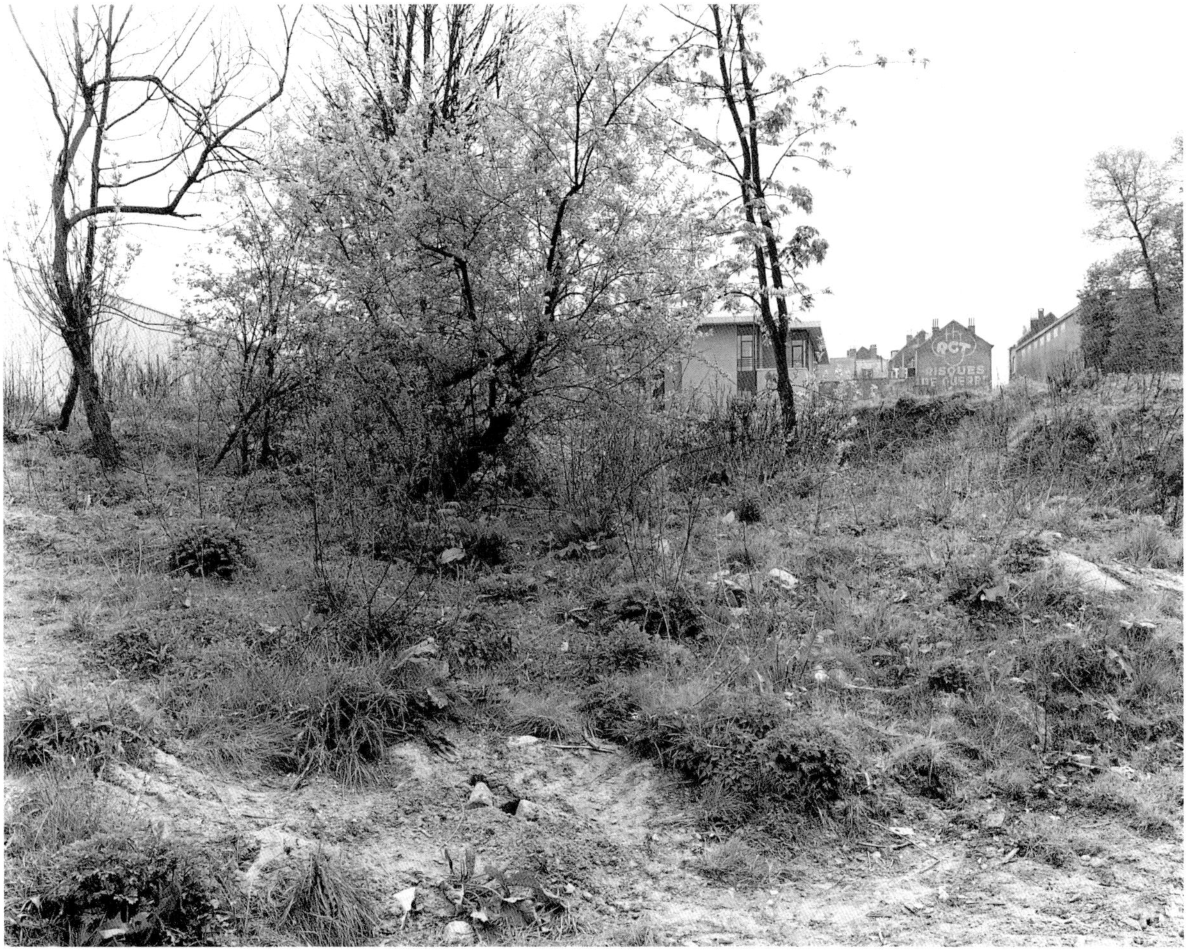

Christian Meynen 'Risques de Guerre' quartier Piardie, Schaerbeck 1991 *silver-gelatin print*

JANE BRETTLE *Scotland*
'Overexposing'

King Street and Port Street, Stirling

PREMIERE

6 OCTOBER – 3 NOVEMBER

'*Overexposing*' deploys the temporal and spatial qualities of photography to question the encoding of gender and dialogues of power within the patriarchally determined history of Western architecture. It creates a synthesis between the viewer's experience of the contemporary city in relation to exterior and interior architectural space. It suggests that our experience of the city is no longer one of architectonic structures, but rather a proliferation of continuous information which reaches us through our television screens and advertising displays. This is ultimately manifested in the television surveillance systems which (re)presents us to ourselves as always on display. In this vein the writer Paul Virilio considers that contemporary time and space has been 'flattened' and the notion of 'duration' abandoned. Past, present and future have been replaced by the photographic experience of under-exposure, exposure and over-exposure.

THE BANNER IMAGES

Leading up King Street and Port Street (opposite above)
The images have been appropriated from a closed circuit television surveillance camera. They have been re-photographed and dyed blue to suggest, or merge with, the sky, to represent infinity. The final pieces are further enhanced, making particular identification a fascinating conundrum.

Leading down King Street and Port Street (opposite below)
These are simple images of the sky appropriated from an architectural photograph and printed in black and white to suggest the apparently 'documentary' approach of the surveillance system.

All the banners are printed on vinyl mesh so that the images merge with the view of the city beyond. Each image is a part of a single larger image to be read across and along the street, suggesting fragmentation and a certain (dis)orientation.

Commissioned by Central Regional Council in collaboration with Independent Public Arts

Central Regional Council

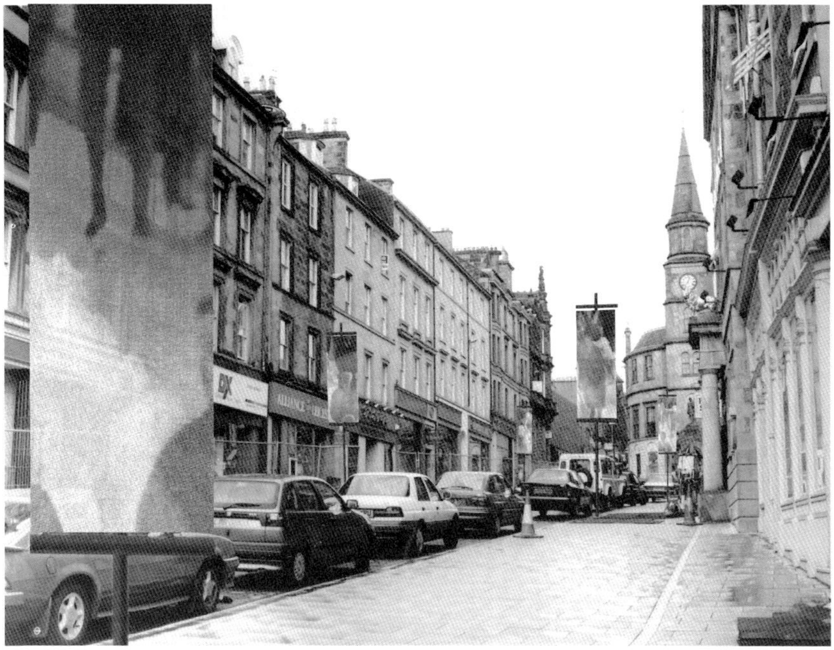

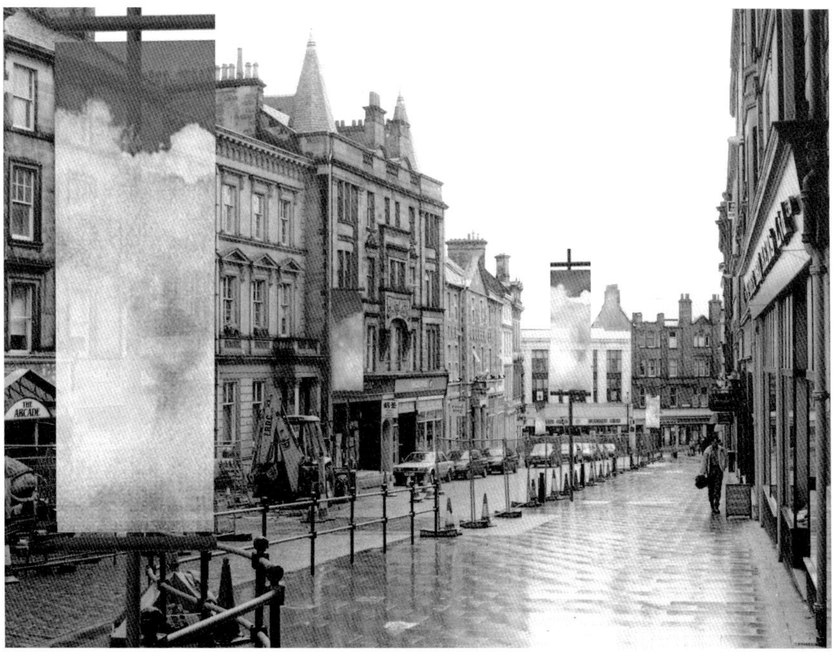

Jane Brettle 'Overexposing' – a simulation 1995 *computer generated artist's impressions*

JOSEPH McKENZIE *Scotland*

Dundee: City in Transition, 1964–66

McManus Galleries

ALBERT SQUARE
DUNDEE

PREMIERE

9 SEPTEMBER – 28 OCTOBER

The ultimate aim of my life, defined as a teacher, a photographer and an artist, is surely to leave on record a lucid and truthful image of what it was like to live through the turbulent twentieth century. JOSEPH MCKENZIE

Dundee – City in Transition is a collection of four hundred and forty one vintage prints. Shown only once in 1966 to mark the opening of the Tay Road Bridge, it was acquired by Dundee Art Galleries and Museums in 1990. It comprises six sections: Building of the Tay Road Bridge; Death of a Station; People in Jute; Women of Dundee; Men and Locomotives; and Impressions of the City.

When Joseph McKenzie came to Dundee to teach photography in 1964, he was immediately struck by the combination of light and urban textures, which lent themselves so well to photography. Like most British cities in a time of postwar optimism and hope, Dundee was beginning to reconstruct for itself a modern identity. Now opened up to the south by the Tay Road Bridge and experiencing a new affluence, Dundee attempted to shake off the legacy of industrial decline. Through zealous slum clearances the population of the city centre communities such as Hawkhill were dispersed to greenbelt suburbs.

Born in London in 1929, Joseph McKenzie was a Lecturer in Photography at Duncan of Jordanstone College of Art from 1964–86. Widely regarded as the 'Father of Modern Scottish Photography', his studies and exhibitions of the Sixties earned him a lasting reputation for versatility, the breadth of his vision and the superb quality of his prints. This exhibition puts a substantial part of the archive on show for only the second time. A new generation can savour the honest realism and humour found in scenes of dereliction, animated street life and, above all, his humane and intimate portraits of Dundee's working people.

Presented by Dundee Art Galleries and Museums

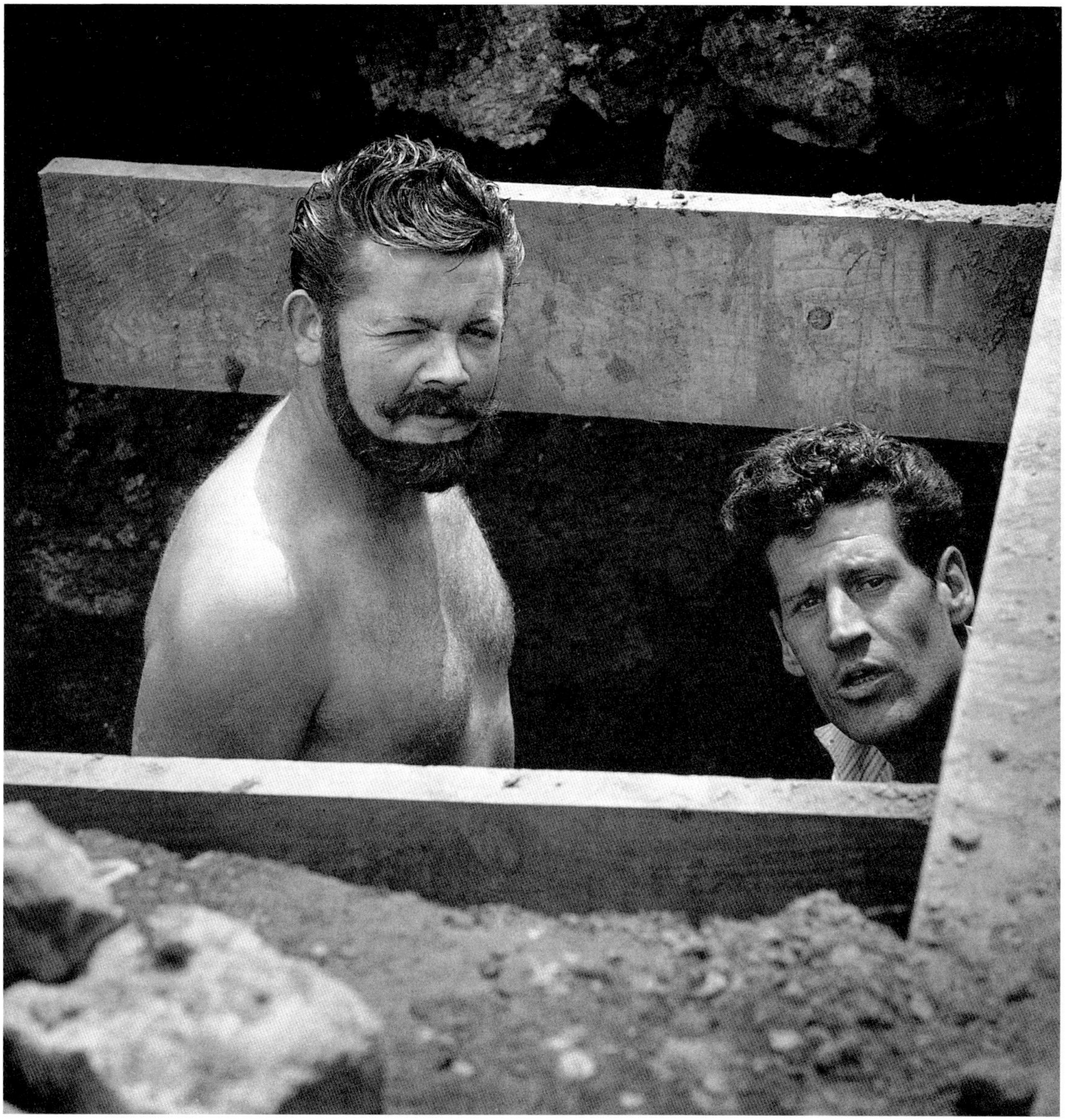

Joseph McKenzie Hole in the Ground c.1965 *silver-gelatin print*

DONNA DE CESARE USA

A Tale of Two Cities: The Rise of LA Gangs in El Salvador

Cranhill Arts Gallery

18 KING STREET
GLASGOW

UK PREMIERE

13 OCTOBER – 5 NOVEMBER

A new Salvadoran generation is growing up with war. The combatants are children and teenagers caught up in Los Angeles gang vendettas. Their parents are refugees who fled the US-backed civil war in El Salvador to seek a better life for their families in the United States. Nearly one fifth of Salvadorans fled their war torn villages to settle in the City of Angels. The reality they encountered was one of drug and gang-infested slums, and their already fragile families began to fall apart. To survive, many Salvadoran immigrant youths joined Chicano gangs like *Eighteenth Street* or formed new gangs like *Mara Salvatruncha*. Mortal enemies, these gangs fight for honour or from hatred whenever they meet.

After the Los Angeles riots of 1992, anti-immigrant feeling in the US grew, leading to a policy of deporting Salvadoran youths. Back in El Salvador these fast-talking American deportees were idolized by local youths who wanted to walk the walk and talk the talk they had come to know through gang movies and rap lyrics. They joined *Mara Salvatruncha* and *Eighteenth Street* and now deadly Los Angeles-style gang wars are being waged by teenagers who have never even been to the United States. In response, the *Black Shadow*, a government-backed death squad has begun to patrol the city, summarily executing the warring youths as part of a policy of 'social cleansing'.

These photographs from the mean streets of Los Angeles and San Salvador attest to the fragility of hope on the margins of both societies. They raise questions about the legacy of war and the realities behind the contemporary diaspora. The social and political realities of the Americas, north and south, are inextricably linked. Difference and distance between the two is no longer relevant.

Presented by Cranhill Arts Gallery in association with Fotofeis

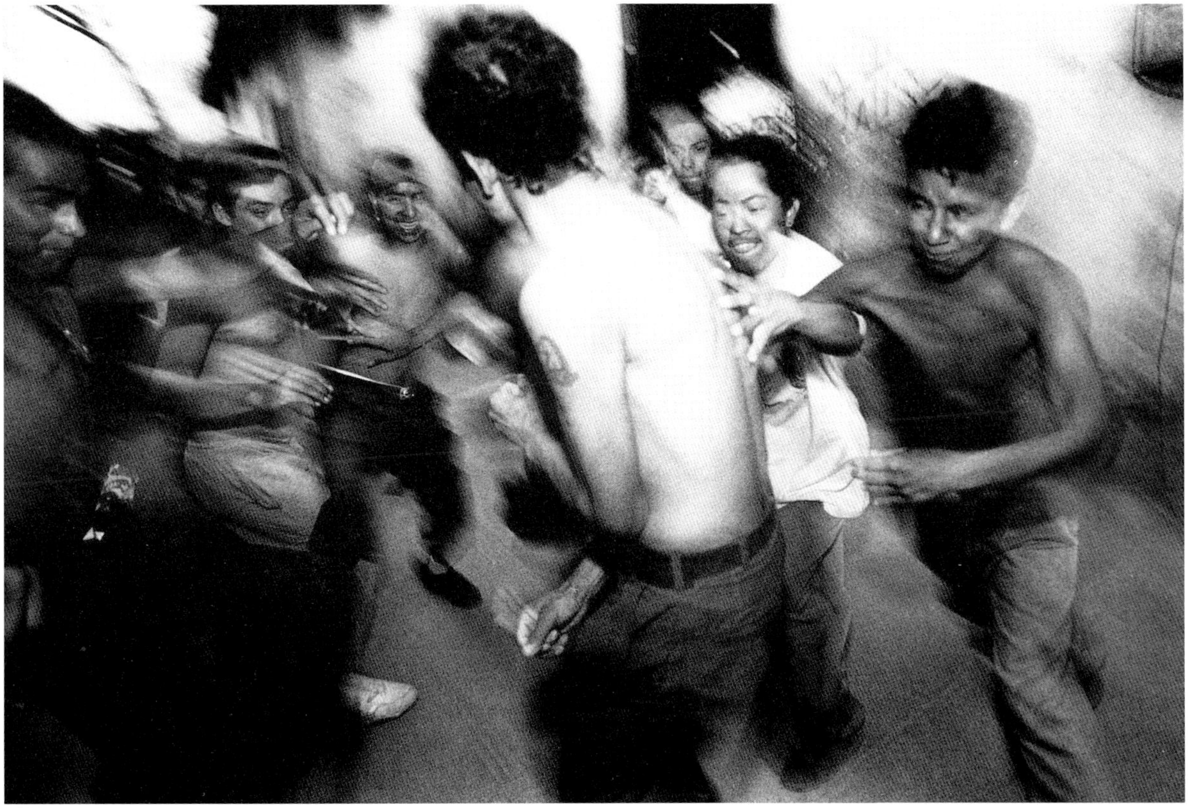

Donna De Cesare Initiation, San Salvador 1994 *silver-gelatin print*

JOHN DUNCAN *Northern Ireland*

Fast Friend Les Dawnson

East Kilbride Arts Centre

UK PREMIERE

OLD COACH ROAD
EAST KILBRIDE

27 SEPTEMBER – 22 OCTOBER

John Duncan produces subtle, allusive and sombre images of his native Belfast. His vision of the city is an alien, depopulated landscape where that which appears at first glance to be ordinary or mundane reveals itself, on closer inspection, to be filled with cryptic detail. Shown in groups of up to five images, these build a complex and multi-levelled narrative.

The work discloses the chaos that every city generates, found in those half-forgotten corners where such raw evidence exists. But the work also alludes to the political tensions in this particular city. A brick wall with hundreds of red-painted hand-prints, abandoned industrial heaters in a back street, a three piece suite on the edge of wood. The images have a sinister drama about them, as if something unpleasant or disturbing has just taken place or is about to happen. The eroding detritus and disregarded symbols of the city provide encoded messages to be interpreted afresh in the newfound freedom which has ensured their very obsolescence. Pushed aside by the ruthless economics and politics of a organism endlessly reconstructing itself, the refuse of yesterday's constructions and habitations tells of past and present as a single, compound and mutable process where identities are relentlessly asserted, obscured and reasserted in new forms.

Presented by East Kilbride Arts Centre in association with Fotofeis

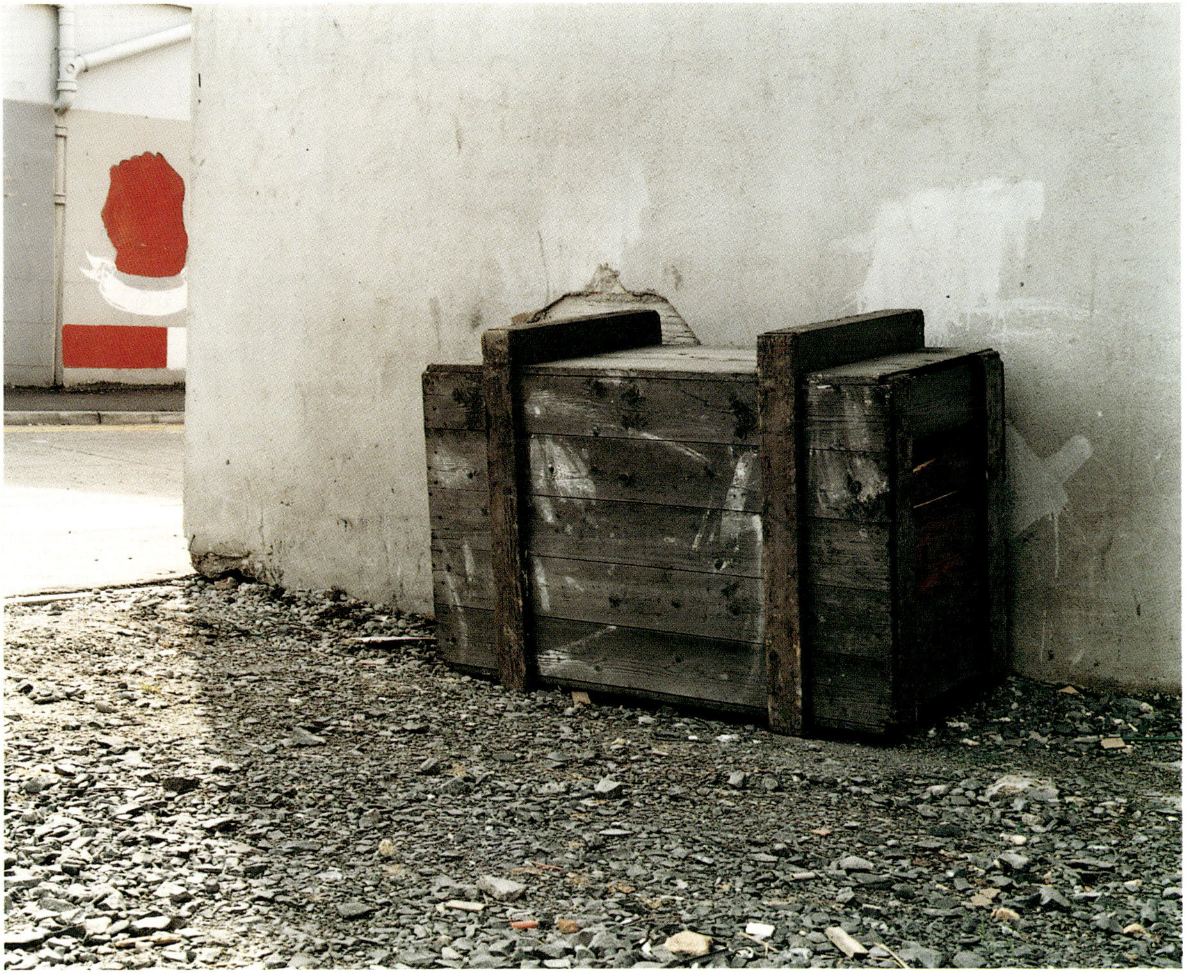

John Duncan untitled 1993 *colour print*

DREAMS THAT MONEY CAN BUY
Indian Studio Photography

Dick Institute

ELMBANK AVENUE
KILMARNOCK

PREMIERE

5 OCTOBER – 11 NOVEMBER

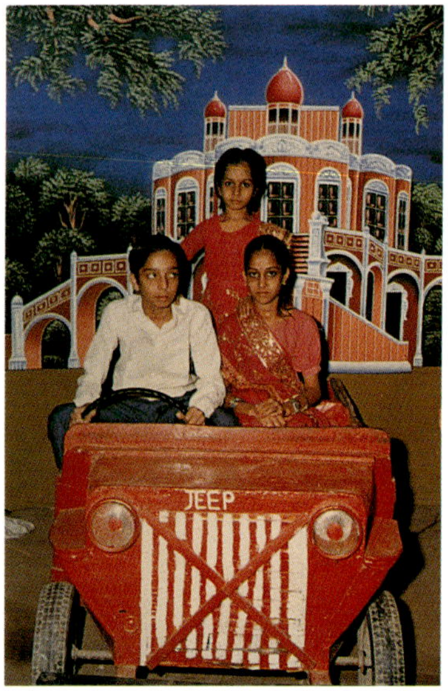

Curated by Satish Sharma

VISITING ARTS

It is impossible to disassociate the history of photography in India from that country's colonial past. The medium's invention coincided with the spread of Western colonisation and as such became a powerful means through which countries and cultures were systematically recorded, catalogued and 'acquired' for the Empire.

Throughout the 20th century, amateur photographic practice was the exclusive domain of British colonials, Indian royalty and the wealthy few. As a medium of expression photography remained beyond the means of the average Indian citizen. Even the advent of Kodak's 'you press the button, we do the rest' cameras did little to open up photography to the majority of Indians and their only access to photography remains the local or itinerant studio photographer.

Employing a pantechnicon of elaborate sets, props and costumes, studio photographers provide a surreal stage for the enactment of fantasies of wealth and power, bringing together the disparate imagery of religion, myth and consumer status symbols. The visual impact of these studio photographs is akin to the epic glamour of the Hindi film industry from which it draws inspiration. Their self-conscious construction runs directly counter to ideals of digital seamlessness and documentary veracity. Rather, the spirit of these images has much to say about the Indian belief in the world as *maya* (illusion) and the view of life as *leela* (divine play).

Although these photographs are universally dismissed, even by their creators, as 'Rotigraphy', within Indian homes they become icons, finding their way into sacred *pooja* spaces. They represent far more than just a banal document of friends and relations, extending their influence into the sphere of family ritual.

The exhibition's curator, Satish Sharma, considers that the visual language of Western 'international' photography belongs to the industrial world. He believes that it is possible to find a more truly national identity in these humble, but quintessentially Indian, studio portraits.

Commissioned by the Dick Institute in association with Fotofeis

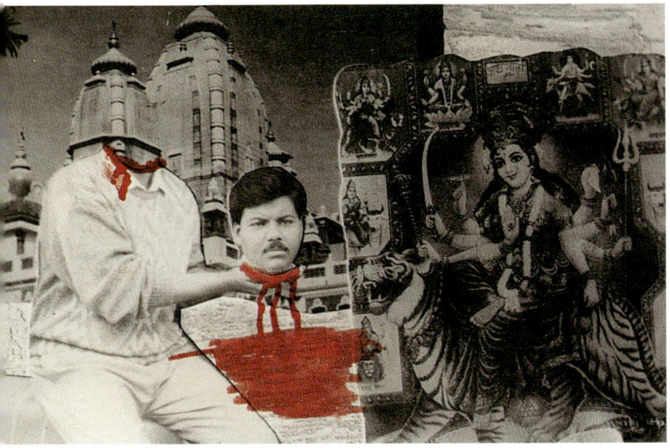

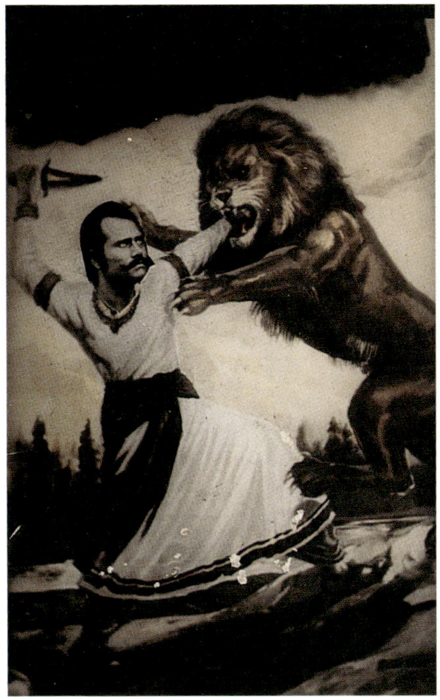

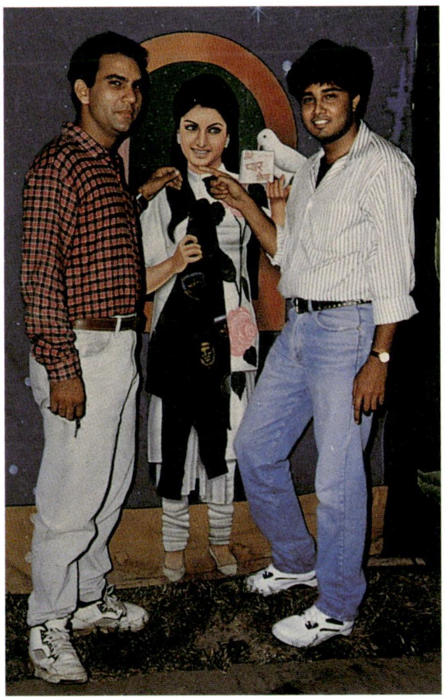

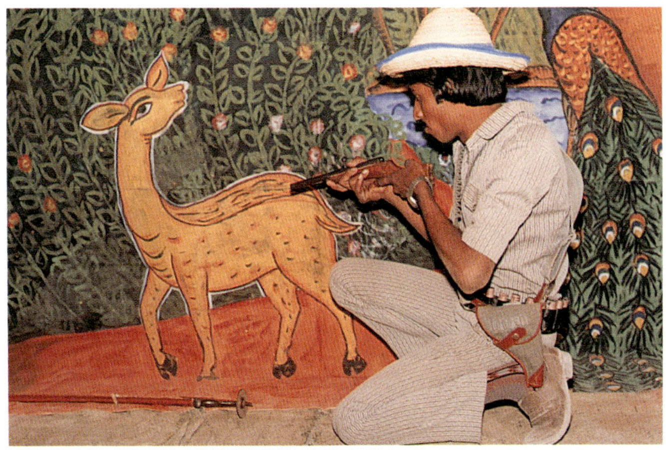

above and opposite Studio portraits from the collection of Satish Sharma

SU GRIERSON *Scotland*

Pollard and Prune

The Gallery

39 WEST GRAHAM STREET
GLASGOW

PREMIERE

7 OCTOBER – 14 OCTOBER

An artist-run project

Glasgow City Council

Cities everywhere have their harshness muted through the introduction of 'nature'; parks, tree-lined avenues, grassy corners, hanging baskets and floral clocks soften our urban landscape. This is nature tamed, contained and restrained until it conforms to our spaces and our aesthetic ideals.

These photographs of urban trees and shrubs which have been intentionally shaped through pollarding, pruning and topiary, emphasise the gulf between their constrained and natural forms. Strongly coloured overlays create a psychological distancing, which, together with a partial loss of focus, produces a sense of unreality. The work draws on photographs taken in Scotland, Belgium, Germany and Tasmania .

Each night, as darkness falls, a video projection will fill the gallery window. In this way, trees in their natural form will be reintroduced into the city.

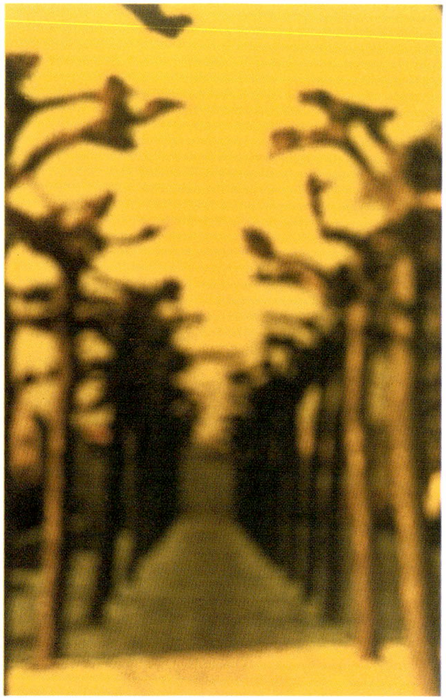

Su Grierson untitled 1995 *colour print*

NIALL HENDRIE *Scotland*

44 Chambers Street, Edinburgh, The World

Royal Scottish Museum

CHAMBERS STREET
EDINBURGH

PREMIERE

6 OCTOBER – 14 JANUARY

The Royal Museum of Scotland is scheduled to open in 1998. Its location in Chambers Street, Edinburgh, will provide new and expanded display for the adjoining Royal Museum of Scotland.

The creation of the new Museum forms one stage in a continuum which links the new building to the old, the historic collections to the contemporary ones and the current building work with the future. This theme is taken and developed in the work of Niall Hendrie. Completed during a year working with the project, this exhibition mixes two sections representing that which is 'implied' and that which is 'applied'. Both develop Niall Hendrie's belief that everything, from the foundations up, is inextricably linked with its function and its environment.

Commissioned by the National Museums of Scotland

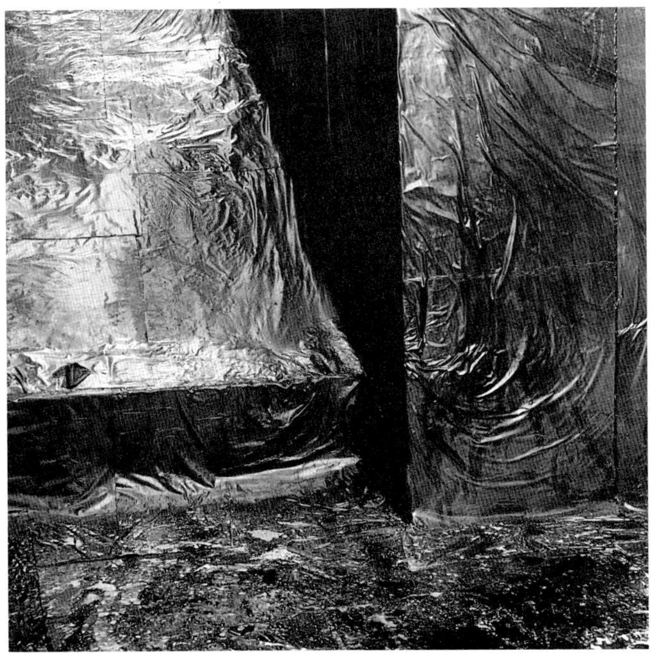

Niall Hendry untitled 1995 *silver-gelatin print*

ROGER PALMER *Scotland*

Coat of Arms

Mackintosh Museum

GLASGOW SCHOOL OF ART
167 RENFREW STREET
GLASGOW

PREMIERE

6 OCTOBER – 28 OCTOBER

There's the fish that never flew
There's the bell that never grew
There's the bird that never rang
There's the tree that never swam

CHILDREN'S RHYME

Coat of Arms comprises a group of approximately twenty black and white photographs, a wall drawing and a text. The photographs were made in Glasgow over a twelve-month period in 1994/95. They are of cast iron reliefs of the city coat of arms which decorate many street-lighting junction boxes. Different daylight conditions, weathered surfaces and various states of obliteration are compared through the emblematic symmetry of each image.

Legends of St Mungo, performer of miracles and patron saint of Glasgow, are remembered in the central shield and in a popular children's rhyme. In this exhibition both of these motifs acquire a new identity as temporary works on the walls of the Mackintosh Museum.

Janitors at Glasgow School of Art wear a jacket with an embroidered badge featuring the civic coat of arms as part of the School's insignia. Displayed above the central stairway which leads to the Mackintosh Museum, is a stylised, three-dimensional version designed by Charles Rennie Mackintosh. Roger Palmer's exhibition brings together the various representations in a building which might be considered Glasgow's 20th century secular cathedral.

Presented by Glasgow School of Art

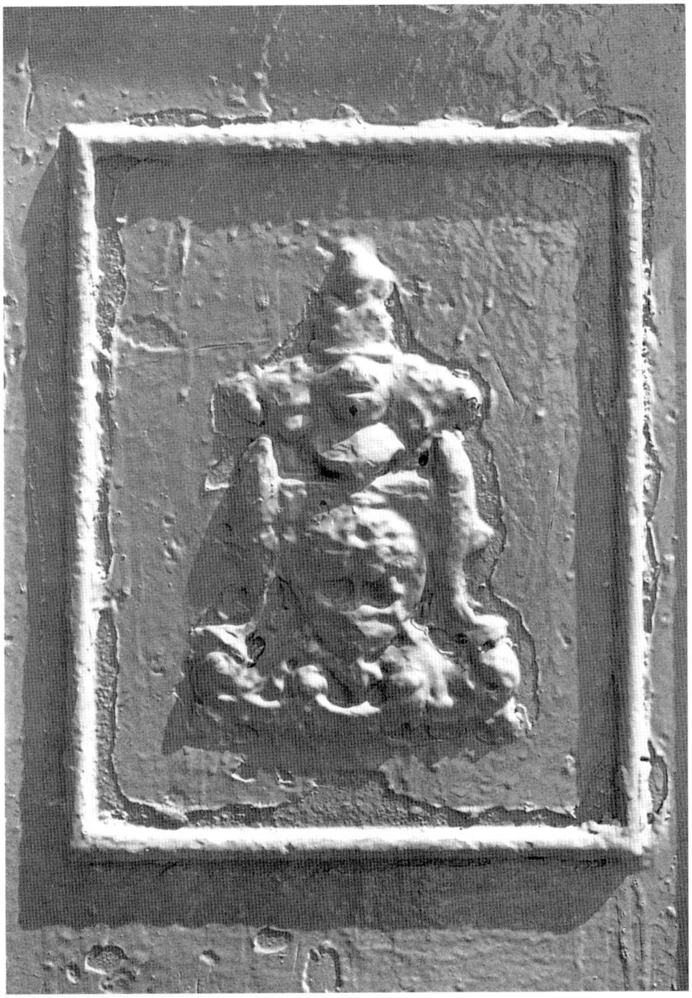

Roger Palmer © Coat of Arms 1994–5 *silver-gelatin print*

DARIO MITIDIERI UK
Children of Bombay

Glasgow Central Station

GORDON STREET
GLASGOW

6 OCTOBER – 20 OCTOBER

Children of Bombay won the first European Publishers Award for Photography from among more than two hundred book projects submitted by practitioners from some twenty European countries. It is an extraordinarily forceful book that focuses on the street children of India's largest city. An estimated thirty thousand children are homeless, living on its streets, under bridges, in railway stations, anywhere they can without being harassed by the police or by criminals. They have no rights, are considered a nuisance and at best are ignored by the majority of people in Bombay. This hazardous position means these young people are very vulnerable; drug addiction, sexual exploitation and criminal gangs are just some of the perils they face.

Dario Mitidieri has covered some of the most significant news stories of the last decade from the Tiananmen Square Massacre through to the fall of the communist regime in Albania. Winner of the prestigious Eugene Smith Award he has also been News Photographer of the Year in the British Press Awards. Both Dario Mitidieri and Dewi Lewis have worked closely with a new charity, *The Railway Children*, established by David Maidment, a senior executive at Railtrack, to support projects which help hundreds of thousands of street children living in and around railway stations throughout the world. Glasgow Central Station is therefore a very appropriate venue to exhibit the photographs.

Dewi Lewis Publishing

An Impressions Gallery touring exhibition presented by Art Exposure Gallery in collaboration with Dewi Lewis Publishing

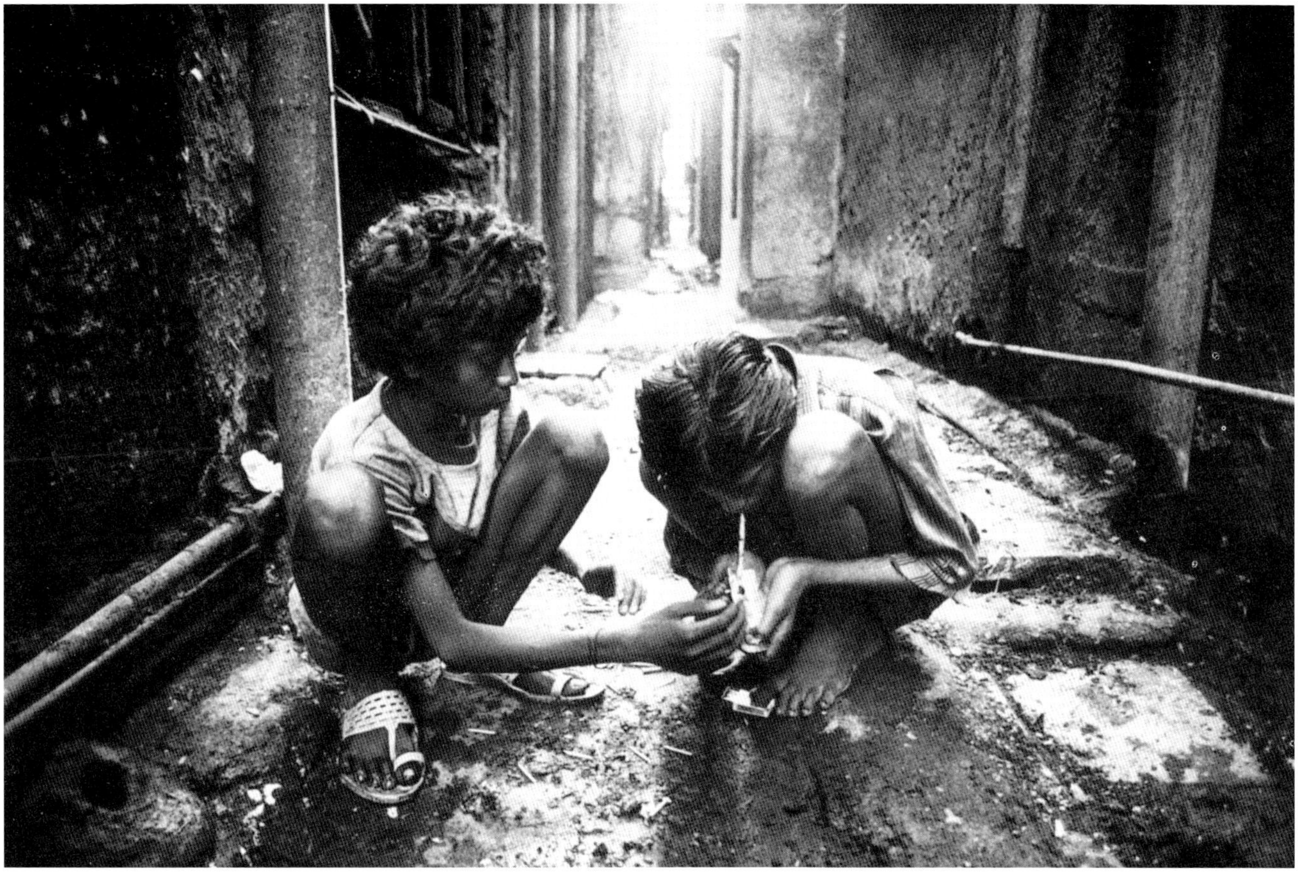

Dario Mitidieri Firoze and Sadik smoke 'brown sugar' in an alleyway in the red light district of Kamatipura *silver-gelatin print*

MARLENE CREATES *Canada*

Language and Landuse, Newfoundland 1994

Collins Gallery

UNIVERSITY OF STRATHCLYDE
22 RICHMOND STREET
GLASGOW

EUROPEAN PREMIERE

26 SEPTEMBER – 21 OCTOBER

Language and Landuse, Newfoundland 1994 was inspired by Marlene Creates' memories of family slide shows containing not only pictures of landscapes but also the signs and plaques from historic sites.

The geography around each of these signs, the territory under the influence of the printed public message, is a place circumscribed by human activity. In each of the assemblages, under the central photograph in a three-part panorama, in juxtaposition to the print and languages of the public sign, the artist has placed a small hand-written panel describing her personal observations and experiences in each place. Below these she places an object which she collected there. The signs she photographs are not about the past, but about the current use of land where infinite changes and events have taken place over the course of time.

Presented by the Collins Gallery

Canada/Newfoundland Cooperation Agreement on Cultural Industries

The Canada Council
Conseil des Arts du Canada

Newfoundland and Labrador Arts Council

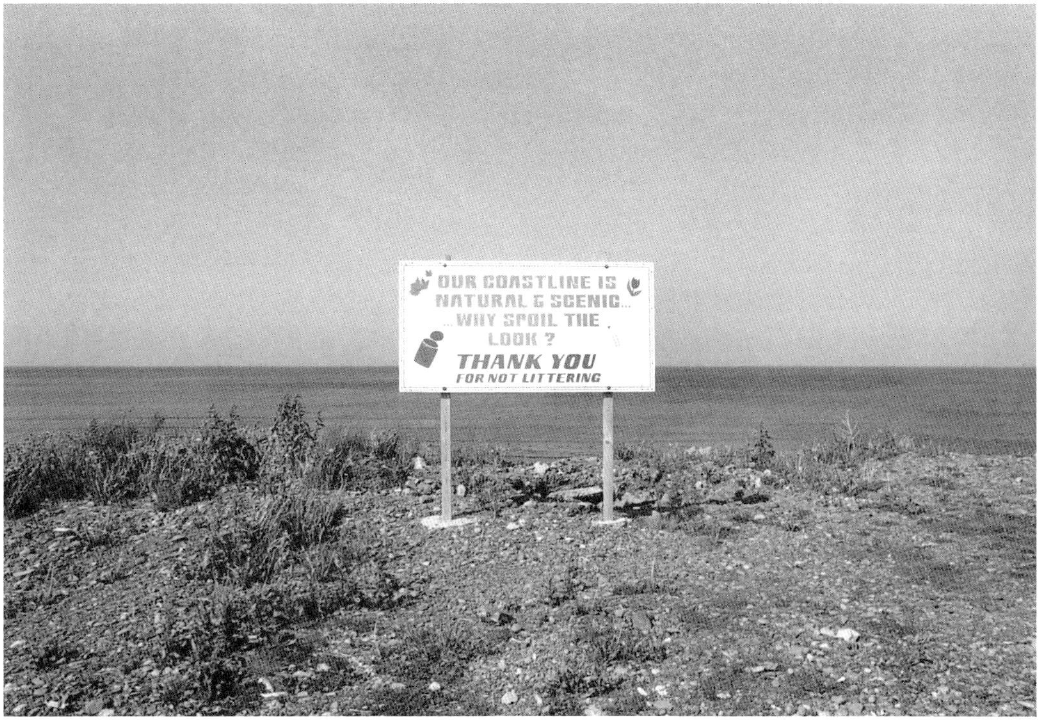

Marlene Creates excerpt from OUR COASTLINE IS NATURAL & SCENIC
from the series Language and Landuse, Newfoundland 1994
assemblage of selenium-toned silver gelatin prints, handwritten text and beach rocks

CHRISTINA McBRIDE *Scotland*

The Grey Patch

Glenacre Shops

GLENACRE DRIVE
CASTLEMILK, GLASGOW

PREMIERE

30 OCTOBER – 5 NOVEMBER

Following her large-scale projection onto the doomed Queen Elizabeth Square flats in Glasgow's Gorbals in 1993, Christina McBride's latest work returns to the theme of urban regeneration. She recently spent a four month period as artist in residence in the Castlemilk housing estate in Glasgow. Here she found much talk of empowering ordinary people to participate in the decision making processes in the places where they live. Christina McBride reflects on the reality that housing is only part of the problem of these crumbling communities where mass unemployment and ill-health are also taking their toll. This new work will centre on a four-storey derelict building in Glenacre Drive, a block of low-rise flats known locally as 'the grey patch', which will be illuminated with projected images and coloured light.

An artist-run project in association with The Arts and Cultural Development Office, South East Area Arts, Glasgow

Glasgow City Council

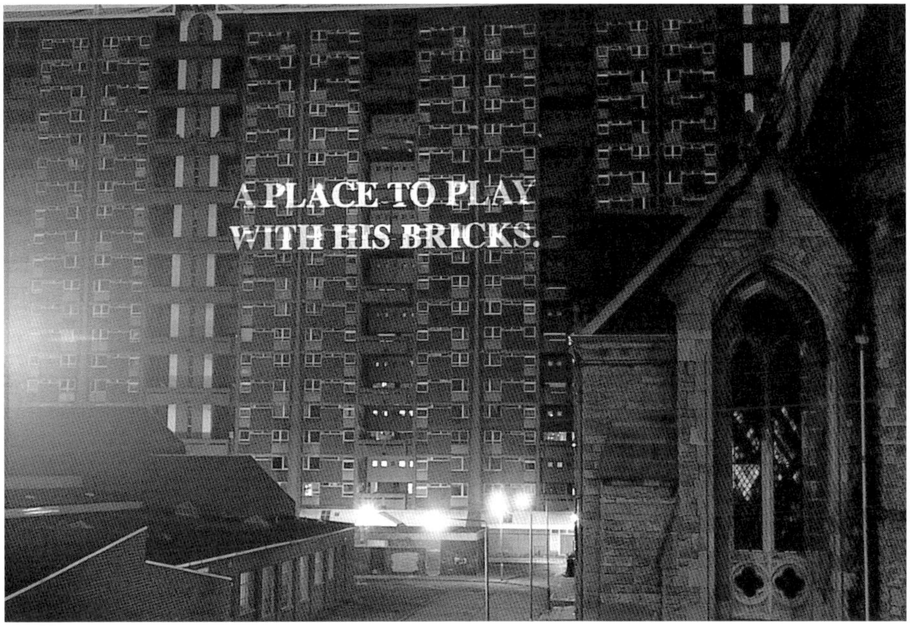

Christina McBride *from* Projecting Gorbals Fotofeis '93 *image/text projections*

COLIN RUSCOE and MALCOLM THOMSON *Scotland*

Dundee 1995 – the City

Tower Galleries

TOWER BLOCK
UNIVERSITY OF DUNDEE
PERTH ROAD, DUNDEE

PREMIERE

5 OCTOBER – 5 NOVEMBER

Malcolm Thomson and Colin Ruscoe continue the long tradition of urban documentary, utilising the high definition of a large-format camera to present a highly detailed view of the city of Dundee as seen from the perspective of an observant pedestrian. Ranging from the docks and the city centre to the peripheral housing schemes, they weave into their compositions the substantial, random and ephemeral details of everyday street life in the Nineties. The result is a finely crafted and honest portrait of the city today.

University of Dundee

An artist-run project

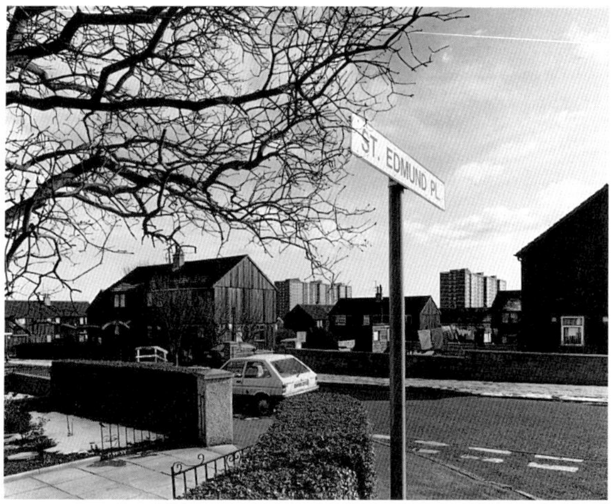

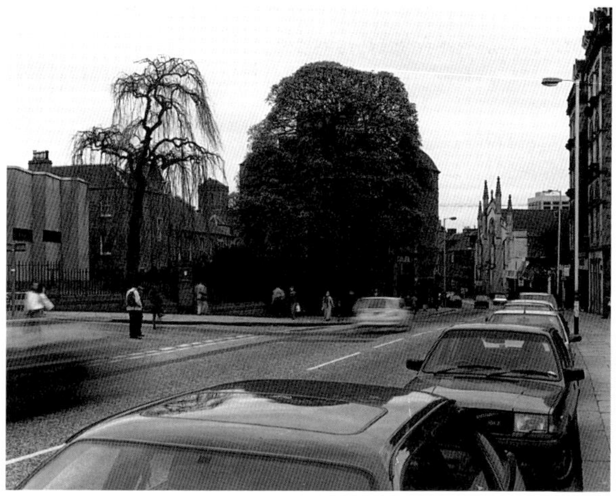

Malcolm J. Thomson and Colin Ruscoe from Dundee 1995 – the City *silver gelatin prints*

ROSS EAKIN *Scotland*

Tribes

The Fringe Gallery

18 CASTLEMILK ARCADE
GLASGOW

PREMIERE

14 OCTOBER – 4 NOVEMBER

Glasgow City Council

This exhibition pursues 'urban tribalism' in and around Glasgow. The groups Ross Eakin photographs include the *Glasgow Gunslingers Association*, *The Clan Wallace Trust*, *The Blue Angels* (Glasgow's Hells Angels), body builders and *Trekkies*. Stylistically the photographs isolate the subject against a neutral background, encouraging the viewer to consider the individual's chosen mode of self-expression.

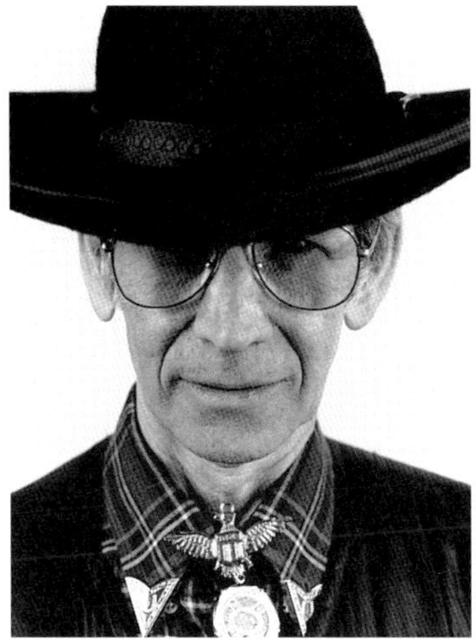

Ross Eakin from the Tribes project
silver-gelatin print

Presented by The Arts and Culture Development Office, South East Area Arts, Glasgow

City

Art Exposure Gallery

19 PARNIE STREET
GLASGOW

PREMIERE

7 OCTOBER – 25 OCTOBER

City at the Art Exposure Gallery is an open submission show in which Glasgow-based artists have been invited to present their individual photographic interpretations of the city. The image size has been specifically restricted to A4 or smaller, resulting in intimate variations on the theme. The participants range from recent graduates to established practitioners. The exhibition is part of the gallery's sixth anniversary celebrations.

Presented by the Art Exposure Gallery

Emergent

It is important in a festival on the scale of Fotofeis to ensure a mix of the established and the famous with the new and unfamiliar. Both are to be found in the preceding sections, but here we present a number of artists whose work is not widely known in this country. There is no theme to this section other than the freshness of their approach and the variety of their talents.

It is also true that not every artist finds their most receptive audience in their own back yard. In placing these dozen exhibitions within the context of an international festival we aim to bring their work to the attention of new audiences and encourage its appreciation by those who live in Scotland and those who visit during Fotofeis.

DIANA THORNEYCROFT *Canada*
a slow remembering

Collective Gallery

22–28 COCKBURN STREET
EDINBURGH

EUROPEAN PREMIERE

10 OCTOBER – 5 NOVEMBER

Diana Thorneycroft makes photographs that investigate personal and universal aspects of sexuality. Informed by feminist theory and psychoanalysis, she has explored the construction of the self, pushing against the twin boundaries of identification and objectification. The honesty of her psychological self-examination has resulted in images that are as emotionally intense as they are illusive and darkly magical.

Diana Thorneycroft constructs evocative photographic images that tease into conscious awareness our hidden desires and memories. To this end, she has developed a process which combines elements of choice and chance, ritual and improvisation. Employing costumes, masks, artificial body parts, surrounded by carefully chosen props and set against theatrical backdrops, she performs before the watchful eye of the camera.

She works in darkness. Her only light source is a hand-held torch with which she illuminates each area of the scene in turn. The blink of the camera's eye is prolonged to become a penetrating, unrelenting gaze into the dark void of the unconscious. Exposure (with all that word can mean) extends into a series of gestures, partly controlled, but open to chance and the guiding hand of intuition. In this way parts of the scene are made visible, whilst others remain cloaked in darkness, inaccessible to all but the imagination.

At every stage in this creative process Diana Thorneycroft is actively opening up her unconscious (and ours) in order to reach the unremembered histories, hidden identities and suppressed anxieties which reside there. An uneasy narrative emerges as individual strands become woven into an intricate, visual fabric – rich, dark and disturbing. The mind discloses its secrets suggestively. As viewers we must also reach into our own imagination, seeking resonant points, projecting personal detail into the blackness of the areas untouched by the artist's torch. In the process of perceiving meaning in these fragmented, suggestive images we must challenge our own psychological censors: we must face our own fears and fantasies, embrace our own daemons.

Manitoba Arts Council

Presented by the Collective Gallery in collaboration with Fotofeis

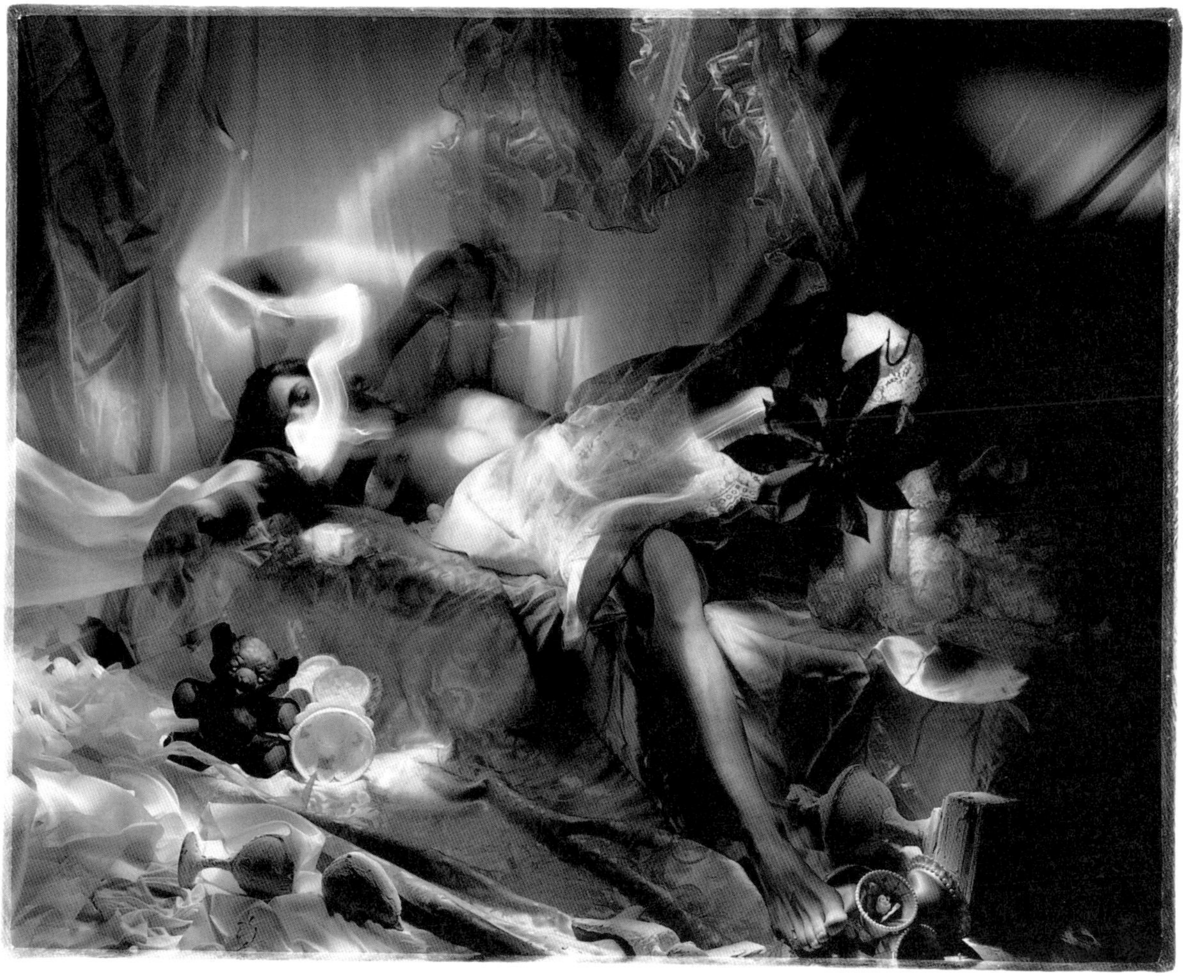

Diana Thorneycroft untitled (and if she wakes) 1994 *toned silver-gelatin print*

BRENDA PELKEY *Canada*

The Great Effect of the Imagination on the World

Gracefield Studios

28 EDINBURGH ROAD
DUMFRIES

EUROPEAN PREMIERE

5 OCTOBER – 11 NOVEMBER

In this work I have attempted to loosen the stricture of 'documentary'. I am interested in addressing the question of what is 'real' and how this 'reality' is changed by individual perception. BRENDA PELKEY

The Great Effect of the Imagination on the World looks at a series of highly personalised, exterior environments constructed in front and back yards in the suburbs of Saskatoon, Canada. These environments have been made by the individuals whose homes the wonderlands surround. They are manifestations of the interior world of the imagination made concrete in the material world. They do not depend on any single, external authority for their style or construction, but rather flow from the unrestrained fantasies of each householder. Each backyard tableau incorporates a set of highly distinctive objects – animals, birds, famous landmarks, religious buildings – many of which have been constructed especially for the purpose. These may be objects from, or reconstructions of places from the individual's past; they may be manifestations of their personal obsessions, or simply fanciful worlds of the imagination.

The theatricality of the places depicted is heightened by photographing at night, illuminating each scene with movie lights. The result is recorded in at least three separate photographs which are then assembled into a panorama. In this way each environment is changed in its representation from its actual appearance.

Brenda Pelkey's objective is to heighten the apparent eccentricity of the householders in creating such scenes within the mundane theatre of the domestic back yard. In doing so the artist seeks, through this embellishing of the actual, to open up the tight conventions and ethics of documentary photography and question the genre's relation to the world as we perceive it.

The Canada Council
Conseil des Arts du Canada

Saskatchewan
Arts Board

University of Saskatchewan

THE SCOTTISH ARTS COUNCIL

John Donnolly Photographic

Presented by Gracefield Studios in association with Fotofeis

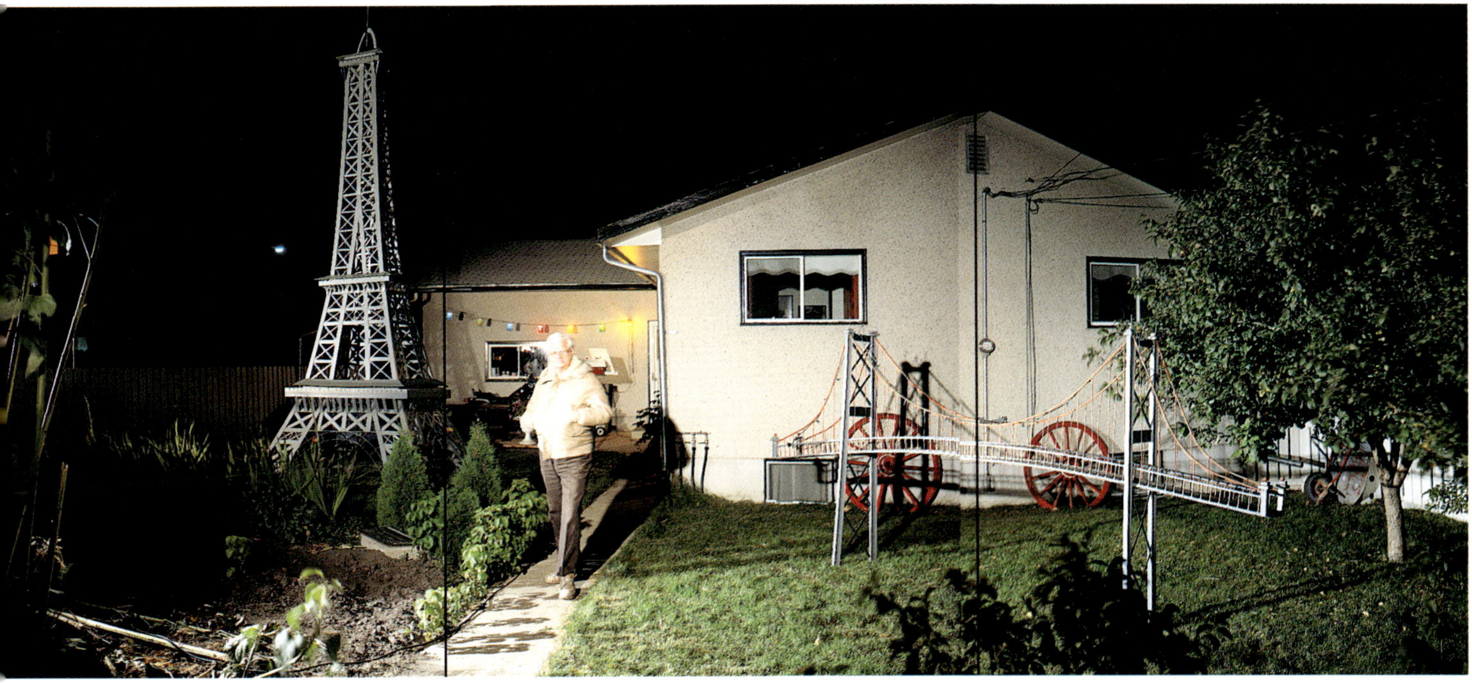

Brenda Pelkey Eiffel Tower and Golden Gate Bridge, Mel Affleck 1988 *three cibachrome prints*

ZOLTAN JOKAY *Germany*
Remembering

Andrew Grant Gallery

EDINBURGH COLLEGE OF ART
LAURISTON PLACE
EDINBURGH

UK PREMIERE

6 OCTOBER – 4 NOVEMBER

There is no perception that is not already subtly permeated by memory and imagination, and no expression that does not depend upon some convention to be understood. Communication is conditional, a hostage, ultimately, to the viewer who weaves meaning from the fabric of his or her own memory, imagination, experience and knowledge. Zoltan Jokay's photographs of children stage the uneasy moment of interpretation within a highly conscious language of pictorial organisation.

Taken in East Germany soon after reunification, Zoltan Jokay's photographs depict each child alone, in her or his street, garden or home. There is neither action nor drama. Each image concentrates on a particular posture, gesture or look adopted unconsciously by the child. The children assume a range of un-childlike qualities. Some seem unnervingly worldly or weary, others defiant, even hostile, others vulnerable.

On longer acquaintance the initial sense of objectivity or distance in the work is shown to be a construction of the predominantly low-angle and frontal camera position adopted by the artist. A new perception of the trust placed in the photographer by the children emerges and with it a sense of his empathy with them. This seeming objectivity, so unassumingly staged, serves Zoltan Jokay to confront the viewer with her or his own subjective responses, with the (perhaps uncomfortable) recognition of our own, adult, projections onto the world of these children. He thus attempts to jolt us into seeing the children 'as they are' and to recognise our interpretations for what they are, too.

Presented by Edinburgh College of Art in collaboration with the City of Edinburgh District Council International Office and Fotofeis.

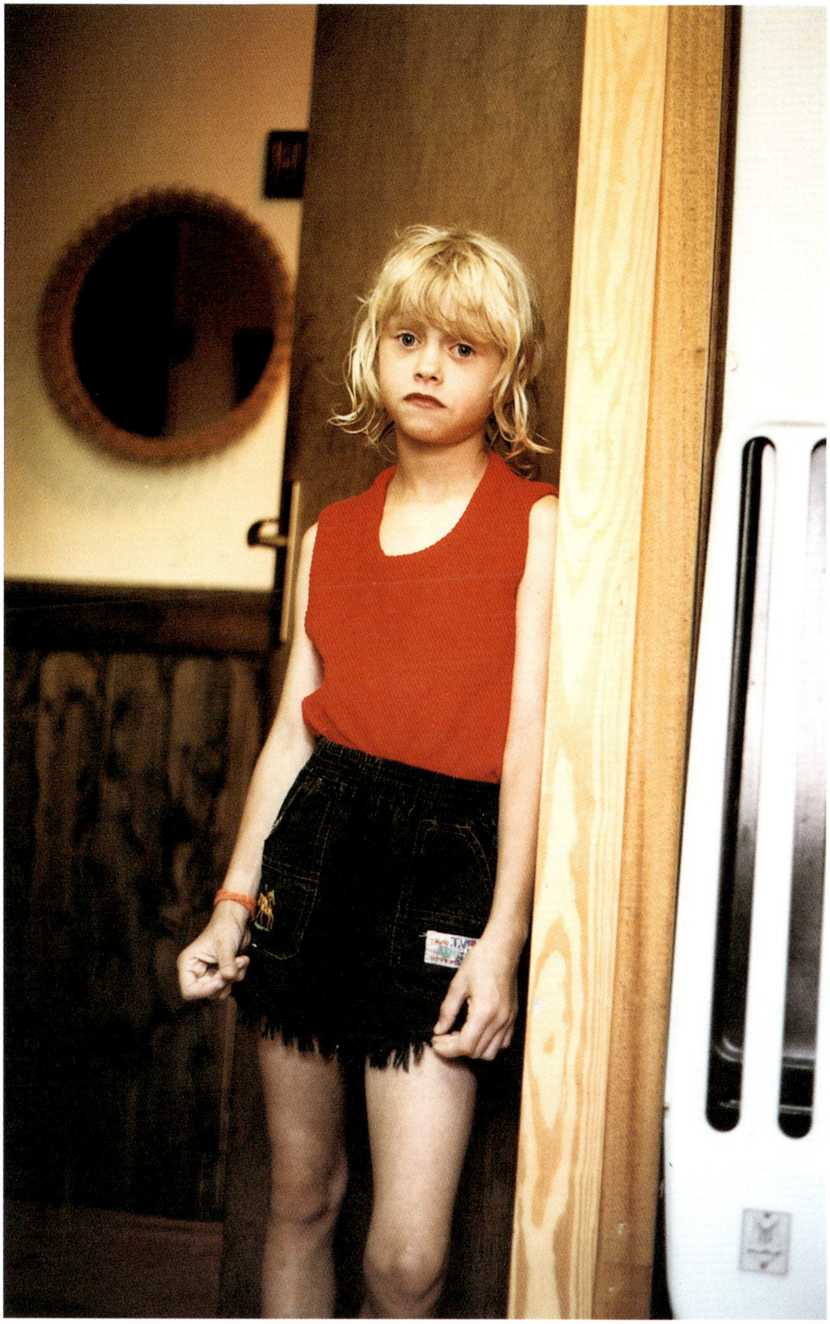

ROSALIE FAVELL *Canada*

Living Evidence

Blue Moon Gallery

36 BROUGHTON STREET
EDINBURGH

EUROPEAN PREMIERE

5 OCTOBER – 5 NOVEMBER

Presented by Fotofeis in collaboration with the artist and the Blue Moon Gallery

Rosalie Favell is a Cree-Metis (cross-blood) from Winnipeg, Manitoba. *Living Evidence* consists of enlarged and inscribed snapshots documenting a lesbian relationship that ended several years ago. Despite their size the images are presented in the style of SX70 polaroids and mounted with photo-corners, a reference to the family album. In the pictures the women appear happy and untrammelled, but Favell adds handwritten text which discloses a more troubled relationship.

Shortly before their first showing, Rosalie Favell's former lover withdrew permission for the images to be shown while she remained identifiable within them. Now married and living in the conservative environment of a Cree community, she did not wish to have this former relationship made public. Rather than shelve the exhibition, the artist decided to work with this situation – to incorporate it within the meaning and 'life' of the artifacts themselves – and make this fear of recognition visible. The crude black tape obliterating her former lover's eyes is like a disfiguring scar, a constant reminder of the wounds inflicted by homophobia.

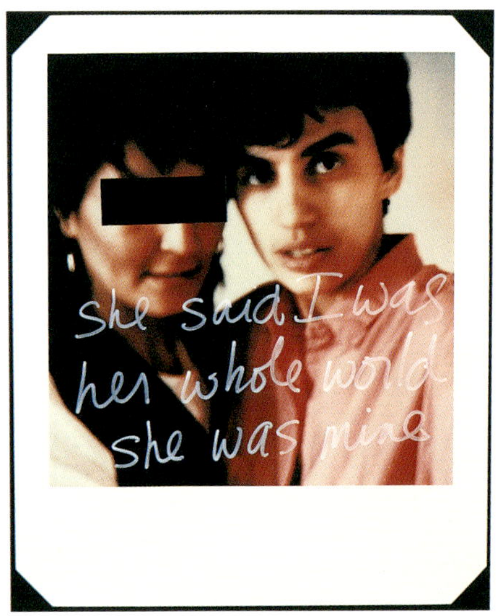

Rosalie Favell untitled # 20 (she said I was her whole world she was mine) 1994
colour print with marker and tape

ELFI FRÖHLICH *Germany*

Staging Authenticity

Newbery Gallery

GLASGOW SCHOOL OF ART
RENFREW STREET
GLASGOW

UK PREMIERE

6 OCTOBER – 28 OCTOBER

The exhibition title *Staging Authenticity* combines two contradictory ideas which affect the credibility of photographic reality. Elfi Fröhlich shifts authenticity to the level of individual sensitivity by 'staging' the chosen subjects. The prime motive of her work, however, is not to demonstrate the difference between so-called 'real' photographs and manipulated ones. Instead, she challenges the viewer's capacity to form visual and verbal associations.

The series of pictures (which she also calls 'musical scores') combine images from various everyday experiences, images of fear or beauty in waking dreams and fantasy. Their original meanings, still discernible in a rudimentary way in the individual elements, vanish in the new pictorial relationships. They do not offer new narratives, however, so much as trigger associations in the viewer, from which new subjectively true meanings tentatively emerge.

Presented by Glasgow School of Art, the Goethe-Institut Glasgow and Institut für Auslandsbeziehungen, Berlin

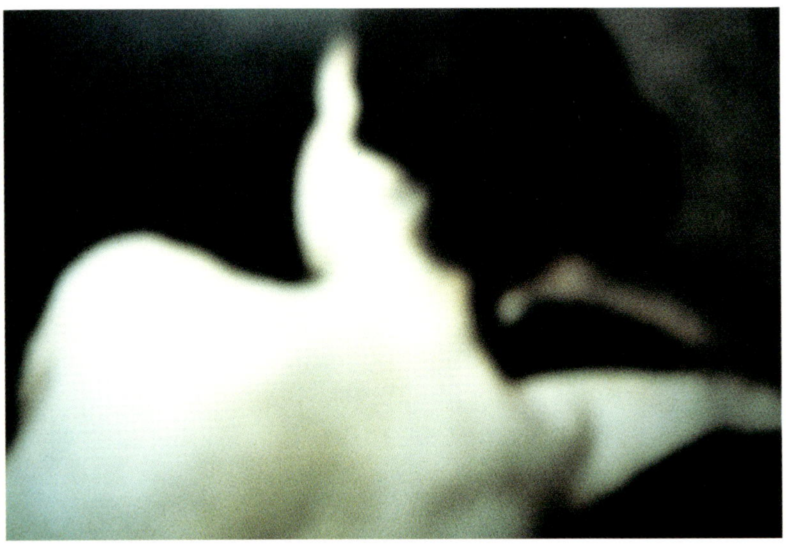

Elfi Fröhlich untitled 1987 *colour print (courtesy of Institut für Auslandsbeziehungen)*

GOETHE-INSTITUT

Institut für Auslandsbeziehungen

Toni Hafkenscheid *Canada / Netherlands*

KJP Gallery

NAPIER UNIVERSITY
61 MARCHMONT ROAD
EDINBURGH

EUROPEAN PREMIERE

5 OCTOBER – 4 NOVEMBER

Toni Hafkenscheid began his 'environmental portraits' in 1989 whilst living in Amsterdam. He was inspired by the views he glimpsed of other people's lives when, at night and with the curtains open, living-rooms can resemble intimate theatre sets. This theatricality is emphasised by the glowing light, which is warm and cosy. By contrast, the lighting in the early pictures these scenes inspired is harsh, artificial and dramatic; the colours are lush. The artist intends the images to be both voyeuristic and seductive – to provide windows onto private moments in the subject's home. In 1991 Toni Hafkenscheid moved to Canada and continued the portraits in a number of the larger cities there.

Although theatrical, the early images still conveyed a sense of authenticity. However, the artist subsequently became more interested in manipulating the scenarios, which lead to the second phase of the work, also included in this exhibition. This phase plays with the edges of fact and fiction in highly narrative works. Using commonplace domestic settings he aims to ground the image in a perception of the real world, but then, quite blatantly sets up dramatic actions which unfold before the camera. The people photographed cease to be themselves, but as actors in these curious domestic dramas, become projections of the artist's own desires, fantasies and fears.

Government of Ontario Ministry of Culture, Tourism and Recreation

Presented by Napier University in association with Fotofeis

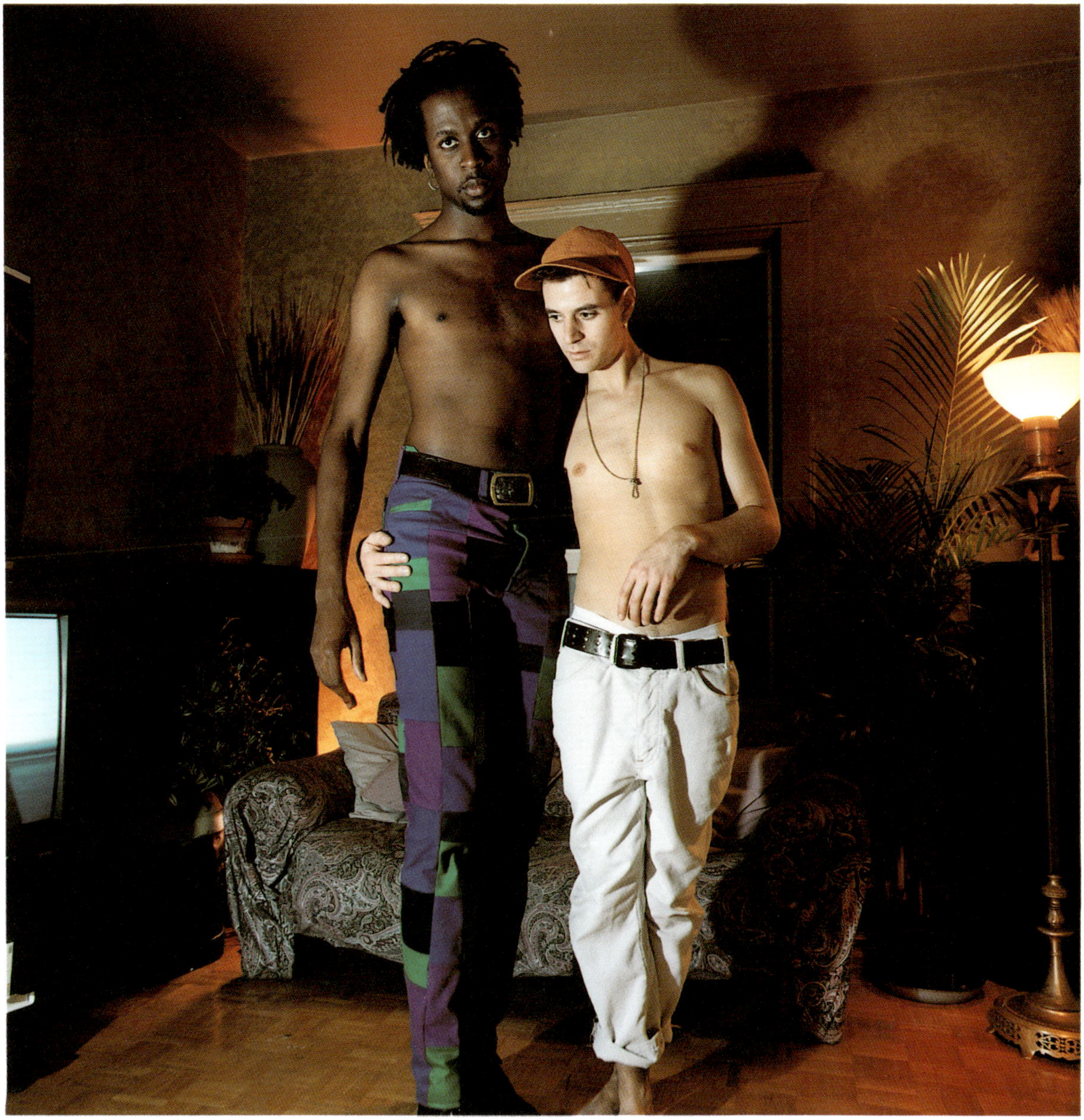

Toni Hafkenscheid Greg and Gordon 1991 *type C print*

THREE TOURING EXHIBITIONS
North East Arts Touring

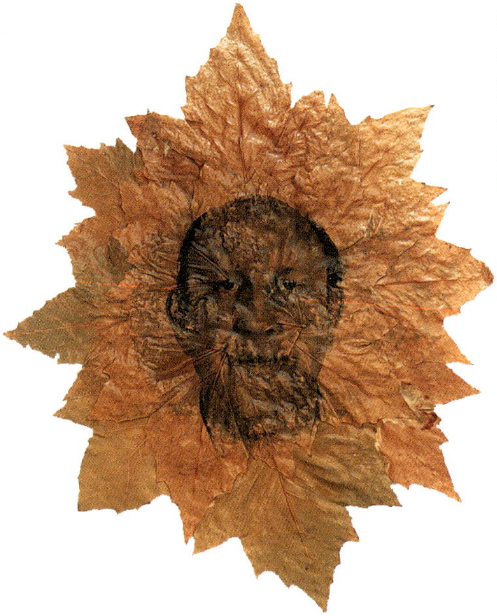

Caroline Blackburn untitled 1995 *photographic emulsion on assemblage of leaves*

ELGIN LIBRARY
GRANT LODGE COOPER PARK, ELGIN

MACDUFF ACADEMY
MACDUFF

THE FOYER, VIEWMOUNT,
ARDUTHIE ROAD, STONEHAVEN

TESCO SUPERMARKET
AND KEMNAY LIBRARY
GORDON

JAMES DUN'S HOUSE AND
THE CENTRAL LIBRARY
ABERDEEN

2 OCTOBER – 23 DECEMBER

ÉLÈNE TREMBLAY *Canada*
Eaux-mortes – Still Waters

EUROPEAN PREMIERE

Élène Tremblay is interested in the way in which our perception of nature is shaped by the artificial construct of an idealized photographic representation. In particular she is interested in the irony that these images proliferate at the very time when so much of the natural world is under threat. Highly coloured and roughly cut into a parody of watery shapes, these photographs of nine Canadian lakes disrupt the comfortable illusion of the interchangeability of photographic representations and the reality of the natural world. In doing so, the artist seeks to question the way in which perception shapes understanding.

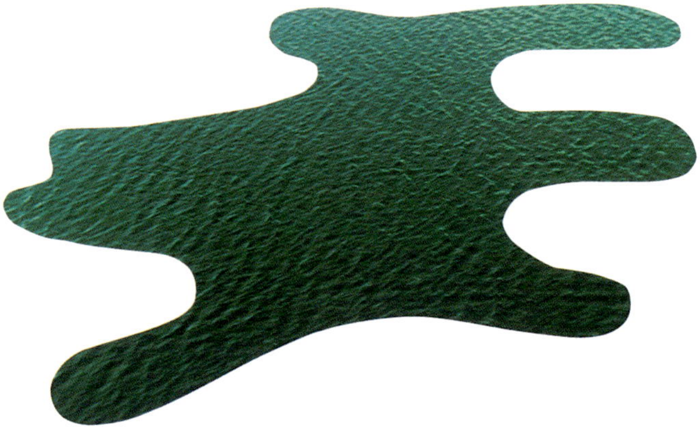

Élène Tremblay Green Lake 1993 *type C print cut-out*

Presented by NEAT in association with Vox Populi, Montreal and Fotofeis

CAROLINE BLACKBURN *England*

The Seven Ages of Man and Woman

PREMIERE

This set of fourteen pictures shows seven men and seven women in an age range from childhood through to old age. Each portrait is printed onto a bed of leaves (glued together to form a mat). In a simple, but evocative association of ideas, the season in which the leaves were picked reflects the age of the person represented; from the child of spring to the autumn of the third age.

Presented by NEAT in association with Fotofeis

ANTONIO CASTILHO *Portugal*

Pencils that I've stolen from my pupils

UK PREMIERE

Antonio Castilho is an art teacher in a junior school in a rural area of Portugal. Over a lengthy period he acquired the smallest stubs of pencils and crayons that some of the children were using to make their drawings and write in their note books. The photographs eulogise these remnants, they are at once both comic and grand, speaking of the hours of patient toil expended as they were whittled away.

Presented by NEAT in association with Fotofeis

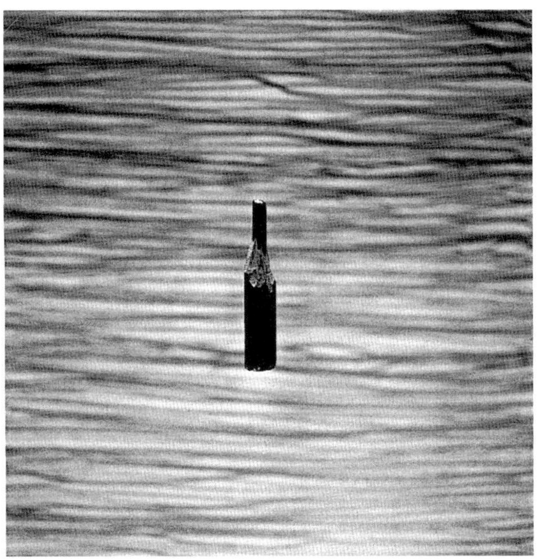

Antonio Castilho untitled 1994 *silver-gelatin print*

ZOFIA KULIK *Poland*

The Human Motif

Francis Cooper Gallery

DUNCAN OF JORDANSTONE
COLLEGE OF ART
UNIVERSITY OF DUNDEE
PERTH ROAD, DUNDEE

PREMIERE

5 OCTOBER – 26 OCTOBER

The purpose of my work is to humiliate the 'spectator' and bring him to his knees. But for whom are you to humble yourself today? There is no god, no leader, no mystery. So who are you to serve? ZOFIA KULIK

Zofia Kulik's large-scale photomontages suggest the immense weight of Eastern European history. They point to the brutal devastation of Naziism; the rise and fall of Communism; the pervasive power of the Catholic Church and the equally painful, euphoric and demagogic transition to democracy. Meticulously composed of hundreds of individual black and white images arranged in complex, formal patterns, her works have been compared to Gothic windows, intricate tapestries or the murals and parade banners of the socialist era.

By her own admission Zofia Kulik was well placed to witness the intricate mechanisms and transformation of such a closed society. Her father was a Colonel in the Propaganda Department of the People's Army of Poland. Her mother was a dressmaker, receiving a daily stream of women to be measured and fitted, each with their stories and opinions of daily life. Later, as a member of the experimental performance duo *Kwiekulik*, Zofia Kulik found her own voice silenced and her passport withheld for engaging in overtly political work.

Even so, Zofia Kulik's work is not confined to political dogma and flat situational statements. She carefully deploys the very structures – aesthetic, social and psychical – which perpetuate ideology. Individual human figures are subsumed into vast 'closed forms' made up of symmetries, symbols and multiple arrangements. She creates an equivocal vision of powerful order which contains no specific identity or focus – seemingly bereft of purpose.

A Zone Gallery touring exhibition presented by Duncan of Jordanstone College of Art in association with Fotofeis

Northern Arts

Funded by THE ARTS COUNCIL OF ENGLAND

VISITING ARTS

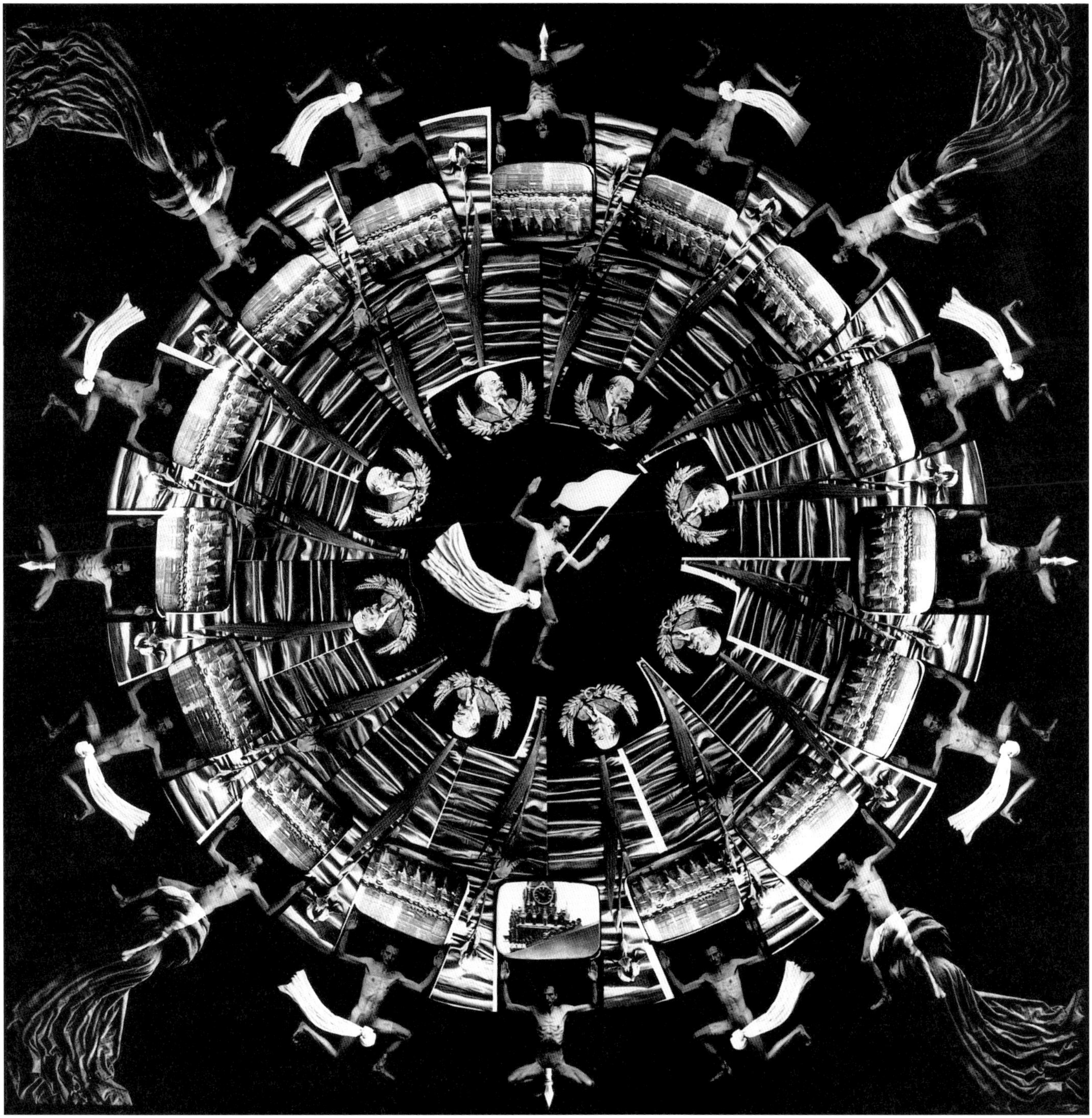

Zofia Kulik Five to Twelve 1992 *assemblage of silver-gelatin prints*

CRAIG MACKAY *Scotland*

Aodannan Air An Iomall – Faces on the Edge

Swanson Gallery

THURSO LIBRARY
DAVIDSON'S LANE
THURSO

PREMIERE

10–13 OCTOBER AND
22–29 OCTOBER

14–21 OCTOBER
SHOWING AT THE MOD,
BRORA

Craig Mackay's portraits of contemporary figures from the world of the arts and politics include the actor Gregor Fisher, the Liberal Democrat MP Charles Kennedy, the poet Iain Crichton Smith, the footballer Duncan Shearer and Mike Scott of the Waterboys. A sense of place and the indigenous Gaelic culture have had a significant influence on the work of these individuals, unifying them in a shared experience of landscape and identity. These portraits of people living, in the geo-political sense, 'on the edge' are a sensitive exploration of this relationship between person and place.

Presented by Highland Regional Council

Caithness & Sutherland
ENTERPRISE

Sutherland District Council

An Comunn Gaidhealach

Sutherland Mod Committee

Sutherland Tourist Board

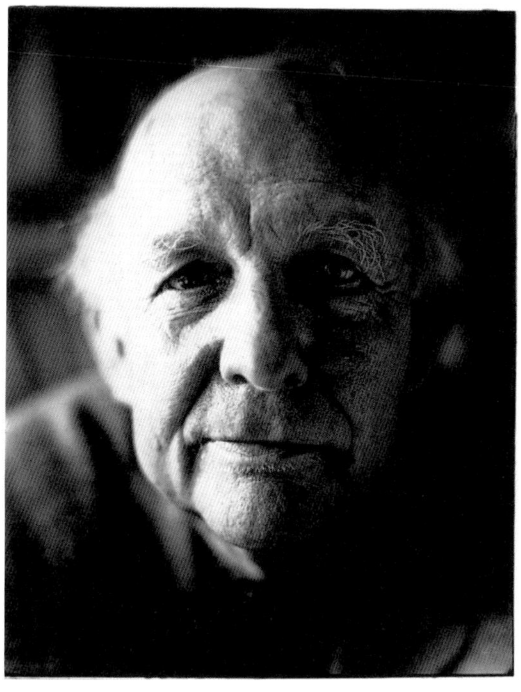

Craig McKay Iain Crichton Smith, poet and author 1995 *toned silver-gelatin print*

SUSANNE RAMSENTHALER *Germany* and HUGH HARWOOD *Scotland*

Common Ground: Travels in Space and Time

Chessel's Gallery

CHESSEL'S LAND
OLD PLAYHOUSE CLOSE
CANONGATE
EDINBURGH

PREMIERE

5 OCTOBER – 2 NOVEMBER

An artist-run project

Bringing together the work of two artists employing entirely different media, this exhibition seeks to explore concepts of travel and history from official hierarchies to personal identity. Hugh Harwood's *Picture History Book* consists of large-format digital colour prints. These are also presented on a computer based multimedia programme where the viewer is free to interact, unfolding and reconsidering written history in her or his own time and order. Susanne Ramsenthaler's work takes the viewer on a journey into the realm of personal history where things are often not what they seem and childhood memories may not be as personal as we had imagined. Together these works take the medium of photography through a range of media from the cyanotype to the digital image.

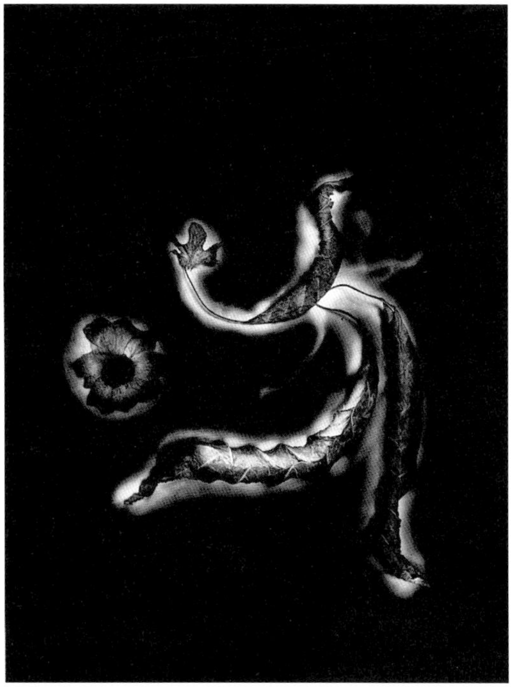

Susanne Ramsenthaler *from* Sarabande 1995 *silver-gelatin print*

Collaboration

The whole of Fotofeis is built upon acts of collaboration, but in this section of the festival we focus particularly on projects where such dialogue and mutual support is central. This collaboration takes many forms, be it between artist and artist, artist and the community, or in the partnership formed when a gallery commissions new work – all are based on the trust one person places in another.

It has been of immense satisfaction for all of us involved in Fotofeis that the festival has been both the catalyst and the context for so many of the projects described in the remainder of this catalogue. They span a remarkably wide range – from the match-making of an artist from Scotland with another from Quebec (which has resulted in an ambitious new sitework in central Glasgow and another to be staged in Montreal later in the year), to an exploration of what it means to be healthy, undertaken in a unique partnership between a health authority, an international arts festival and the community.

DAVID MICHAEL CLARKE *Scotland* and PIERRE ALLARD *Canada*
Trans Action Public

The St Enoch Centre

ST ENOCH SQUARE
GLASGOW

PREMIERE

6 OCTOBER – 28 FEBRUARY

Initiated by Glasgow-based artist David Michael Clarke, *Trans Action Public* is a collaboration with Pierre Allard from Montreal. The artists had never met before they were brought together through the agencies of Fotofeis in Scotland and Oboro in Quebec specifically for this project. David Michael Clarke was interested in exploring not only the challenge of making site-specific work, but in working on a truly collaborative basis with a partner of whom he had no previous knowledge and who would bring different cultural referents to the project. *Trans Action Public* is thus the fruit of a series of negotiations: between artist and site, and between artist and artist.

They began their artistic blind date with a one month period of exchange in each city. Based on their reactions to one another, their respective cultures and the sites, they devised two public interventions. After a two-month production period, the first work has been sited within Glasgow's St Enoch Centre. Large-scale photograph-based banners are complemented throughout the mall by smaller works which together invite the public to redefine their relationship with a space that is purpose-built for commerce. The second intervention will build on the Glasgow project, and will be staged in Montreal in January, 1996.

Trans Action Public will not only explore human relations to the complex environment of the city, but also intercultural relations and the creation of art in the space which embraces cultural difference.

An artist-run project produced in Scotland by Breathe and in Quebec by Oboro, developed in collaboration with Fotofeis, Festival of the Visual Arts '96, and UK City of Architecture and Design 1999

Glasgow City Council

THE SCOTTISH ARTS COUNCIL

Québec

The Hope Scott Trust

The British Council

Scanachrome

B&S VISUAL TECHNOLOGIES LIMITED

BELL'S

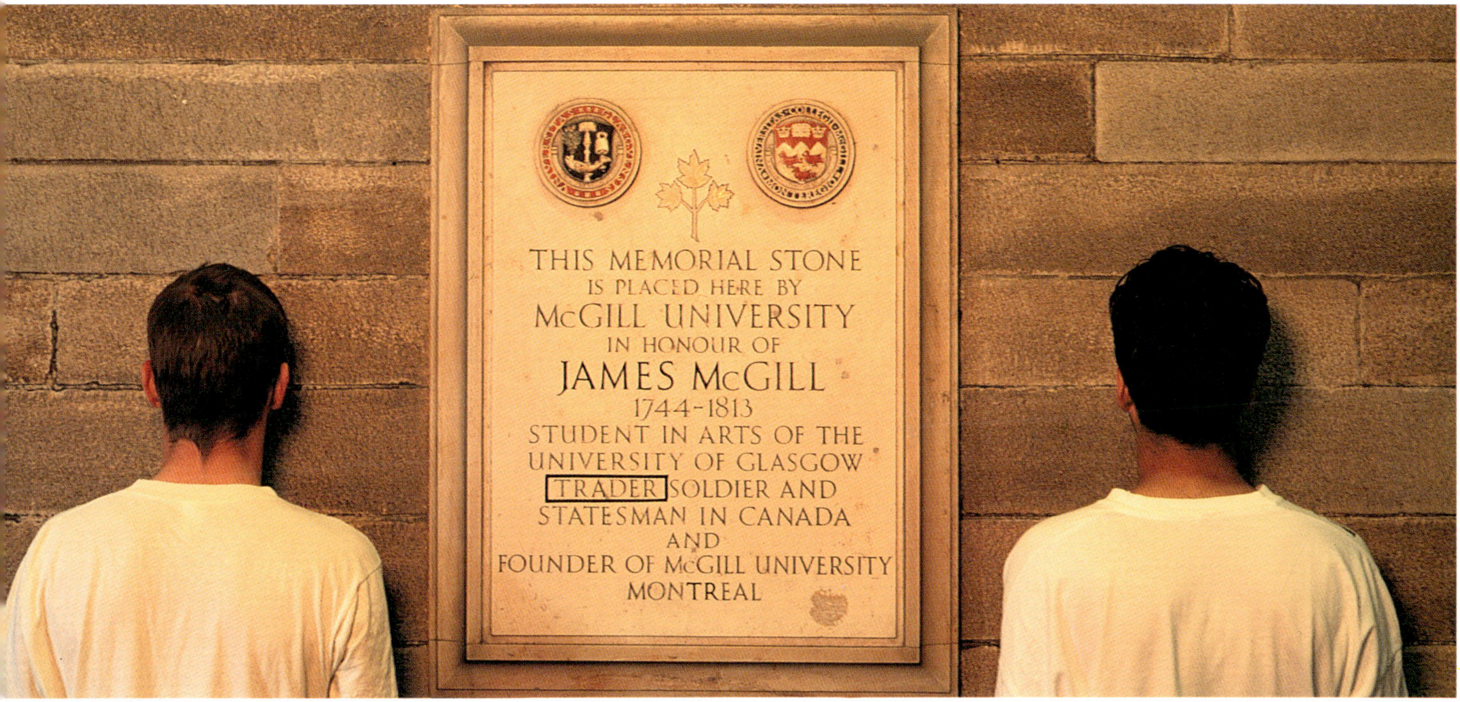

Pierre Allard and David Michael Clarke Trans Action Public 1995 *colour transparency (work in progress)*

RORY DONALDSON *Scotland*
Boiling Petroleum

Aberdeen Art Gallery

SCHOOLHILL
ABERDEEN

PREMIERE

30 SEPTEMBER – 5 NOVEMBER

Tradition and innovation have always been fiery bedfellows but where there is conflict there is always energy and creativity. RORY DONALDSON

The contrast between old and new, the indigenous and the imported, is the underlying concept in the construction of *Boiling Petroleum*, and the immiscible relationship of oil and water is perhaps its dominant metaphor.

As a student, Rory Donaldson spent four years in Aberdeen and in this project works with imagery that reflects his strongest perceptions of the city, above all reflecting the twin cultures of the fishing and oil industries. Given that both are intimately bound to the sea, their place in the culture of Aberdeen could hardly be more different, or their impact on the city more profound.

The work utilises a variety of different media, including photographs arranged in grids, large black and white prints, *scanachromes* and computer-aided design to construct densely-layered images which use the oil industry as a visual metaphor to reflect upon the complex and contradictory effects of the industry on local culture and identity. The installation of the exhibition further explores the possibilities of fragmentation and friction by placing works directly against the gallery walls whilst layering one work over another. By partially obscuring and combining seemingly antithetical images and ideas, Rory Donaldson reflects upon the challenge of trying to mix oil and water.

Subsidised by City of Aberdeen

THE SCOTTISH ARTS COUNCIL

Commissioned for Fotofeis '95 by Aberdeen Art Gallery with the assistance of the Scottish Arts Council

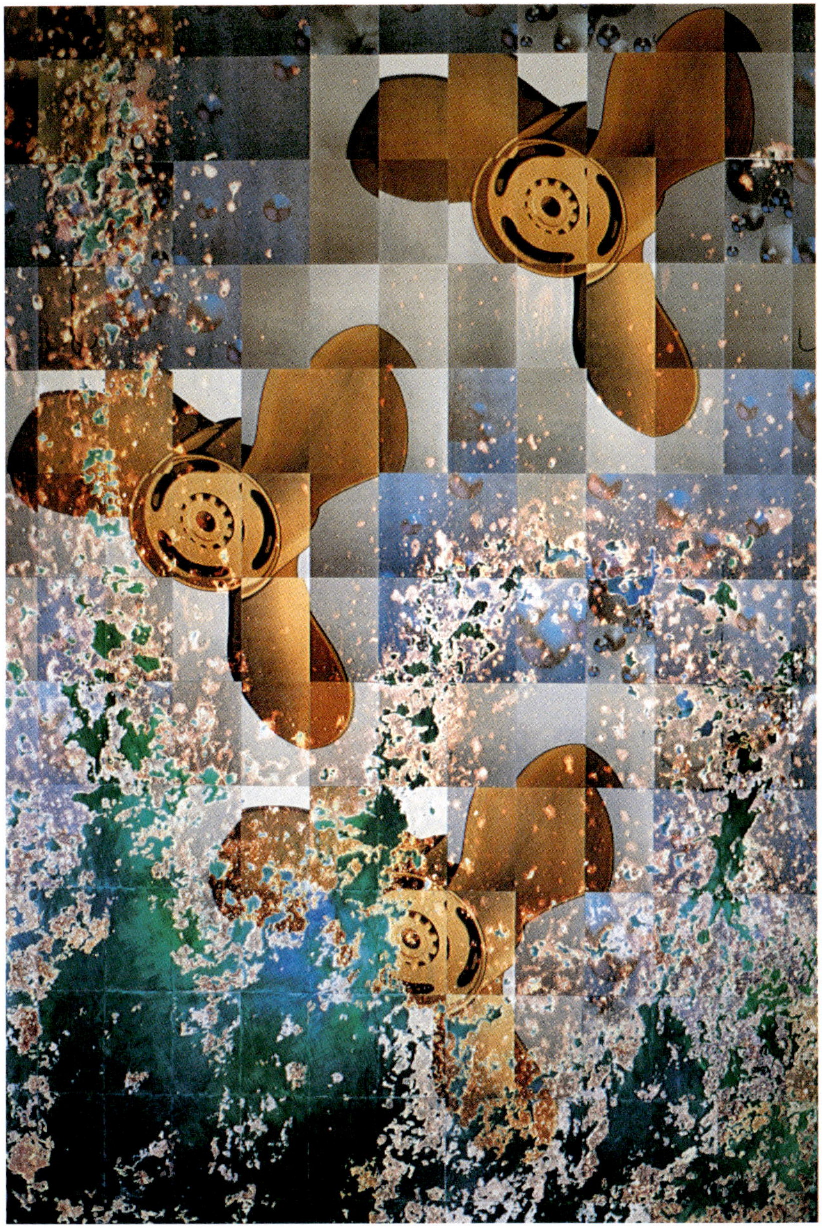

Rory Donaldson part of Boiling Petroleum 2 *1995 mixed media photowork*

LESLEY PUNTON *Scotland*

where deer sleep

Aberdeen Art Gallery

SCHOOLHILL
ABERDEEN

PREMIERE

7 OCTOBER – 5 NOVEMBER

A space, an emptiness, often seems to me to have greater emotional and poetic weight than a direct representation of an actual object. And photography has the capacity, in a unique way, to draw together time, trace and memory. Photography, you could say, is unique in the way it gives presence to absence, an idea which is crucial to my working practice. LESLEY PUNTON

The photographs in *where deer sleep* may seem at first sight to be featureless, but closer inspection brings to view a subtle play of light which reveals an image of flattened grasses softly stirred by the wind. The grasses have a rhythmic, dance-like movement that draws on the photographic surface like a fine pencil on paper. The surface becomes a rich and sensual plane for contemplation.

The series has its origins in the discovery by the artist, while walking over moorland in the West Highlands of Scotland, of areas of flattened grass where deer had spent the previous night. She became interested in them as imprints on the landscape of the missing bodies, transient marks which gradually faded during the course of the day to leave no record of the animals' passing. As traces of an absence, they evoked a melancholy poetics of time and loss, which she reinterpreted by taking most of the photographs in the low light of dawn and dusk, at the same time offering the viewer an intensely intimate record of weather conditions and times of day.

Commissioned for Fotofeis '95 by Aberdeen Art Gallery with the assistance of the Scottish Arts Council

The artist acknowledges the kind help and support of Kay and Bobby Shearer.

Subsidised by City of Aberdeen

THE SCOTTISH ARTS COUNCIL

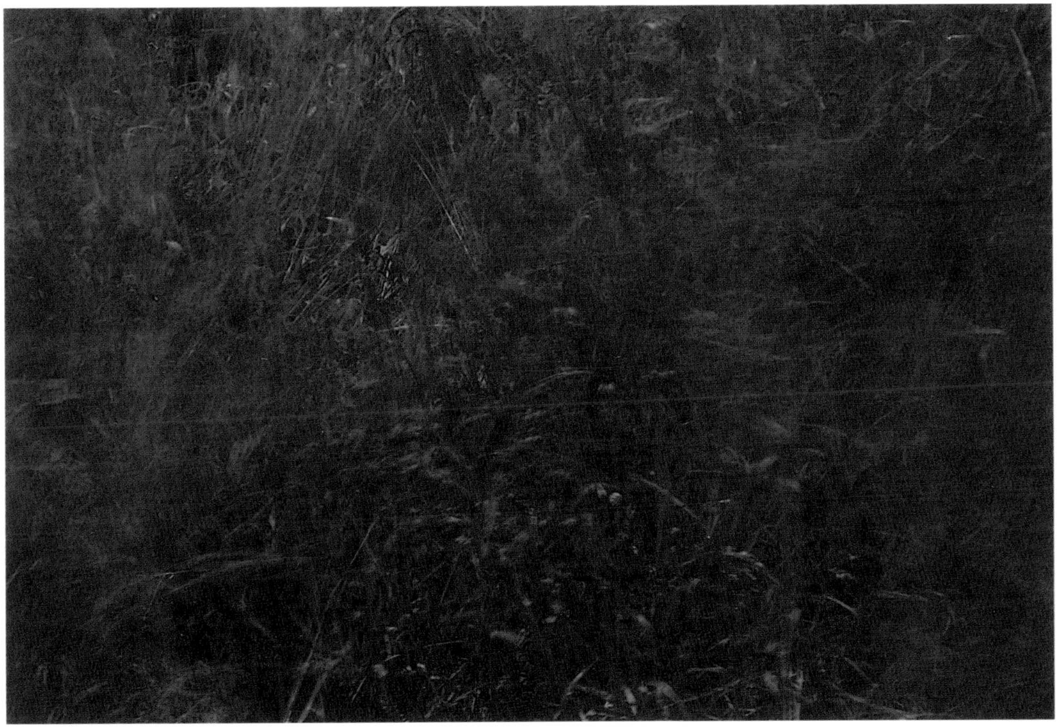

Lesley Punton *from* where deer sleep 1995 *toned silver-gelatin print*

FOTOFEIS '95
Community Programme

It is part of the philosophy of Fotofeis to integrate the international with the local. The festival's community programme plays an important role in involving people from a diverse range of backgrounds and across a wide geographic spread. Community projects such as those described below help to fix cultural activity within the social fabric – to remind us that art is part of life and not the plaything of a privileged minority.

Whereas many exhibitions focus on the artefact – the finished work – community projects exploit and celebrate the *process* of making art. In these community projects it is at least as important *how* the artworks were made as *what* they are, for it is in the act of making work that the expressive and communicative powers of artistic activity come to be learned and understood. The benefits are twofold as participants begin to discover new modes of self-expression and a deeper appreciation of the visual arts.

Strathclyde Region

Building on the success of the Strathclyde Schools and Community project for *Fotofeis '93*, a similar range of groups have been involved in the 1995 festival.

Fragments of Light is a lively exhibition of work by the elderly residents of Cowglen and Blawarthill Hospital. The exhibits span a wide range of photo-based media including projections, polaroids, film and photocopies and are the result of a year-long collaborative project between Art in Hospital (Glasgow) and Street Level Gallery and Workshop. At the Hunter Street Work Centre, artist Mark Pawson has been running a series of workshops in photocopy art for adults with learning difficulties. The artist (who is featured in the exhibition *Fairy Tale in the Supermarket* described on page 16 of this catalogue) travels worldwide showing work and distributing artists' books. The work made during these sessions ranges in scale from small postcards to huge wall hangings.

The artist Janie Nicoll (whose own public artworks are described on page 19 of this catalogue) has been working with seven teenagers from Irvine and Kilmarnock on a project managed by Kilmarnock Social Work Department. Their unusual project involves copying images onto acetate and fitting them into a series of perspex boxes which are themselves arranged into an internally lit sculpture. Adults attending the Strathclyde Refugee Centre will also be working with Janie Nicoll on their own project for *Fotofeis '95*. The Robert Owen Centre in East Kilbride is also taking part.

Five schools are involved in the Strathclyde project. Children at Ayr Academy have been building a vast scenic collage from scores of individual photographs. Prestwick Academy are also working with Janie Nicoll to explore the architectural features of the town. Their work will be manifested in such unusual forms as tee-shirts, photo-sculpture and murals. Hunter High School and Maxwellton Primary School in East Kilbride are currently preparing projects as this catalogue is being written.

Children on the island of Tiree, off the west coast of Scotland, have been working with the artist Hilary Stirling and Graham Paterson, a tutor from the Visual

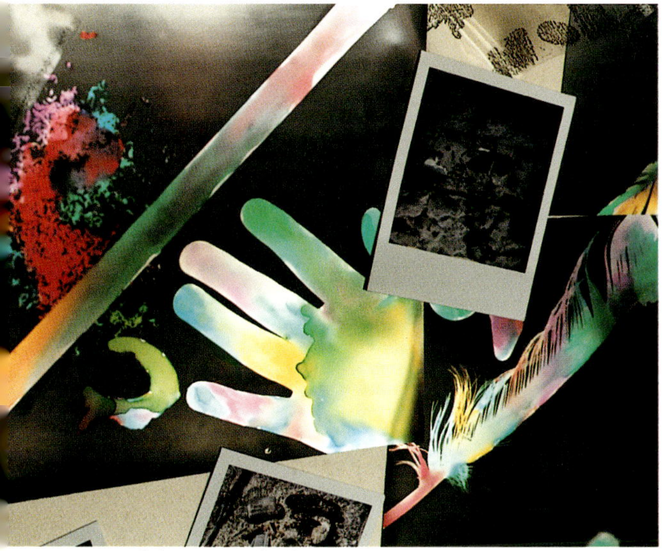

Work from Tiree School project

Arts Studio in Glasgow, on an adventurous five-day project on the theme of 'cast away'. Working on the beach with the sand, seaweed, rocks, driftwood and bottles found there they have made complex mixed-media works. At the end of the project each child placed a personal note and a picture into a bottle and 'cast it away' into the sea.

Many of the works made as part of the Strathclyde Schools and Community project will be on show at the Strathclyde Arts Centre in Glasgow during Fotofeis.
Supported Strathclyde Regional Council

MOTHERWELL DISTRICT

As a collaborative project between *Fotofeis* '95 and *Motherwell Music Festival* the `Pop Portraits' community project used both the photographic and the screenprinting facilities at Motherwell Leisure's *Artworks*, based in Wishaw. These intensive workshops introduced young people to new visual art skills as they worked together to create banners featuring their favourite pop stars and rock heroes. The large, brightly coloured banners are being displayed during *Fotofeis* '95 and will feature in the 1996 Motherwell Music Festival.

Since *Fotofeis* '93 the profile of photography in Motherwell District has been on the up and up. Workshops and exhibitions organized by Motherwell Leisure revealed the depth of skill and imagination of the local photographers. Launched in February, the Photographer / Young Photographer of the Year Competition 1995 has confirmed this talent and the resulting exhibition is on show at Viewpark Library, Viewpark and later at Craigneuk Community Centre, Wishaw.

BACK TO THE BLACK? is an exhibition by freelance photographer Mark Jackson showing at Bellshill Cultural Centre. This exhibition focuses on the Monktonhall Colliery near Edinburgh. After the miners strike the Coal Board decided to run down the colliery and by 1992 only seventeen men were still employed there. In June of that year the Monkland Consortium, a group of one hundred and sixty-seven Scots miners who each invested £10,000 redundancy money, bought the colliery and saved it. Over the twelve month period, Mark Jackson has produced a unique record of the resilience and determination of a group of workers at a colliery which has survived political and economic attack and is now one of only two deep mines remaining in Scotland.
Supported by Motherwell District Council

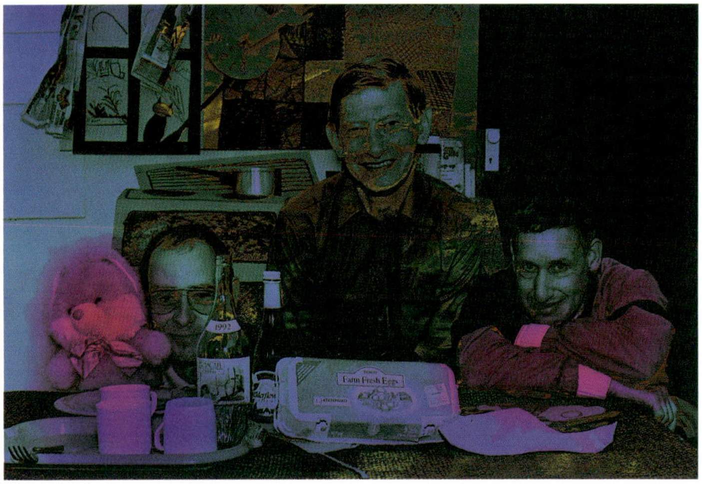

City of Aberdeen

Established during the Council restructuring in 1990, the Arts Development Section of Aberdeen City Council has gradually created a programme of arts activities in the city including a number of well-subscribed photographic workshops. Initially run from make-shift darkrooms at community centres and in redundant buildings, these have gradually fused together founding dedicated areas in schemes such as WhiteSpace, an arts venue near to the centre of Aberdeen, and the Powis Multi-Arts project based at a flat at the heart of a zone of high unemployment. Other groups meet under the auspices of Grampian Regional Council in Community Education Centres and the Workers Education Association, whose participants at the so called Reachout centre make use of another District Council darkroom.

Although funded by a variety of bodies with quite different strategic goals and working from places with considerable geographic distance between them, there has always been a steady exchange of ideas, staff and users. The Powis Multi-Arts project, for instance, first exhibited under the Fotofeis banner two years ago and will be showing this year how the work has progressed; one of the original exhibitors from this project now runs the photographic aspect of the Reachout project.

The exhibition *Canned-Id Camera* showing at James Dun's House, Aberdeen during *Fotofeis* '95 is made up of work from these projects. It is a complex mix of images, issues and imagination from the daily lives of people in Aberdeen.

Supported by City of Aberdeen District Council

Magnus the Print Bus

Magnus the Art Bus is a mobile resource in the Highlands of Scotland. As part of *Fotofeis* '95 Magnus brings photo-silk-screen printing into the lives of hundreds of young people who would not otherwise be able to take part in the festival. With the help of a professional artist, Magnus is spending a month touring Caithness and Sutherland in the north of Scotland. The aim of the project is to excite and stimulate the participants by producing objects that they can use: T-shirts, badges, printed carrier bags, postcards and so on. This project is a collaboration with the Highland Printmakers Workshop and builds on ideas explored in the exhibition *Fairy Tale in the Supermarket* described on page 16 of this catalogue.

Supported by Caithness District Council, Sutherland District Council, Caithness & Sutherland Enterprise, the European Commission's Leader II project and Scottish Hydro-Electric plc

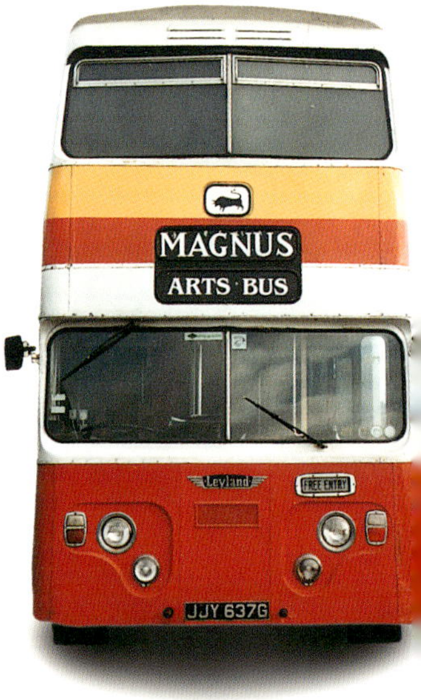

above left *work from* Canned-Id Camera, *Aberdeen*

above right *Magnus the Art Bus*

Lothian Health

What makes us healthy and what makes us sick? How can health services respond more appropriately when people need help? What in our society needs to be changed if we are to lead healthier lives? Can photography persuade planners what needs to be done?

These questions have been explored by ten community groups in Lothian using photography as a way to present their ideas and experiences. The people involved have a wide variety of interests and all were supported by funds from the Health Promotion Department of Lothian Health.

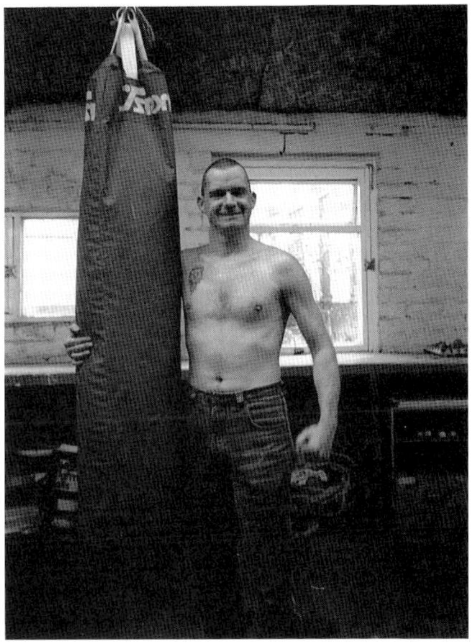

A group that meets at the Cowgate Day Centre looked at how being homeless affects health, and what a healthful day is like. Deans Community Club and members of Oasis Women's Support Group have depicted their experiences of mental health problems, and what the support groups mean to them. People at the Orchard Centre in Bonnyrigg have used a variety of photographic techniques to explore what being healthy is all about. Men's health is the subject chosen by another group.

The group Bosnia Now has worked on images exploring the experience of becoming a refugee. Women living in Blackburn and in Pilton have looked locally at what in their environment makes them healthy and sick. The experience of a group of deaf women has been explored through photography. Young people at the Open Cafe Project have investigated the effectiveness of housing improvements on the lives of the residents of Muirhouse.

Improving health involves us all. Those who have worked on this project hope that the exhibition will inspire everyone – including those who plan our health services – to think about what it means to be healthy.

Supported by Lothian Health Promotion

Kinlochleven Project

The Kinlochleven project is a 12 week artist residency to be undertaken by Kinlochleven Community Ltd in collaboration with Fotofeis with the assistance of Highland Printmakers Workshop.

The project is designed for an artist who uses both photography and screen-printing in their work. The developmental aspect of the project is especially important as it aims to mesh with the larger plans for the village to exploit its natural assets as a means by which to address the inevitable changes precipitated by imminent closure of the aluminium smelter, which was once the major employer in the village. Set at the head of a narrow loch, Kinlochleven is positioned in an area of outstanding natural beauty on the West Highland Way. Consequently the aim is to develop its potential as a walking and tourism centre. This project is part of plans to further enhance the cultural life of the village and encourage the nascent arts groups that already exist there. The project aims to generate a legacy of skills and equipment in the village to be built upon by arts providers in the Highland Region and by the village itself.

Supported by The Lochaber Arts Partnership, Leader II, Scottish Arts Council and Alcan

above *Men and Health Photography Group* Macho? or Mocking?

Photo-Link

The Photo-Link project was initiated by the artist Kenny Bean and links children in Nepal and Scotland. The children learn from each other about their respective cultures by swapping images depicting their everyday lives. The project, which was first featured in the community programme for *Fotofeis* '93 has now been running for three years and has involved hundreds of children.

Early in 1995 Kenny Bean travelled to Nepal to run workshops for the children there. The workshops proved so popular that he set up a permanent darkroom for use after he left. Since then the darkroom has been moved to Kathmandu to enable children there to make photographic enlargements. A group of eight year olds took home a disposable camera and recorded their family life. Their photographs are on show at Stockbridge Library along with photographs from a number of earlier Photo-Link projects.

Supported by the Scottish Arts Council

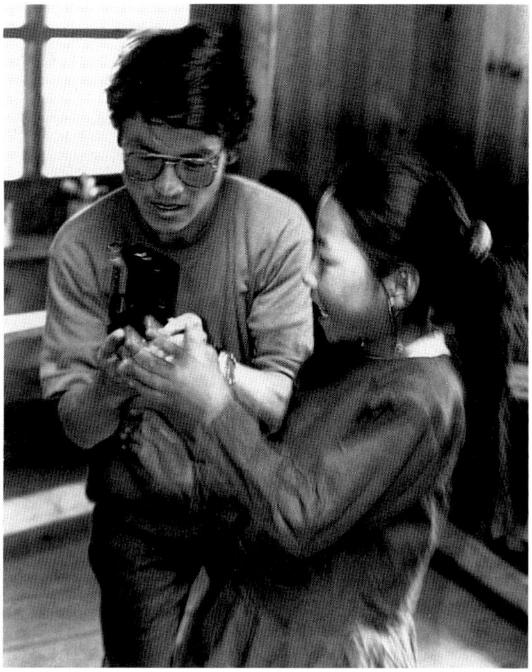

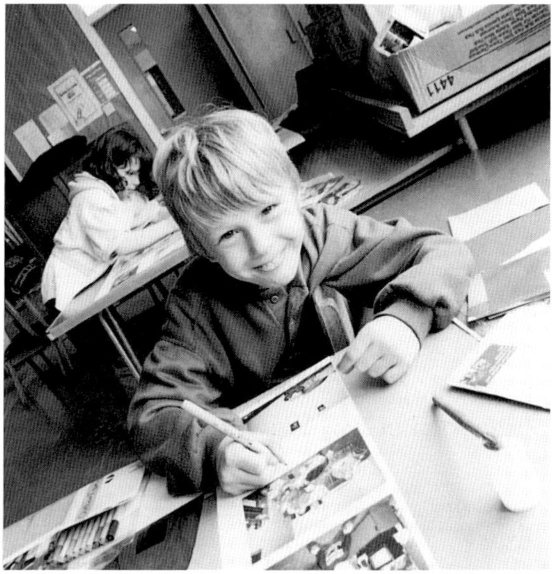

Tayside Region

Three community projects have been arranged for *Fotofeis* '95 through the Community Education Service of Tayside Regional Council. In Forfar a group of girls have created a photomontage expressing their perceptions of life in the town, while another group, this time of elderly people, take their own view on the same subject. Senior pupils at Arbroath and Forfar Academies are working on a project via fax machine links with foundation students at the Kent Institute of Art & Design. Together they are exploring the playful and creative potential of this item of office equipment for cultural exchange. This activity is part of a larger project run by Zone, a multi-media event for young people in Maidstone.

Supported by Tayside Regional Council
Zone supported by Maidstone Burgh Council, CCPM, Canon, Kent County Council Arts & Libraries

above left *Fotofeis '93, Fort Primary, Edinburgh*
above right *Fotofeis '95, Lukla Primary, Nepal (photos: Kenny Bean)*

Perth and Kinross District

Children in Perth and Kinross District have been going one better than taking holiday snaps this summer when they joined a free two-day arts workshop at Perth Museum and Art Gallery in August. The resulting pictures are showing at the A. K. Bell Library in Perth from 4th to 18th October. Eight to twelve year olds worked with artist/photographer, Catriona Grant, and the Writer in Residence, Robert Allan Jamieson, to combine words and images on the theme of migration. Simple photographic techniques involving cyanotypes, typefaces and creative writing were incorporated into two and three-dimensional forms to convey the theme in its widest sense.

Supported by Perth & Kinross District Council

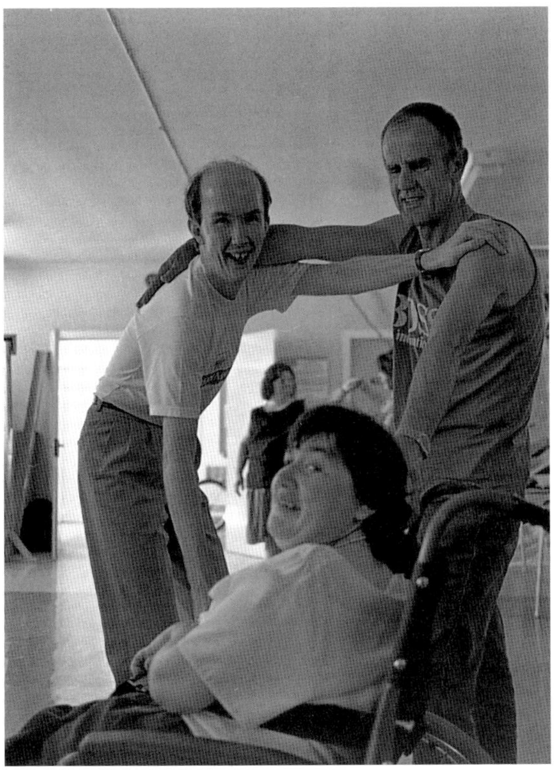

International Artist Exchanges

The artists on exchange are part of two separate, but equally strategic initiatives.

In Edinburgh, the artist Zoltan Jokay comes over from Munich. A real dialogue is beginning to develop between Edinburgh and Munich through their twinning agreement. Following the first exchange in 1993, the curator of photography at the Munich City Museum, Ulrich Pohlmann went on to curate a large exhibition of Scottish Photography, *Revisions*. The second exchange was effected through the offices of the City of Edinburgh District Council International Office working with the City of Munich, and in particular through Elaine Ballantyne and Ulrich Pohlmann. The exchange will also enable an Edinburgh-based artist to go to Munich in 1996.

Zoltan Jokay is a well known German photographer, winner of several prestige awards. He has shown at the Folkwang Museum Essen and recently had a one-person exhibition at The State Museum in Munich. He will be in Edinburgh throughout *Fotofeis* '95.

Glasgow welcomes two young artists from Lisbon, Luisa Ferreira and Mario Valente. Researched with the support of a *Go & See* grant from *Portugal 600*, the exchange is funded by Glasgow City Council Department of Performing Arts, the British Council and the Gulbenkian Foundation. The artists will be in the city for six weeks, making contact with artists in Scotland and creating their own work. Towards the end of their stay they will make a small presentation about their work.

In 1996 two Glasgow artists will travel to Portugal for six weeks to undertake a reciprocal project.

above *Woodlands Hospital, Aberdeen (photo: Sean Burn/Maverick)*

Objects, Places, Mental Health and the Community

Highland Printmakers Workshop & Gallery

20 BANK STREET
INVERNESS

PREMIERE

30 SEPTEMBER – 5 NOVEMBER

Adviser: Jim Neville

Presented by Highland Printmakers Workshop & Gallery

This exhibition is the result of a series of workshops run by Highland Printmakers Workshop and Gallery. Four mental health day centres in Highland Region acted as hosts for these workshops. In them people were asked to consider objects and places that were of significance to them and to attempt to define their feelings about their past, present or future environments. The intention was to create a forum for people to consider and express the changes of circumstances that they and many people in the mental health community are currently experiencing. Each workshop explored a different photographic process under the tutelage of Michele Lazenby.

Each of the photographs selected for the exhibition is accompanied by a text describing the reasons for the choices made within the photograph and the significance of the portrayed image to the life of the photographer. Accompanying the exhibition is archival material and a number of everyday objects relating to Craig Dunnain – the main psychiatric hospital for the Highlands – an institution built in the 1880s that is now in the process of decline. A number of works by people living at the hospital will be on display in the Applied Arts showcases at the gallery.

HI~ARTS
HIGHLANDS & ISLANDS ARTS LTD

Hugh Deans Trust

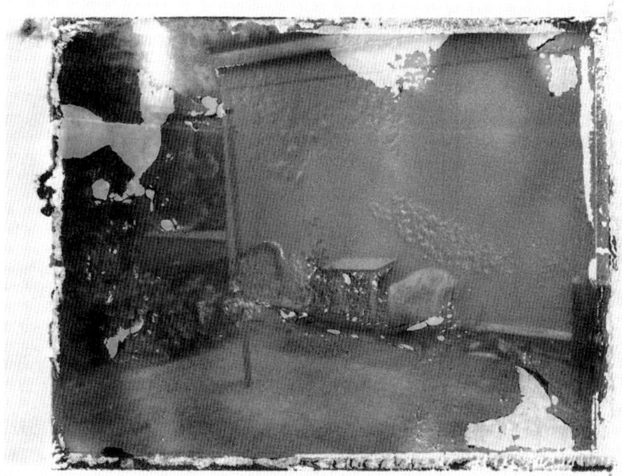

from Objects, Places, Mental Health and the Community 1995 *polaroid transfer (original in colour)*

Power, Love and Housework

Contact Gallery

GRINDLAY COURT CENTRE
GRINDLAY STREET COURT
EDINBURGH

PREMIERE

9 OCTOBER – 5 NOVEMBER

MICHELLE COZZI

AILEEN FENDER

DAVID HOLLOWAY

IAN LYON

DOROTHY MCLEOD

MOIRA MCLEOD

WILLIAM PORTER

EUAN WRIGHT

Power, Love and Housework is the culmination of a project which began during spring 1995 at Grindlay Court Centre, a day centre which provides services for adults who have learning disabilities. The Project involved two professional photographers, Margaret Mitchell and Lucy Hicks, working alongside a group of eight people from the Centre. Based on identity and self image, the project has provided the participants with an opportunity to explore self-expression within a photographic context. Each member of the group was invited initially to look closely at her or himself, to think about their likes and dislikes, fantasies and realities. From this they have created photographic self-portraits which reflect their individual identities and personalities.

Within this theme of identity and self-image various aspects of their lives have been explored, ranging from issues of independence and power to romantic idealism and love. Montages, cyanotypes, liquid light and computer-based images have provided a range of media through which the participants have expressed their ideas.

Presented by The Grindlay Court Centre

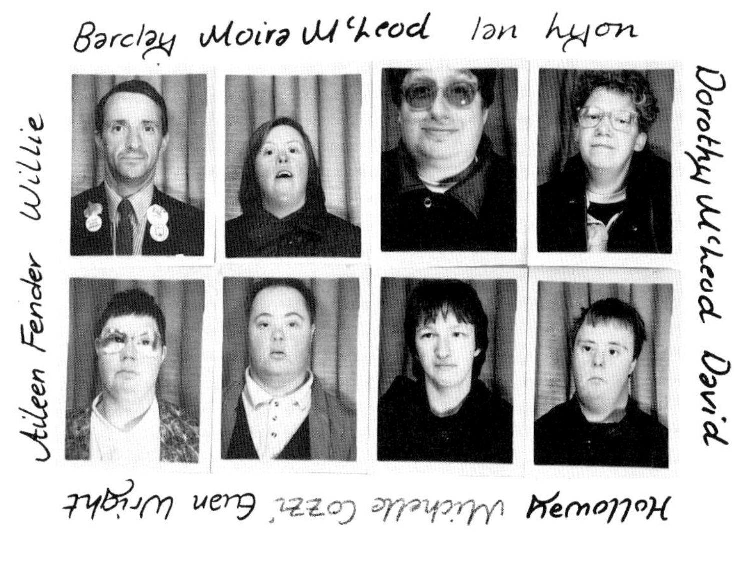

from Power, Love and Housework 1995 *photo-booth prints and handwritten text (original in colour)*

Coordinated by Margaret Mitchell and Lucy Hicks

Lothian Regional Council Department of Social Work

Ilford

THE CARIB PEOPLE OF NORTH EAST DOMINICA

Yet We Survive

An Tuireann

STRUAN ROAD
PORTREE
ISLE OF SKYE

PREMIERE

5 OCTOBER – 5 NOVEMBER

Curated by Mary Walters

THE SCOTTISH ARTS COUNCIL

The Carib people of North East Dominica are the largest group of indigenous people remaining in the Caribbean melting-pot. There are Caribs also in St. Vincent, Trinidad, Belize and Guyana – linked in the late 20th century by a fierce sense of survival which is currently nourishing a renewed cultural identity.

During the summer of 1993, a basic training programme in photography and sound recording was delivered to a group of young Dominican Carib people by trainers from Slide Workshop, Scotland.

The training was linked to the current programme of cultural revitalization and was implemented in partnership with Development Alternatives, a Dominican non-government organization. All images, text and recordings in this exhibition were produced by Carib people, working around a daily schedule of banana farming, fishing, copra production, fetching water, cooking and family life.

Presented by Slide Workshop in association with Fotofeis

Organisation of Amercian States

Afro-Caribbean-Pacific Foundation

Caribbean Conservation Association

Caribbean Council of Churches

Cable and Wireless

Dominica Coconut Products

Christian Aid

Help the Aged

Geest

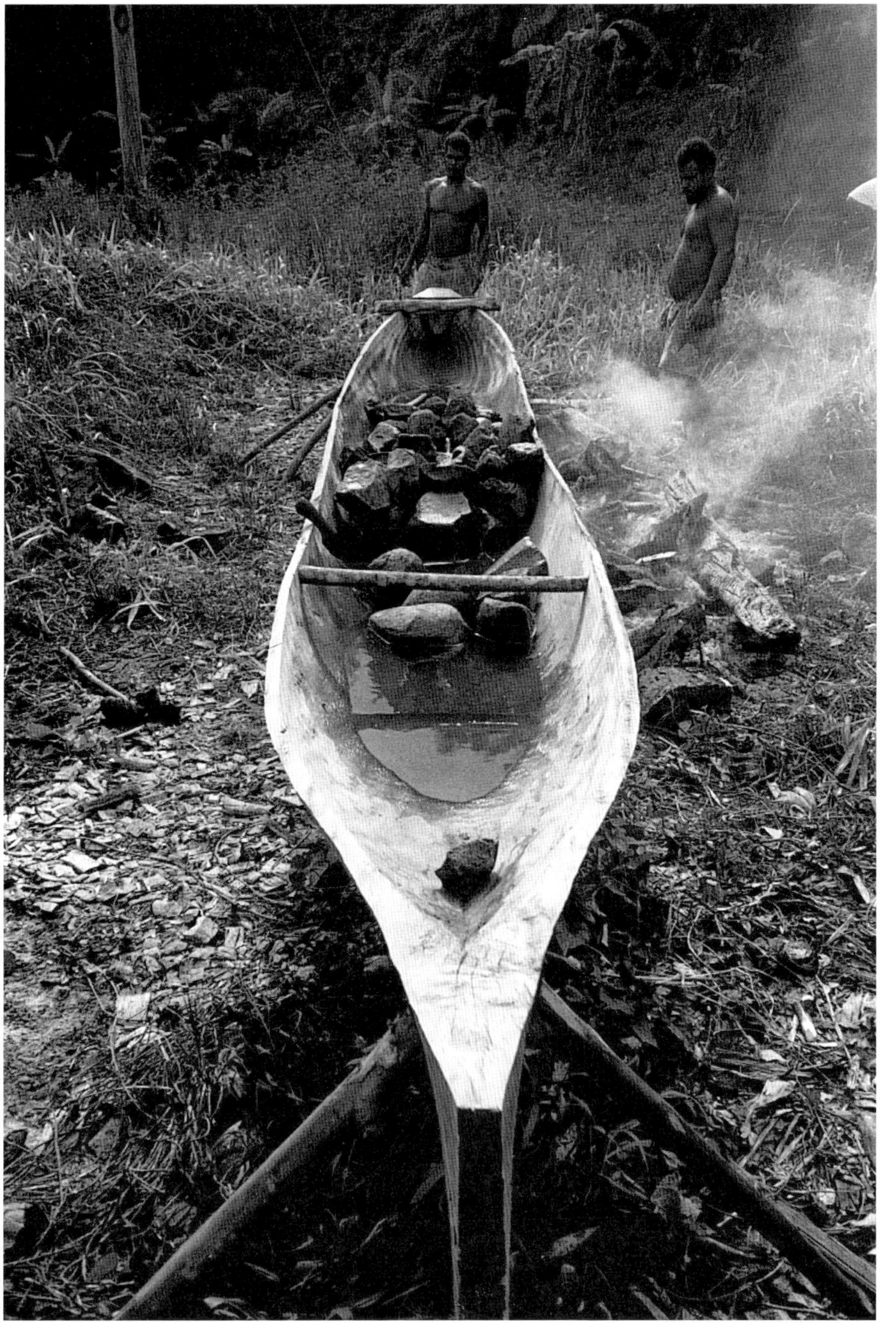

John Valmond, boat-builder, Carib Territory, Dominica *silver-gelatin print*

SAM MAYNARD *Scotland*

An Sgoth

Bonhoga Gallery, Weisdale Mill

WEISDALE
SHETLAND

6 OCTOBER – 5 NOVEMBER

An An Lanntair / Eòlas touring exhibition presented by Shetland Arts Trust

The exhibition follows the construction of the last sgoth (pronounced 'skaw') – a 32 foot traditional long-line sailing boat developed for fishing in the turbulent waters of the Atlantic and North Minches of Scotland.

Built over a ten month period in 1994 by John Murdo McLeod (a master boat-builder from Ness in the north of Lewis) and his assistant Angus Smith, the project records the traditional boat-building methods.

As the boat grew, so did community support and involvement. It represented a return to the simple cycles of life: the cutting down of a mature tree, the building of a new boat, the passing on of old skills to young hands. By the time of the launch in early December 1994, An Sgoth had come to symbolise a revival of traditional culture in the Gaidhealtachd.

The exhibition records in parallel the human and the technical aspects of the story. A seven minute time-lapse animation documents the boat's construction. This is projected onto the boat's sail in the centre of the exhibition space.

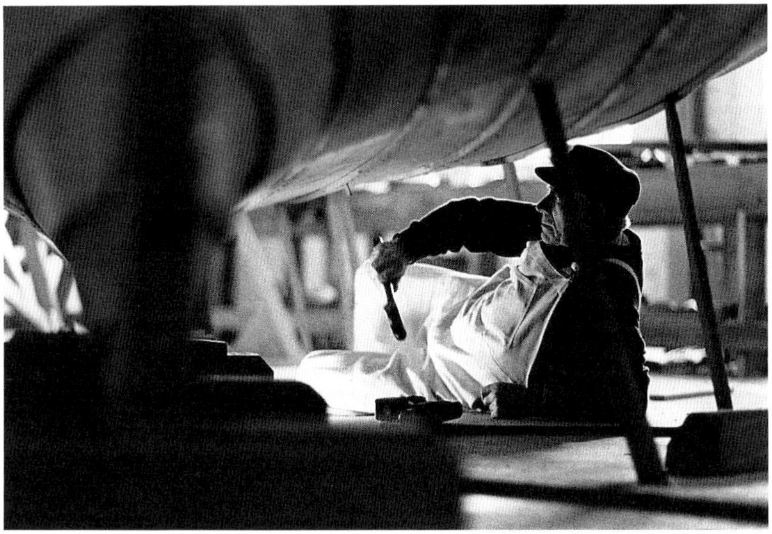

Sam Maynard untitled 1994 *silver-gelatin print*

ANNE ELLIOT *Scotland*

Tight Knit

Newcastleton

ROXBURGHSHIRE

PREMIERE

9 OCTOBER – 5 NOVEMBER

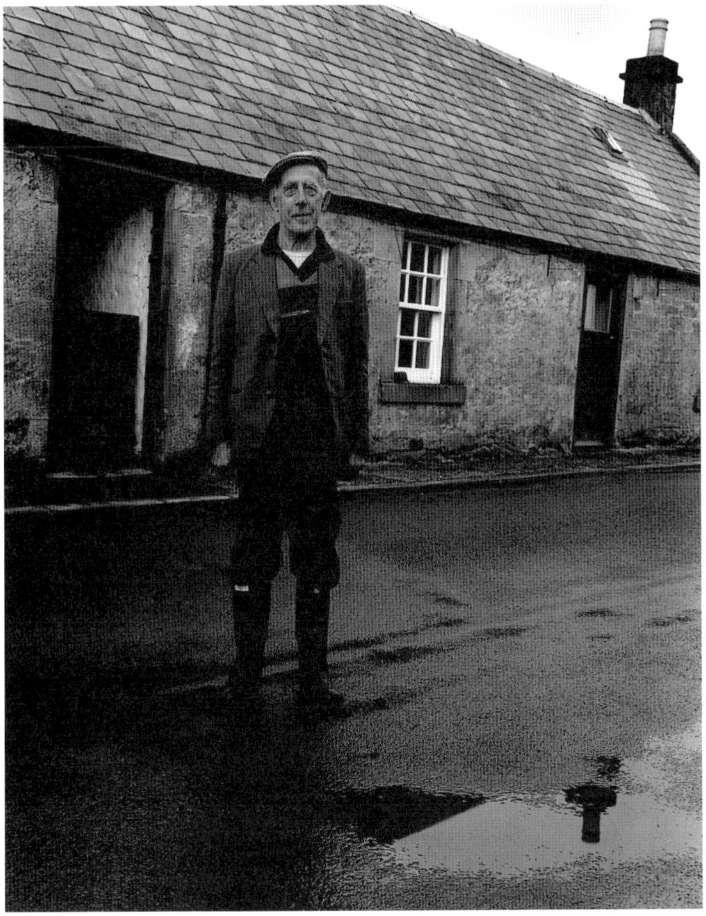

Anne Elliot untitled 1995 *silver-gelatin print*

Tight Knit is a series of photographs made in the Newcastleton area of the Scottish Borders over the last three years. Public visibility is heightened with images presented on specially created temporary billboards and in the windows of a disused shop. They are portraits, their format inspired by early photographic postcards and the photographs of a local photographer who worked at the turn of the century, Dr. Evans. The photographs are accompanied by factual records of people 'in their place': dates, names and addresses start to hint at a form of official registration.

An extension of *Tight Knit* is the compilation of *A Photographic Document*. As a reference book its aim is to hold photographs of every resident in the village grouped by household – approximately four hundred homes. Of equal interest to the local community and the wider audience, *A Photographic Document* could be considered a large 'family' album. It will be permanently housed in the Heritage Centre, Newcastleton, from 1996.

An artist-run project

Chimera

Maclaurin Art Gallery

ROZELLE PARK
MONUMENT ROAD, AYR

5 OCTOBER – 29 OCTOBER

The Chimera was a fire-breathing she-monster of Classical mythology, a fabulous amalgam of lion, goat and serpent. In modern language, the word chimera is used to describe anything that is wildly fanciful. It has become a symbol of vain imaginings, of unrealistic dreams, and of extravagant fantasies. Using photographic processes, the six artists in the exhibition navigate visionary and whimsical areas of the imagination, constructing fantastical journeys to idyllic places, challenging accepted histories and fables, exploring dream-worlds, self-image, desire, womanhood, and motherhood.
Based on a text by Cheryl Reynolds

Presented by the Maclaurin Gallery

EMMANUELLE WAECKERLE
MAGALI MOREAU
SUE ANDREWS
HELEN KITSOS
HEATHER JOHNSTON
LANA WONG

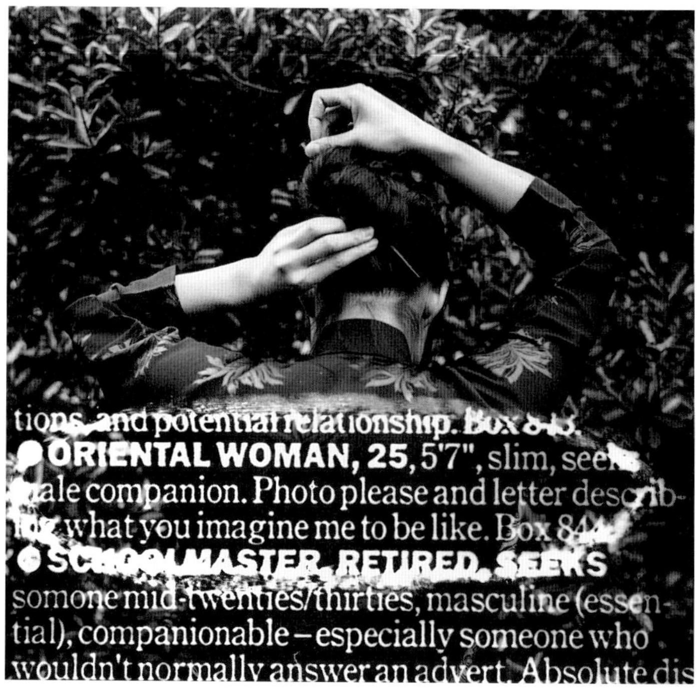

Lana Wong Mis(s) Orient 1994 *installation detail*

Photogenetic

Curated by Maud Sulter, *Photogenetic* features twelve artists who use photographic sources and media to explore issues centred on the colonial past and the use of photographic evidence to inscribe history. In challenging the notion of photographic truth and its power to record women's experiences, the exhibition challenges ethnocentric discourses of marginalisation and notions of otherness.

Each artist has taken photographic documents as source material for a commentary on their lives and cultural heritage.

A Street Level Gallery touring exhibition

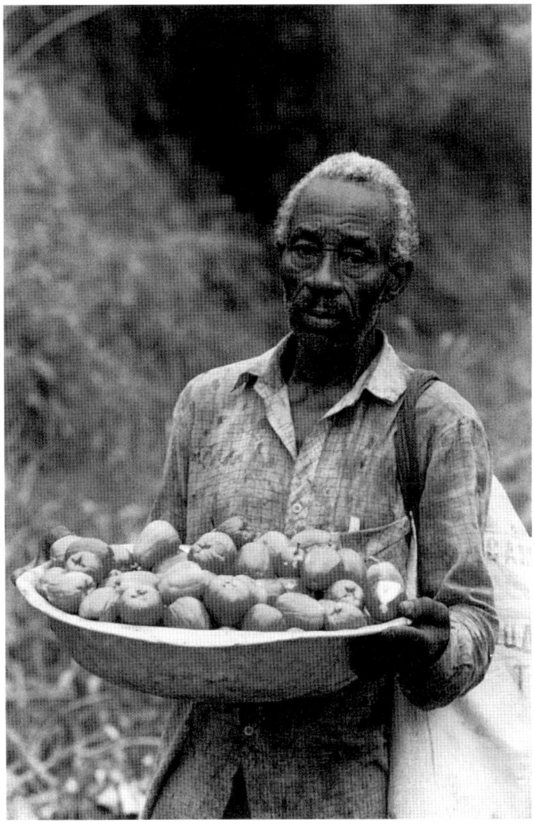

Angele Etoundi Essamba Vendeur de Pommes Sauvages *(original in colour)*

MHAIRI DUNLOP *Scotland*

Portrait Studies

PREMIERE

Commissioned for Fotofeis '95 by the Maclaurin Art Gallery

A recent graduate of Glasgow School of Art who has since specialised in television, Mhairi Dunlop worked with Anton Corbijn and his associates, becoming deeply interested in his work and ideas. *Portrait Studies* is an exhibition of a series of drawings derived from Anton Corbijn's photographs and executed in a strictly photo-realist manner.

Children in Focus

Museum of Childhood

42 HIGH STREET
EDINBURGH

PREMIERE

29 SEPTEMBER – 25 NOVEMBER

Curated by Susan Hutchings

Presented by the Museum of Childhood

Children in Focus offers a fascinating insight into the changing face of childhood from 1860–1960. The photographs, drawn from the Museum's collection, range from formal portraits for display on the mantlepiece to family snaps of seaside holidays and days in the garden.

Photographs play an important part in the work of the Museum, offering a wealth of information about the lives of children over the past 150 years. Visitors are encouraged to come forward with any photographs of children from 1930 onwards which could be added to the Museum's archive.

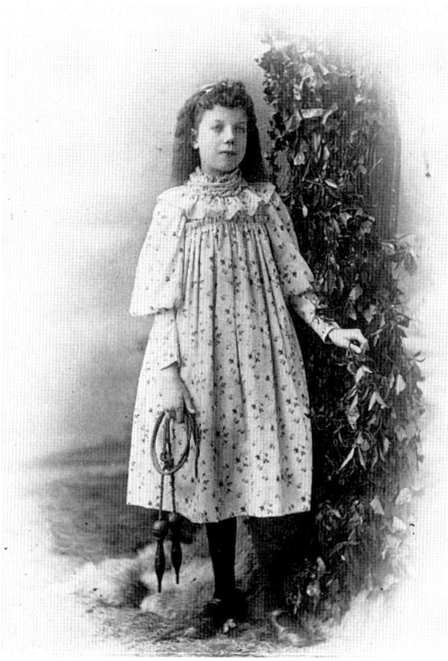

Unknown untitled [girl with skipping rope] *undated black and white print*

WITEK MOJSIEWICZ *Poland*

Arbuthnot Museum

ST PETERS ROAD, PETERHEAD

UK PREMIERE

5 OCTOBER – 4 NOVEMBER

Presented by the Arbuthnot Museum

Few people have experienced the unique underwater world captured by Witek Mojsiewicz in the vivid detail shown in this exhibition. Comprising thirty-six colour prints, the exhibition aims not only to make the viewer aware of the beauty and diversity of marine life in our deep waters, but also the dramatic richness of colour, shape and texture obtainable by macro photography. The exhibition will be of interest to everyone concerned with the marine environment and the relationship of man to the sea which provides the livelihood of many people in this area of Scotland.

ALEXANDER GUNN *Scotland*

Uisdean

Nairn Library

68 HIGH STREET
NAIRN

2 OCTOBER – 17 OCTOBER

Uisdean focuses on the traditional life and contemporary disintegration of the fishing communities of the North East of Scotland. Alexander Gunn combines photography and sculpture using found objects with strong connotations of Scottish sea-going culture, traditional fishing industry materials and photographs directly related to the artist's own family history.

In a series of large wooden box constructions the artist powerfully conveys the daily life struggle of the Highland fishing communities as experienced by successive generations.

Presented by Highland Regional Council

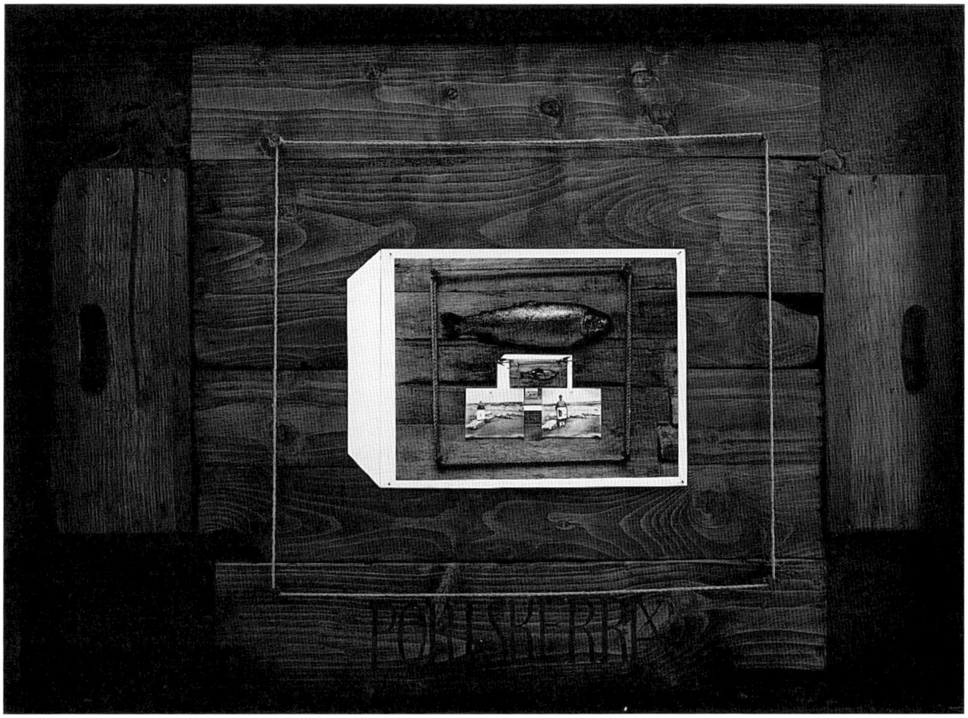

Alexander Gunn untitled *mixed media*

Funders and Sponsors

Fotofeis gratefully acknowledges the generous support of the following funders, sponsors and donors:

THE SCOTTISH **ARTS** COUNCIL

Glasgow City Council

City of Aberdeen

EDINBURGH
THE CITY OF EDINBURGH DISTRICT COUNCIL

Highlands & Islands
ENTERPRISE

ALL·ROUND There's Culture STRATHCLYDE

LOTHIAN health

Health Promotion Department

European Kaleidoscope Fund

The British Council

VISITING ARTS

arts & tourism SCOTLAND

LEADER

Assisted through the European Commission's LEADER II project

HI~ARTS

HIGHLANDS & ISLANDS ARTS LTD

Grampian Regional Council

Tayside Regional Council

EDUCATION DEPARTMENT

Caithness District Council

Sutherland District Council

Caithness & Sutherland ENTERPRISE

Lochaber Limited

Lochaber Arts Partnership

THE ROBERT GORDON UNIVERSITY ABERDEEN

NAPIER UNIVERSITY

Edinburgh COLLEGE *of* ART

School of Fine Art, Glasgow School of Art

CALOUSTE GULBENKIAN FOUNDATION

Esmée Fairbairn Charitable Trust

Russell Trust

Binks Trust

Canadian artists supported by

The Canada Council
Conseil des Arts du Canada

CANADIAN
HIGH COMMISSION

Québec

CONSEIL
DES ARTS ET DES LETTRES
DU QUÉBEC

Ontario Arts Council

Manitoba Arts Council

Saskatchewan
Arts Board

Newfoundland and Labrador Arts Council

Government of Ontario Ministry of Culture, Tourism and Recreation

Montreal City Arts Council

Canadian/Newfoundland Cooperation Agreement on Cultural Industries

University of Saskatchewan

AIR CANADA

Sponsors

BECK'S

MAJOR FESTIVAL SPONSOR

S·H·A·W

MARKETING AND DESIGN LTD

B&S VISUAL TECHNOLOGIES LIMITED

Canon

SEi

SCOTTISH EXPRESS INTERNATIONAL

norbord highland

fujifilm Professional

ALCAN

Festival Board, Staff and Advisors

BOARD OF DIRECTORS OF FOTOFEIS

Ciaran Monaghan *Chair*
Jane Brettle
Matthew Dalziel
Robert Greenhalgh
David Jamieson
Robert Maclennan MP
Jane Rigby
John Waddell *Company Secretary*
Michael Wolchover

Observers:
Andrew Nairne and Susan Pirnie *Scottish Arts Council*
Robert Livingston *HI Arts*

FESTIVAL STAFF

Alasdair Foster *Director*
Ken Gill *Head of Programme*
Jackie Shearer *Head of Programme Support*
Rosemary Blight *Secretary*
Eric McBain *Accountant*
Mari Little *Head of Communications*
Eve Navarro *Hospitality Coordinator*
Philippa Johnston *Press Officer*
Caralin Montgomery *Administrative Assistant*
Kas Robson *Information System Programmer*
Ursula Cleary *Volunteer Programme Assistant*
Dominique Cameron *Volunteer Community Assistant*
Rich Hardcastle *Volunteer Events Assistant*
Grant Crain *Volunteer*
Penni Dolan *Volunteer*
Duncan Ganley *Volunteer*
Thomas Jenner *Volunteer*

FESTIVAL DESIGNERS

Shaw Marketing & Design Edinburgh

RESEARCH PLACEMENTS

Jamie Pagan *Database Feasibility Study*
Noelle Campbell *Fotofeis Tour Feasibility Study*
Amber Knight *Market Research Study*

ADVISORS

David Bruce *Funding Advisor*

The following have assisted Fotofeis under placements arranged through Business in the Arts Scotland:

Richard Musson of Scottish & Newcastle plc advised the development of the festival marketing strategy

John McElwee of Marks & Spencer and Dylan Paterson of Jenners advised on Customer Care Training

SELECTION PANELS

The following artists and curators helped with the first stage of selection of work for *Fotofeis* '95:
Martine Beugnet
Jane Brettle
Matthew Dalziel
Lorraine Grant
Sara Munroe
Simon Starling

Luisella d'Alessandro *President, Fondazione Italiana per la Fotografia, Turin*

Pool Andries *Curator, Museum voor Fotografie, Antwerp*

Diana Augaitis *Director/Chief Curator, Walter Phillips Gallery, Banff*

Frederick Baldwin *President, Fotofest International, Houston*

David Balsells *Director, Primavera Fotogràfica, Barcelona*

Ruth Benzacar *Director, Ruth Benzacar Galeria de Arte, Buenos Aires*

Evgeny Berrezner *Art Director, Museum of Photographic Collections, Moscow*

Dr Vladimir Birgus *Katedra Fotografi, FAMU, Prague*

Pierre Bonhomme *Chargé de Mission, Mission de Patrimoine Photographie, Paris*

David Brittain *Editor, Creative Camera, London*

Susan Daniel *Director, Oriel Mostyn, Llandudno*

Deborah Ely *Director, Australian Centre for Photography, Sydney*

Ute Eskildsen *Museum Folkwang Fotografische Sammlung, Essen*

Paul di Felice *Editor, Café Crème Editions, Luxembourg*

Susan Fereday *Director, Centre for Contemporary Photography, Melbourne*

Joan Fontcuberta *Artist and Editor, Photovision, Barcelona*

Allen Frame *Independent Curator, New York*

Christine Frisinghelli *Editor, Camera Austria, Graz*

Sabrina Fung *Sabrina Fung Fine Arts, Hong Kong*

Frits Gierstberg *Exhibitions Curator, Nederlands Foto Instituut, Rotterdam*

Monte Greenshields *Director, Photographers' Gallery, Saskatoon*

Marek Grygiel *Director, Mala Galeria and Curator of Photography, CCA Ujazdowski Castle, Warsaw*

Martha Hanna *Curator, Canadian Museum of Contemporary Photography, Ottawa*

Yuko Hasegawa *Curator, Setagaya Art Museum, Tokyo*

Amanda Hopkinson *Independent Curator and Critic, London*

Ewa Hornowska *Curator of Photography, Video and Film, National Museum, Poznan*

Maaretta Jaukkuri *Chief Curator, Museum of Contemporary Art, Helsinki*

Pirjo Lampea *Director, Northern Centre for Photography, Oulu*

Peeter Linnap *Artist and Curator, Tallin*

Karen Love *Director, Presentation House, Vancouver*

Jan-Erik Lundström *Director, Fotografiska Museet, Stockholm*

Václav Macek *Director, Fotofo Photographic Foundation, Bratislava*

Andreas Müller-Pohle *Artist and Editor, European Photography, Göttingen*

Amanda Nevill *Head of Museum, National Museum of Photography Film & TV, Bradford*

Suzanne Nicholas *Assistant Director of Education, International Center of Photography, New York*

Alison Devine Nordström *Director, The Southeast Museum of Photography, Daytona Beach*

Virginia Perez-Ratton *Director, Museo de Arte y Diseño Contemporaneo, San José, Costa Rica*

Rui Prata *Director, Encontros da Imagem, Braga*

Christine Redmond *Director, Gallery of Photography, Dublin*

Pam Roberts*, Curator, Royal Photographic Society, Bath*

Michael Sand *Editor, Aperture, New York*

Rona Sela *Curator of Photography, Tel Aviv Museum of Art, Tel Aviv*

Satish Sharma *Independent Critic/Curator, New Delhi*

Pirkko Siitari *Northern Centre for Photography, Oulu/Jan van Eyck Akademie, Maastricht*

Sara Stevenson *Curator of Photography, Scottish National Portrait Gallery, Edinburgh*

Gilane Tawadros *Director, INIVA, London*

Ann Thomas *Acting Curator (Photography), National Gallery of Canada, Ottawa*

Finn Thrane *Director, Museet for Fotokunst, Odense*

Georges Vercheval *Director, Musée de la Photographie, Charleroi*

Hripsimé Visser *Curator of Photography, Stedelijk Museum, Amsterdam*

Bas Vroege *Curator and Editor of Perspektief, Rotterdam*

Peter Weiermair *Frankfurter Kunstverein, Frankfurt*

Paul Wombell *Director, The Photographers' Gallery, London*

Index of Venues

Index of Names

Figures in **bold** denote illustrations

Names in *italics* indicate curators and coordinators

Acknowledgement

Fotofeis '95 has involved the combined efforts of many individuals and organisations. To all those who have been involved, to all those who have helped and advised, who have given their time, their encouragement and their expertise, we offer our sincere gratitude. Without you this festival would not have been possible. Thank you.